Praise for *A Year in Beer*

"Insightful and entertaining! This book celebrates beer from every conceivable angle. Guided by Jonny's spritely charm, exploring the world of beer is a total delight—I warmly recommend joining him, ideally with a glass in hand!"
—Olly Smith, wine expert, TV personality, author and columnist

"The book is a sheer joy. Jonny's brilliance is to bring beer and its many methods of production to the attention of drinkers in a manner that's not preachy. It's like sitting down in the pub with a new friend who tells you, in a conversational manner, things about the liquid in your glass that you didn't know before. In common with Jackson's *Beer Companion*, it will endure and continue to delight people for years to come. Now, it's a bit warm today. Where's that bottle of Harvey's Imperial Stout?"
—Roger Protz, *Protz On Beer*

Praise for *Beer School*

"Good fun, funny, interesting and you never quite know what's coming next."
—Mark Dredge, author of *Craft Beer World*

Jonny Garrett

THE MEANING OF BEER

How Our Pursuit of the Perfect Pint Built the World

HANOVER
SQUARE
PRESS

HANOVER
SQUARE
PRESS™

ISBN-13: 978-1-335-23083-6

The Meaning of Beer

First published in 2024 by Allen & Unwin in the UK. This edition published in 2024.

Hanover Square Press
22 Adelaide St. West, 41st Floor
Toronto, Ontario M5H 4E3, Canada
HanoverSqPress.com

Printed in U.S.A.

For my daughter.

THE
MEANING
OF BEER

Introduction

Not how we made beer, but how beer made us

Every night when my dad got home from work, he'd kiss my mom, ask what my brother and I were watching on TV (usually to little or no response), and head straight upstairs.

There he'd change out of his work uniform of branded polo and chinos, and into his home uniform of unbranded polo and chinos. He'd then thud back downstairs and hit start on the microwave to reheat whatever we'd eaten a few hours before. Finally, he'd go to the fridge, pull out a stubby bottle of lager and settle at the kitchen table. He'd only ever have one beer, but in my misty-eyed recollections he never skips it. It was the routine; his signal that the workday had ended—as vital as the meal he had it with, as the kiss for my mom, as the begrudging communication from his heirs.

For such an important moment—maybe the best moment of the day—he didn't invest much in it. My dad is hardly a gourmand, but he knows his wine in an "oooh Gavi di Gavi!" kind of way. He's certainly never served red with fish, and likes to discuss that fact. But the opposite is true of his beer drinking. Despite having a bottle every darn day, he stuck to the bottom-shelf stubbies: lagers our family fondly came to call French Piss. I don't know if Bière d'Or was his favorite, or if my mom simply shopped at Tesco more than any other supermarket, but the gold label, chunky bottles and flimsy cardboard crate shaped like a *Robot Wars* entry destined to go out in the first round are burned into my memory.

When I was young I'd sometimes be charged with loading the basket at the bottom of the fridge with more, and when I was a little older I was allowed to crack open the bottles for him, sniffing suspiciously at its strange grainy aroma. I took my first tentative sip in my early teens. One evening my older brother had—to his and my surprise—been left in charge of the house along with some friends. Naturally, being in charge at the age of sixteen meant drinking beer and watching films with an eighteen certificate. The fact that I was only thirteen didn't seem relevant as he handed me a bottle and said, "Don't get drunk." That wasn't a problem—the beer was awful, and I struggled to get through one 8 oz. bottle. Bière d'Or is barely introduced to hops when it's brewed, but it was bitter enough to claw like fingernails at my juice-weaned palate. I sipped half-heartedly at it, feeling the bottle go warm in my clammy hands and wondering why my dad would put himself through this every weeknight.

Of course, that mystery revealed itself pretty quickly, as it does with most teenagers. My dad's green stubbies became the lubricant for many drunken barbecues and illicit house parties as I pinballed my way through my teens, and Bière d'Or now holds a very special place in my heart. When I visit my parents these days, I insist that there's a stack of French Piss in the fridge ready for my arrival.

I'm telling you this admittedly indulgent story for a very important reason. Civilization certainly didn't start, or even really continue, at my kitchen table—not the way the Garretts eat. There were no great inventions or cultural moments inspired by Bière d'Or there, either. But my dad's ritual is the bedrock upon which my love of beer was founded, and I bet you have a similar story. To me, beer has always retained the key purpose it had for my dad. It's not just a quick drink or a way to wash down a microwave meal: it's a period on the day—a moment that may seem small if you're sitting opposite my dad, but takes on a global significance when you think that on our suburban road, tens of people were doing exactly the same thing at the same time. In bars throughout my hometown there were hundreds more sharing that moment. Around the world, as 5 p.m. hit each time zone, millions would pop caps and lean back, sharing in the collective sip and sigh of a day done that stretches back millennia.

My point is that since civilization began, beer has played a vital role in how we experience and process the world, even during childhood. My dad's routine sparked synapses in my brain that connect beer and relaxation, beer and food, beer and work, beer and home, beer and family. My pubescent misadventures bonded beer irrevocably to adventure, to friends and to love. Most of my best memories involve it in some way—from finishing school to celebrating my master's, from starting my first job to painting the walls of my first house, from my first date with my wife to our wedding. And that personal significance needs to be multiplied by the billion: by everyone who has ever lived and everyone who ever will, because beer (which is to say an alcoholic drink made from fermented cereals) has been with us for at least 13,000 years—and will outlast everyone alive today.

It's not just the personal stories that are timeless, either. Something of such cultural significance requires huge means of production. An inconceivable amount of human ingenuity and endeavor, of adventure and trade, of experimentation and research went into making the French Piss my dad unwound with every night. Some anthropologists believe that the nomadic tribes that roamed the earth 13,000 years ago only settled to grow cereals for beer and bread. There's archaeological evidence that refining the brewing process was humanity's first great engineering project, with epic breweries found in the ruins of ancient societies. We built the first commercial compressed-gas refrigerator exclusively to keep our beer cold, and laid railways to take it to new places as quickly as possible. The process of pasteurization was perfected to ensure beer didn't spoil and led to the discovery of bacteria's role in infections. The isolation of yeast, key to all bread baking and even biofuel production, was done in the name of brewing. Beer was the keystone of early civilization, then spurred humanity on its endless scientific advances. We'll fully explore all this throughout this book, but clearly beer is one of the most important discoveries we have made as a species. In fact, there are academics who believe—like I do—that the control of fermentation is as important to human development as the discovery of fire.

Not a Real Job

You wouldn't know that to look at how we treat it or talk about it, however. As my dad's blasé approach shows, while the traditions of fine wine are held in the highest regard, beer's central place in the world seems to be its undoing. Far from being an artisan endeavor, to most people it's a daily inevitability that sits on shopping lists next to the dish soap. This delicious drink, through which the entire history of humanity can be traced, has become a homogeneous corporate product, the significance of which few give a second's thought to. It's this fact that has spurred me on the journey I've taken for this book, and indeed inspired my career as a broadcaster and writer.

My job has taken me across the globe in search of exciting flavors, but like everyone else my love of good beer started in my local bar. I was fresh out of university and flush with my first paycheck as a journalist. A sunny Saturday stretched out in front of me, and I wanted to try something different: something bold and exciting. Standing at the bar, I looked past the standard lager taps of my teens and saw a giant hammer at the end. It loomed out of the beer fonts in lieu of a normal tap handle. Along its shaft were written the words *Long Hammer IPA*. I couldn't not order it.

The bartender pulled the foot-long hammer down in a great arc. Clear amber beer and creamy white foam cascaded out of the tap, and as he passed the glass over to me the head spilled luxuriously over the side. That first sip changed my world. Citrus oils swam across my palate; pine needles pricked the back of my tongue; caramel stuck to my teeth. I was intoxicated in so many ways—by the alcohol, the heady aromas, the biting bitterness, the mystery of where it all came from. How was this beer so radically different from the faux lagers I'd grown up choking down?

That pint, as well as three more that followed it, sent me on the adventure I've been on for over a decade—traveling the world to discover all the flavors that malt, water, hops and yeast create when put together in the right order, at the right temperatures, and at the right time. On the surface it seems like a very simple process: warm water is mixed with malted grain to create a sugary liquid, which is then boiled with hop flowers to add flavor and bitterness, before yeast is added to eat the sugar and release alcohol. But as I've proven many times through my home-brewing exploits, making good beer is a lot more complicated than that. As I looked to unlock brewing's secrets, I read every book I could afford and toured every brewery I came across. I tried every sample and asked every question I could think of. I learned of remarkable beer styles and drinking cultures—the lambics of Belgium, the farmhouse ales of Norway, the diverse lagers of Bavaria and Bohemia, the soft and bittersweet cask ales of the UK, and hop-saturated IPAs of the West Coast. As I fell deeper down the rabbit hole I started blogging about it, then filming it, then finally writing my own books. The aim was to convince everyone to drink better beer—to help people have the same experience that I did with that pint of Long Hammer. Over the years, however, my motivation has shifted.

Unless you're a politician or an arms dealer, you've probably never had to justify your job. But I have to every time I use the phrase *beer writer*. Usually I face the same stock questions—How do I make money ("I don't, really"), Do I get lots of free beer ("Yes, there's very little room for food in my fridge"), or Isn't that just a fancy phrase for *alcoholic* ("Have you been talking to my mother?")? The most common one, however, is "Is that really a job?" The first hundred times I laughed it off with some variation of "Well, someone keeps paying me." But increasingly I'm asking myself that very question. As I hit my thirties I started to wonder where my career could go from here, how many times I could tell the same stories. Most importantly, when my daughter was born, I asked myself what I was doing to improve the world she was growing up in.

There are no joke answers to those more introspective questions—so on my trips I started to ask about not just the beers, but the people. And not just the brewers either—the locals, the farmers and the families. That led me to track down and interview historians, anthropologists and politicians to piece together how certain beers, breweries and styles came to be, and what their place in the world was. Slowly I built up this picture of humanity entirely through the lens of beer, and my favorite drink took on much more significance. I began to see it not as a lovely addition to daily life, but as a central part of it.

Everywhere I looked I started to see beer's impact on the world. I've explored the archaeological site of one of the world's oldest commercial breweries, and talked to the prince of Bavaria about his family's ancient purity law. I've attended China's Oktoberfest some 6,000 miles from Munich, and followed the spread of lager throughout the world. I've gone to one of the UK's incredible British Indian pubs and visited the most northerly brewery in the world. I've toured a secular brewery in a church in Stockholm, and the devout, monastic breweries of Belgium. I've dug into the history of a brewery that defined Czech identity when the nation was occupied, first by the Nazis and then by the Soviet Union, as well as the epic Budweiser Brewery in St. Louis, where a German brewer helped build the very idea of the American dream. I've toured the historic laboratory where yeast was isolated in the 1800s and spoken to scientists who, 150 years later, are using those yeasts to treat diseases and tackle climate change. These are just some of the adventures we're headed on in this book: from how beer helped kick-start humanity, right through to how it might just save it.

Like I said, on the surface, beer is just malt, water, hops and yeast. That's how most beer books define it, and how beer writers often structure their stories. This is not one of those books. This is not a book about how beer is made, but about how beer made us.

Chapter 1

Civilization

Or how beer built our first cities and cultures

The origin of beer is much debated for the simple reason that it happened so very long ago. There's no written record of it because it predates writing, and though humans were speaking by then, voices leave no trace in the archaeological record. Instead, as we hunt down the earliest evidence of brewing, we're left brushing at dirt, carbon-dating dust and analyzing scrapes in rock invisible to the human eye.

When we do study an era in which beer is written about, it's mythologized. Popular scientists, historians and beer writers seize upon evidence and anecdotes that support their worldview. Pretty much every beer book that has ever been written, and indeed ever will be written, contains some kind of reference to Mesopotamia, a thing called the Sumerian tablet, and a poem written about the goddess Ninkasi. Usually it will follow it up with something about how the pharaohs paid the people who built the pyramids in beer. You've possibly heard variations of all these things and, well, this book will be no different, save for the fact that I have now lived it—I have dipped my toes in the sands of Egypt, held their pottery in my hands, and met archaeologists looking to change our view of ancient brewing and civilization itself.

It's my profound belief that without our eternal, close relationship with beer, society would have evolved to be a very different, much poorer place. Brewing ranks among music, language, religion, sport and cuisine as the things that set us apart from our closest relatives (primates that is, not your boring uncle). But until recently it was just that—a belief. And like most human beliefs, it was probably based on confirmation bias. Wanting to be right is as innate to our species as our love of beer. More than that though, when you spend your life intently studying something, it's natural you might inflate its importance.

Which is why even my closest friends, who are used to me indulging in pint-swinging generalizations, tend to roll their eyes when I get on my soapbox/beer crate. I've waved my brewing bibles at them, sent links to obscure Wikipedia pages, and got in round after round to buy myself more time, but it always gets the same response. Apparently, secondhand information presented by a "glorified beer PR person" (that one hurt a bit) doesn't constitute a valid revisionist history of our entire species.

That's because my friends are well-adjusted, well-educated people with practical jobs: broadcast engineers, academics, teachers, social workers, programmers. When their parents explain what their kids do, they say it with pride, safe in the knowledge there will be no awkward follow-up questions or looks of pity. It was these faces, along with the rolling eyes of my dearest friends, that I thought of as I booked my tickets to Cairo.

From Grave to Cradle

Egypt does not contain the oldest evidence of brewing. By the time you read this there might be a new one, but currently the title belongs to Israel, and a place called the Raqefet Cave near Nazareth.

This cave was once inhabited by a prehistoric group of people called the Natufians. The Natufians were mostly hunters, but at Raqefet they foraged wild grains such as barley and wheat, then brewed beer using techniques so advanced that it's almost inconceivable it couldn't have been developed even earlier: their ancient brewery takes the form of several divots dug into the floors and boulders of the cave, in which archaeologists found not just traces of grains but of enzymes that implied those grains were malted and broken down in water—the first step in the beer brewing process, known as *mashing*. From the lacerations on the stone, it's presumed they malted the grain in the floor basins and stored it in the boulder ones. On the brew day, they mashed the grain in the floor divots, then fermented them (covered with a slab) for a few days until ready. Archaeologists have even found strands of tightly wound wicker baskets in the boulder basins that would have contained the ingredients or even the finished beer.

Now for the big reveal: carbon dating puts the residue at Raqefet at a monumental 13,000 years old. When these people were brewing, woolly mammoths roamed the earth and we were still in the last Ice Age (it seems the beer jacket is a very old invention indeed). This time period is remarkable for more than just the number of zeros, though. It means that beer was likely the first example of humans intentionally making alcohol: wine was first made about 5,000 years later, and we didn't start distilling spirits for nearly 12,000 years. Even more importantly, if beer was made this early, it potentially predates two incredibly important things: bread and civilization itself.

Let's start with the former. Archaeologists, anthropologists, food writers and beer writers all disagree about which was invented first—beer or bread. Without getting into it too much, the earliest records of each come within 1,000 years of each other and in neighboring countries (Israel and Jordan). The reason for the debate is that whichever came first likely inspired the other, because their ingredients are almost identical—grain and water, with one being baked and the other being stored. Telling the two apart 13,000 years later is pretty tough, and it's important to say that some academics believe only bread was made at Raqefet, with any alcohol being a by-product.

There are two compelling arguments against this, however. The first is that there's clear evidence the grain was germinated—a process that releases lots of fermentable sugar that's vital to making beer but superfluous to bread baking. Given that malting took days to do and was tricky to get right, you'd only do it if you really needed to. Secondly, whatever was going on in the basins seems to have played a ritualistic role as well as a production one: the cave also features flower-lined graves and animal bones that suggest funeral-related feasting and drinking. This spiritual or religious side to beer is a connection we'll see throughout human history, and to me it confirms the divots at Raqefet held a lot more than just dough.

I suspect that as we find earlier evidence of brewing and baking, the methods for each will get simpler and simpler until beer is pretty much unbaked bread and bread is pretty much just baked beer. Working out which came first might be beyond our technology. There's a very strong argument, however, that brewers may have invented leavened (risen) bread. In Nicholas P. Money's excellent book, *The Rise of Yeast*, he suggests that the most likely cause of the first bread rise was an accidental splash of yeasty beer or frothy yeast from a ferment. To my mind it could just as likely have been the intentional use of beer as the water for the dough.

It's not unreasonable, though, to ask why beer was even being made so long ago. If you got your hands on some grain, bread would have been much quicker to make and arguably more filling. The reality is that humans need liquid more than they need food: you can go a few weeks without eating, but more than three days without water and you'll be on the brink of death. So beer killed two birds with one stone—it was filling and nutritious but also staved off thirst. A little kicker for our ancestors (and incredibly around 700 million people today) was that the available water wasn't always safe to drink—stagnant water can get infected with nasty bacteria and viruses that might kill you nearly as quickly as not drinking at all. Alcohol, however, is an antiseptic, so beer was very likely to be sanitary, making it the ancient world's safest source of liquid. This is why beer was so pervasive, but its cultural significance likely comes from another reason...a reason we consider even more important today: it gets you drunk.

Now, being a little buzzed wouldn't have been entirely new to humans who tried beer for the first time. Fallen fruit is rotted by a combination of bacteria and fungi including yeast, so it's very likely our ancestors would have gathered and eaten semirotten "floor treats" that were a good few percent ABV. If that sounds gross, beer 13,000 years ago wouldn't have tasted particularly great either—probably sour thanks to the other microbes that would have got in with the yeast. It would, however, have been predictable, safe and even storable. If it was a strong enough batch, it might have made our prehistoric brewer feel rather good about themselves. Their cheeks would have flushed, their pupils dilated, their inhibitions been suppressed. They might have found the sudden courage to grunt at their crush, or try that new dance move around the campfire. After telling all their friends about this amazing discovery, I assume the tribe experienced their first Big Night Out and immediately started planning next weekend's.

I'm being a little trite there, but there's overwhelming evidence from disparate ancient societies that beer was a central part of all kinds of social, religious and ritualistic occasions. All over the world we find evidence of beer at the center of feasts, of brewing and beer offerings to the dead near prehistoric grave sites, and remarkably diverse recipes and processes to turn grain into alcohol. For example, before Raqefet's brewing process was explored around 2018, we thought that Jiahu in China, where people combined broomcorn millet with moldy grains and herbs, might have been the origin of beer about 8,500 years ago. In most of these locations, however, we only have the implication of beer: the warm, morning dregs of the party. The earliest recorded example of humans *talking* about brewing beer comes from a fertile part of Iraq once called Mesopotamia—a wide band of fertile land that follows the Euphrates and Tigris Rivers. It's just a few thousand miles from Raqefet and is often referred to as the cradle of civilization.

Try to Be Civil

Before Beer—a bit like Before Christ but more important—the earth's population mostly consisted of sporadic tribes of nomads or semisedentary people like the Natufians. There was the odd permanent settlement, but a life of foraging, herding and running away from dangerous animals kept most people moving. In ancient Mesopotamia, people hunted and gathered across the land, foraging food where they found it and rarely staying in one place for long. But then, around 5000 BCE, something changes and a group we know as the Sumerians settle. We're not talking natural caves like Raqefet, here. We're talking about permanent buildings in organized towns with social hierarchies, religious customs and even forms of governance. We're talking civilization.

Until a few decades ago, the earliest evidence we had for brewing came from these Sumerians and so many academics pondered if the advent of beer and civilization were intertwined; if the discovery of beer compelled people to settle in one place. The theory went something like this: the ancients loved this new drink—how it filled their stomachs and gave them inner peace that must have been hard to find in their wild, dangerous world—but to make it they needed a lot of grain, more than they could forage. So when they found fertile soil already growing cereal, they cultivated it and built a life there.

There are multiple issues with this idea. Most significantly, we now know that beer had been intentionally made for at least 7,000 years by the time the Sumerians rested their weary legs, yet the Natufians did not build a civilization anything like the Sumerians did. A more likely explanation is that humans had learned a huge amount about building shelters and preserving food, while rapidly increasing in number as they imposed themselves on the landscape with their increasingly sharp arsenal of weapons. It's also worth noting that as the Ice Age receded, winters were getting less harsh and people had to travel less to stay warm and find food.

So while beer instigating civilization itself would be a very romantic and convenient story for this book, it's more likely that civilization instigated the need for lots more beer. It was already as important as any solid foodstuff in terms of sustenance and culture, but in a world without currency, beer had also become a key way of paying for labor and other products. As such, historians now believe that while brewing might not have founded civilization, it was almost certainly one of the first concerns of those who did. Not only that, but it's considered a key reason we domesticated grain—so perhaps we'll settle for beer inventing arable farming.

Early evidence for this comes from a series of Sumerian tablets found in what's now Iraq, but carved between 5000 and 1500 BCE. Sumerian is the oldest known language, and its speakers were pretty rigorous record keepers—perhaps because they learned that alcohol tends to make you forget things. Among these amazing tablets is essentially the world's first payslip, resembling a cartoon strip in which symbols for beer (a jug with a pointed bottom) and food (a head eating from a bowl) are totaled up by what look like thumbnail marks. Many of these tablets were forms of accountancy, and the Sumerian system—

based on twelves and sixties (sexagesimal) instead of tens like our (decimal) system—even set the precedent for the sixty seconds we count in a minute. So you could argue that the trading of beer 6,000 years ago is responsible for our very sense of time.

Beer was far more than just currency and food to the Sumerians though—they had a saying that went *He who does not know beer does not know what is good.* In the Sumerian poem "The Epic of Gilgamesh," about a Sumerian king trying to achieve immortality, beer is listed as one of the things that make us human, alongside sex, food and oil rubs (the latter is a little unexpected, but it all sounds like a nice afternoon anyway). From this and many other sources we know that drinking beer was both a daily routine and a religious ritual. During feasts to honor the gods, statues of Sumerian deities would have been "fed" beer— indeed the Sumerian word for *banquet* is *kas-dé-a* which translates as *the pouring of beer.* Into another tablet is carved a poem to their goddess of brewing, fertility and harvest, Ninkasi. It takes the form of a literal recipe for Sumerian beer, describing how it starts with the making of bread, before the fermenting of the spent grains with honey and water in tall clay vats that also filtered beer.

Perhaps *filtered* is a strong word, because another tablet depicts Sumerians drinking the beer from giant pots with long straws. Presumably they did so to reduce the amount of grain you swallowed, allowing them to drink straight from the fermenter, which every beer geek will tell you is the best way to consume beer. It all sounds a little "goldfish bowl cocktails" for me, but the upshot is that we can probably credit brewers with the invention of the straw, which came in all kinds of forms, from simple bamboo to solid gold. The oldest ones found (this time in Maikop, Russia, from around 3500 BCE) were so long that they were originally thought to be tent poles, but after tests of the residue inside we can only presume they were ornate drinking tubes. They were long enough that they'd allow up to eight people to drink from the same pot, which was handy because at some point, the populations of our early civilizations would have grown so large that feeding people became a major problem.

Initially it would have been everyone's job to provide food through farming, hunting and gathering, but as cities sprang up, new careers were created that had nothing to do with food production: laborers, builders, messengers, warriors, teachers, priests, politicians. They all needed to be fed and paid—even the politicians—and according to John W. Arthur, an archaeologist and professor of anthropology at the University of South Florida, beer was fueling all of this as food and currency. Without beer, you couldn't have persuaded or supported the people building the cities, upholding its traditions, expanding its territory and making scientific advances.

In his remarkable book *Beer: A Global Journey through the Past and Present*, Arthur claims that brewing marks some of the first great advances in engineering, particularly biological. Brewers were learning that certain vessel shapes and sizes yielded better beer, and even that specific fermenters were better than others. They would have put this down to a deity like Ninkasi blessing select ones, but by choosing to reuse the so-called blessed vessels, they were in effect selecting healthy yeasts from healthy fermentations. Doing so would have improved the quality and consistency of the beer, as well as having a long-term effect on the evolution of yeasts in the area. It's a technique humans have used for millennia in food production and farming: selecting the best examples of grains, fruits and vegetables to grow from seed the next year.

By 1800 BCE, which is when the "Hymn to Ninkasi" was written, there were breweries in Sumerian outposts all along what would become the Silk Road trade route that linked Asia and the far eastern parts of Europe. But barely 1,000 miles to the west, at the far end of that route, stood one of the most remarkable ancient buildings ever discovered: a brewery that would tower over not only all Sumerian ones, but most modern ones too. It was a founding feature of a civilization destined to become the most advanced and fascinating in the ancient world. It was built around 3000 BCE, and in 2024, I stood above its ruins.

I say above them because when I visited Egypt's Abydos brewery, about 100 miles north of Luxor, it was under several yards of sand. This is how the brewery spends most of the year in a bid to protect its structures, artwork and pottery from the outside world. I'd been attempting to visit the brewery for nearly two years, and just weeks before I was intending to head out I got the dispiriting news that the site would not be dug up in 2024. After downing a few beers and smashing some of my own pottery, I decided that it didn't really matter. After all, this is not a book about how beer is made. It's about how beer made us, and much of what this brewery laid the groundwork for is still out in the open. Including the pyramids.

Call to Prayer

I'm not sure how anyone sleeps in Luxor. It's a bustling, sandy city that snakes alongside the Nile, nearly 440 miles south of Cairo. Tourists might take a once-in-a-lifetime river cruise to get there, but I was on a tight schedule and took a late-night flight. I arrived tired and hot, and despite downing two bottles of Sakara lager was kept wide awake by the blaring of car horns, blowing of the air-con, and at 2:30 a.m. an almighty ship's horn from the Nile. That seemed to silence the cars (or perhaps put them in perspective) and I slept until the call to prayer at 5:15 a.m., which served as the alarm for my 6 a.m. departure for Abydos.

The city was still buzzing when I came out of the hotel to meet my guide Ghada. She motioned me into a white Toyota

Corolla where my driver Gerges said, slightly cryptically, "Welcome back," and immediately pulled out into oncoming traffic.

That's not a criticism, that's life on the roads in Egypt: lanes are a guide, horns a conversation, indicators mere flirtation. The laws got looser as we left Luxor behind and reached the wide-open roads of the rural Nile valley. Most of them are still under construction, so we weaved our way down them, reversing up unpaved slip roads and braking hard for the more obvious bumps and potholes. Every few miles we'd slow down to snake through roadside settlements, some no more than farmsteads built on the rubble dug for the road and others just corridors of shantylike shops slinging pottery, flatbreads, drinks and vapes. Mopeds, tuk-tuks and donkey carts were the preferred modes of transport—all worked harder than they were designed to be with their drivers unapologetic about taking up the whole street.

As the dusty dawn lifted, the silhouettes of the desert plateau became visible in the distance, showing how deep and sudden the Nile valley is. Up to the cliffs are palm trees, sugarcane, banana groves and housing; but above them is nothing but rock and sand stretching out to Libya in the west or the Red Sea in the east. They say that Egypt is the gift of the Nile—that it could not exist without it—and that's abundantly clear. Nearly the entire population lives within a few miles of its banks, and it's been that way since at least 3000 BCE.

Back then there was probably more of a system, though. The floodplain was wider on the eastern shore, so that's where most people settled. Because the sun also rose on that side, it became lore that it was the side of the living, while the tombs of ancient Egypt are all found on the west bank, where the sun sets. Abydos is on the west.

It's very possible you've never heard of the place. Abydos lacks the wow factor of the Pyramids of Giza and the density of temples and tombs that makes Luxor essentially an open-air museum. It's also in the absolute dust dune of nowhere. Its biggest draw is the temple of Seti I, commissioned by Seti himself around 1280 BCE and completed by his son, Ramesses II—both among the greatest kings Egypt ever saw (Ramesses lived to over ninety, reigned for sixty-six years and had at least eighty-eight children). The temple has two of the most incredible hieroglyphics ever found—one in the roof that looks a lot like a helicopter (and has been the source of much wildly inaccurate time-travel-based speculation); and the Abydos King List, a corridor upon which ancient scribes painstakingly carved out the unique emblems of all the Egyptian kings Ramesses considered legitimate (despite the role of pharaoh being God-given, it seems the priests and royal families had plenty of say too). It's a dizzying work of art, and its epic span is too big to take in even with your back against the opposite wall. The list stretches two millennia, right back to the man who united Egypt and laid the ground for everything that came after.

His name was Narmer. Or maybe Menes. Probably both. Egyptian kings get a little hazy toward the start because they had both royal names and civilian names: Menes appears on the King List, but Narmer is credited with the military conquest of the south over the north. The fact they seem to be contemporary suggests they were one and the same. Whatever his name, this man was more than an accomplished warrior. He was a visionary who innately understood what was needed to unite and rule such a huge swathe of land: an understanding he passed on to his descendants. Ancient Egypt was the first nation-state in humanity's history, and one that—save for some pretty violent wobbles—lasted more than 3,000 years. Narmer's approach was based on three things that the pharaohs (and indeed all dictators) have relied upon since: authority, awe and propaganda. The brewery at Abydos accomplished all three.

At *Gunpoint*

Ghada and I had just finished touring the Temple of Seti, and were blinking in the sunlight wondering what to do next. I'd spent two years chasing down the field director at Abydos, Dr. Matthew Adams of New York University, sending so many emails I risked a restraining order. Every time he replied he was as excitable and interested in this book as anyone I've met, but as a world-leading archaeologist, replies were few and far between. We'd managed a Zoom call, but what I really wanted was to visit the site—to see and hear everything firsthand. At the end of our call he said it was perfectly possible, but then went radio silent again.

And so I threw caution to the wind, estimating when he'd be back in Egypt and booking some eye-wateringly expensive flights. Just days later, he emailed to say the brewery would not be dug up that season due to the proximity of war in Gaza. Perhaps I should have given up at that point, but I had a very expensive air ticket and a very cheap hotel booked. When I explained this to his colleague Dr. Wendy Doyon (who also must have considered legal action after all the Instagram messages I sent her), she was adamant we should still meet if I got on the plane.

Quite *where* we would meet was the mystery Ghada and I were trying to solve, standing at the back of Seti's temple. Abydos is not a small archaeological site, and with phone signal letting me down she approached a heavily armed guard to see if any American archaeologists happened to be around the corner. Incredibly, he nodded and said he'd take me. Ghada decided to go for a coffee at the site café and leave me to it, so I trotted off with my new machine-gun-toting friend literally, directly and unabashedly into the desert.

As we walked, newspaper reports of my demise started writing themselves in my head: "YouTuber lost in desert: parents

in de-Nile." After five minutes of dusty hiking and faltering
conversation we reached an impressive-looking dig. Every face
looked up in surprise save one, who was clearly the manager.
Unfortunately that man was not Dr. Matthew Adams. He explained that Matthew was, in fact, about a mile or two farther
into the desert. I looked hopefully (but nervously) at the policeman, who mimed driving a car.

Back we trudged to the Temple of Seti, and having tipped him
for the effort I headed back inside to find Ghada. On my way I
noticed a carving of a man offering wheat and grapes to a god
and, as anyone would, stopped to take copious photos and videos
for social. While doing so I became aware I was being watched.

"Hello," the man said.

My brain went into overdrive. What rule had I broken, what
convention had I forgotten—was it because I was filming? In
classic British fashion, I pretended I hadn't heard.

"You are looking for Mr. Adams?"

My poker face faltered.

"He called me. My colleague Ahmed can take you to him
now."

I cast my eyes about for Ghada. Had word got around that
there was a bearded white guy you could walk into the desert
for five minutes, turn around and get a tip?

"I am the director for the archaeological site of Abydos," he
added, holding out a hand for me to shake. I felt a little shame
creep up my neck as I took his hand and introduced myself.

We met Ahmed outside, and flanked by another machine-
gun-laden policeman headed to the café, where a surprised-
looking Ghada must have wondered what on earth I'd done.
Soon we were back in Gerges's car, thudding and squeezing our
way through modern Abydos to the northern part of the site.

On the edge of town, the desert dunes started suddenly and
Gerges was unable to go any farther. Ahmed, the policeman and

I climbed out of the car and started walking toward the horizon again. While we hiked, Ahmed explained what he did at Abydos, most recently helping the American team identify the various bones left at the temples. As he did so he pointed at a white protrusion in the ground.

"There's one," he said, brushing the sand away. "Human." The policeman gave a start.

I clocked another one, clearly the ball of a hip joint, and picked it up.

"Yes!" he cried, taking it, and placing it at his hip and then in his pocket. The policeman was wide-eyed, on the verge of saying something.

"Very old," Ahmed said reassuringly, in English so I got the joke.

We crested a dune and finally something I recognized came into view: a huge mud brick ruin with gently sloping walls. The Shunet El Zebib is a funerary temple—essentially a place people could visit to worship and mourn a dead king (the tombs themselves were only for the dead). It was built during the king's reign and, once complete, offerings would be made during epic rituals, with all the gifts going on to the next life to await the king.

"I'm at the temple!" I messaged Wendy excitedly, hoping for signal.

"Which temple?!" came the exasperated reply, and I realized what a shockingly stupid thing this is to write in a place like Egypt.

After some back-and-forth Wendy told us to stay put, which we did next to a car-sized pile of gray pottery shards. I'd barely registered them when two people came over the brow of a dune.

"In real life, at last!" said Matthew, grasping my hand and launching straight into his favorite topic: how beer built ancient Egypt.

Beer and Brick

Shunet El Zebib is the only ancient funerary temple left standing (and it's had a lot of help), but it's far from the only one at Abydos. In fact, where we were standing is arguably the most sacred and important funerary site in the ancient world. While the tombs in the nearby cliffs are nothing compared to those at the Valley of the Kings in Luxor, nowhere else are the funerary temples so close together or so old. Somewhere underneath our feet was Narmer's, perhaps the first of its kind. His was built around 3100 BCE, and similar ones were built here for centuries— Shunet El Zebib was built for King Khasekhemwy and might be the youngest, around 2700 BCE.

Clearly, a funerary temple built and used for rituals long before the death of a monarch has more of a role to play than simple mourning. It was part of Narmer's plan to amaze his subjects; to convince them that he was not only king but a demideity capable of feats (and worthy of worship) equivalent to that of the gods. The rituals held here would have shocked the common person with their opulence, decadence, scale and—in modern terms—wastefulness. The bones of hundreds of courtiers sacrificed to go with their rulers to the afterlife have been found around the site, alongside enormous boats that were buried here (despite the site being 6 miles from the Nile). If that seems incredible, it's nothing compared to the amount of beer that would have passed through.

Just like in Mesopotamia and many other parts of the world by Narmer's time, beer was a staple food in Egypt. Pretty much every Egyptian king's tomb or temple references beer and bread being taken to the afterlife, and even common people were often buried with a supply of booze for the great house party in the sky. But the scale at which it was offered here, at the start of civilization and the heart of Egypt's funerary tradition, is so epic as to be inconceivable.

"It really is beyond belief, but the archaeology is what it is and we need to make sense of it," says Matthew. "I never expected to be a beer guy, but as part of my work to understand these early kings I knew we needed to look at this site."

The archaeology he's referring to is the thing buried a few hundred yards away: a brewery so vast that it leaves all but the biggest modern breweries in the shade. It takes the form of eight huge, hollow structures, each over 32 yards long. Between the walls of each are wedged the remains of forty clay vats that each contained a total of 1,500 or 1,900 gallons—meaning a batch capacity across all eight structures of around 13,200 gallons (about 88,000 pints). These vats would have been filled with Nile water and emmer wheat, a local variety that grew in the fertile valley. Wood was fed through holes in the outer walls, then lit before a roof was fitted and the fire was left to go out over many hours. The heat killed bacteria and caused the chemical reaction that releases the sugars, then the yeast (wild or placed by a brewer, we don't know yet) would get to work in the warmth of the afterglow. Once fermented, the beer was put into large pots with pointed ends that could stand up in the sand, and stoppered with mud. It was the shards of these dark pots that I stood next to while waiting for Matthew and Wendy. Thousands upon thousands of shards, found pretty much in that spot, 5,000 years after they were tossed out.

Despite what it sounds like, most Egyptian beer was made at home by the common people: industrial-scale brewing was rare this early in human history. There are a few Egyptian breweries that predate Abydos, but none are even close to its scale, and its size isn't even the most remarkable thing about it. While several mounds of serving pottery were dug up, just one single drinking cup has been discovered so far. It was found by Matthew himself in one of the brewing vats, and must have been dropped by a brewer who was sampling the beer.

"It was a wonderful moment," says Matthew. "I held that

cup in my hand and thought about the person who dropped it 5,000 years ago, holding it the same way to see if the beer met his expectations."

What this implies is that, unless people were necking it straight from the pots, no one was actually drinking this beer. So what was happening to it? Matthew's theory is one of elimination: the beer must have been an offering in the temples. He believes it was poured onto the ground where it would await the king in the afterlife, as part of the epic funerary rituals.

If that sounds like a waste, it's worth remembering how devout the ancient Egyptians were: for them the afterlife was a certainty, which is partly why archaeologists found no obvious evidence of struggle in the remains of the sacrificed courtiers. But these rituals had a second purpose—one for this life. That purpose was shock and awe. Consider how the tiny pots of beer made by Egyptian commoners at home would have compared to this giant brewery making 88,000 pints at a time. The smoke must have been visible for miles when it was lit, and the beer must have flooded the temple when it was poured out. Then remember the supply chain—the tons of wheat that would have been required as well as the thousands of workers and acres of land to produce it; the water that would have been carried from the Nile or a canal dug specifically to reach the brewery; and finally the epic fires fueled by wood, which was in very short supply in this fledgling desert nation. Tests of the residues in the beer jars show that the beer was flavored with anise and pomegranate—expensive and heady ingredients. There's no doubt that this brewery, and the tales of it that would have spread up and down the Nile, was created to impress upon Narmer's disparate people how powerful their leader was.

"They are using beer to define the nature of kingship," says Matthew, his voice breaking a little as he hammers the point home. "To demonstrate materially that the king operates at a superhuman level; to say, 'This is what I am capable of. Look on my works, ye mighty, and despair!'"

We see similar tactics in all kinds of ancient and modern dictatorships, and we'll discuss a few in this book (particularly the Wittelsbachs of Bavaria), but the Egyptians were the early masters of it, and Narmer its originator. The importance of the brewery in terms of creating authority should not be understated. It was one of the first publicly funded buildings in Egypt, and the incredible amount of administration, labor and resources required is seen by some academics—most notably Matthew—as a direct inspiration for all the nation's great architectural works.

"You can draw a direct line from the brewery through to the Pyramids of Giza," says Matthew. "Exactly the same skill set made the pyramids possible just a few generations later: logistics, labor mobilization, marshaling of resources and administrative capacity."

Those at Giza were not the first, of course. It started with the step pyramid of the Pharaoh Djoser, which was built around 300 years after the brewery at Abydos and bears a striking resemblance to the Shunet El Zebib. Djoser's is only 74.1 yards tall and layered like a wedding cake, but the straight-sided pyramid slowly came to be as techniques improved—culminating in the Great Pyramid of Giza around 2570 BCE. This one, built as a tomb for Pharaoh Khufu, reached 160 yards and was the tallest building on earth until the Eiffel Tower was finished in 1889. In *The Rise and Fall of Ancient Egypt*, historian Toby Wilkinson estimates that if construction began on the day Khufu took the throne, a stone would have been laid, on average, every two minutes for it to be finished by his death. The scale—and cost—of this logistical and human endeavor is hard to comprehend. As we tried to do so, stood looking at the comparatively simple Shunet El Zebib, Matt reminded me, "It was the need for beer that created that skill and infrastructure."

It paid for it too. You see, Egyptian brewing didn't just serve as a model for big projects or historic inspiration—like in Mesopotamia it literally fueled the labor force of these great public works. There was no currency in ancient Egypt until the Greeks came along in the third century BCE, so until then wages were paid in what those workers needed—namely clothing, bread and beer. The laborers working on the Great Pyramid were given roughly ten pints of weak beer a day to slake their extreme thirst and give them the calories to keep working. We know this because the Egyptians kept records of the costs, and because the tombs of some workers who died during construction were recently discovered, and all of them had beer for the afterlife.

"In all Egyptian history there are two needs that are universal: bread and beer," explains Matthew. "They are named again and again and again in Egyptian texts, but also in religious terms: what the gods need, what your king needs, what your dead relatives need in the next life."

Without brewing as an engineering project and architectural challenge, and without beer as currency and part of the daily diet, it's possible the pyramids may have never been built. Barely a century after the Great Pyramid was completed, it was decided that tombs were safer and easier if built underground, and incredible burial systems such as the Valley of the Kings were created. At these later sites the Abydos brewery's impact feels less significant, but it can still be seen in both the hieroglyphics on the sarcophagi and the monumental effort and administration involved. Abydos may be one of the oldest archaeological sites of ancient Egypt, but it is at the cutting edge of academic research on the topic thanks to the brewery and its associated temples. It is the place where what we know as ancient Egyptian culture began. If you want to understand how the most advanced and famous ancient civilization came together, you now have to consider that beer was at the heart of it—both practically and philosophically.

"It had this workaday aspect but it also had this deep, deep cultural value that it doesn't have in the modern world, where people don't give it that respect," says Matthew.

After we parted in the dusty desert and I headed back to find a presumably half-baked Gerges, I reflected on how beer's place in the world today compares with that of ancient Egypt. Many Indigenous people in Eastern Africa and South America still rely on beer as a foodstuff, but in the developed world it's purely for pleasure. I don't think that diminishes its importance, and hopefully you'll agree by the end of this book, but Matthew's on the money in at least one respect: the religious element of beer is all but gone.

There is, however, one small religious sect that still understands the fundamental importance of beer, and indeed relies on it as much as the ancient Egyptians. Oh, and while most of their breweries would pale in comparison to the one in Abydos, they happen to make some of the best beer in the world.

Blessed Beer

Throughout history, science has slowly eroded the idea of religious intervention or significance in what humans experience. The ancient Egyptians believed the sun was a god called Ra, who was responsible for all life. We now know it's an 864,000-mile-wide hydrogen and helium fireball, formed as a solar nebula collapsed on itself around 4.6 billion years ago. It's still responsible for all life on earth, but its spiritual element is somewhat diminished by the hard facts we've discovered.

The same has proven true for the things humans make, and beer is no different. Over several thousand years we came to realize that we had a lot more control over brewing than we'd given ourselves credit for.

If we head north from Egypt, or west from Israel, and into

Europe (which is the way civilization spread), we see beer and brewing blossom and develop faster than ever—whichever god was presiding over it. When we picture ancient Greece we are more likely to think of wine, but we know they were germinating then kiln-drying wheat and barley to brew beer as early as 2100 BCE thanks to discoveries at Argissa, about an hour south of Mount Olympus. Images from pottery and the presence of several stone tools implies that the process had come a long way even from Narmer's time.

The Romans weren't famous for brewing either, but Pliny the Elder (CE 23–79) describes it happening in Britain, France and Spain, while Tacitus calls beer "horrible" somewhere between CE 56 and 120. When they retreated from northern Europe a few hundred years later, brewing proliferated in homes across Britain, Belgium and Germany. In Anglo-Saxon England, alewives—that is, women making beer in the kitchen alongside cooking food—made most of the beer. Those that were most adept at it would even tie a branch to a pole outside their home to let friends and potential buyers know good beer was available. This is the origin of the British public house, and would have had everything to do with the skill and equipment of the brewer and little to do with rituals, blessings and faith.

But while the gods' responsibility for making it faded, the practical link between beer and religion took longer to break—particularly in Christian regions. This was because beer was so vital to the nourishment and survival of the population that Christians were allowed to drink it during religious fasting. Perhaps just as importantly, however, religious establishments needed to fund themselves.

Aside from the women making it at home on their stoves, the other main source of beer in Middle Ages Europe were the monks who made it for themselves and the local community.

Perhaps significantly, the roots of monasticism are actually found in Egypt, which largely converted to Christianity during its time under the Roman Empire. Some earlier converts had started to withdraw from society to dedicate themselves to the pursuit of holiness, and the most famous of these was St. Anthony of Egypt (c. CE 251–356), who attracted a great number of followers through his personal example of simple living and praying. A biography of his life is credited with spreading the concept of religious enclaves, and today he's regarded as the Father of Monasticism.

I'm not sure whether he was brewing during his time in the desert, but beer production became a central part of all denominations of monasteries. That was handy because at their peak, monasteries were huge communities, with some employing dozens or even hundreds of laypeople to keep the place running and produce things that could be sold. Along with things like cheese and cloth, beer production helped fund and shape Christianity right up until the Reformation in the UK and later revolutions in mainland Europe.

Many of the world's oldest surviving breweries have roots in monasticism, including the oldest of them all, Bavaria's Weihenstephan, which was supposedly brewing in 1040 and likely long before that too. Selling beer would have helped feed the monks and doubled as a recruitment and conversion tool by bringing people in for feast days to give the monks a chance at some good old-fashioned Bible-thumping. While it was wine that was featured in Jesus's miracles and the Last Supper, beer still features in the Bible—as you'd expect, given the book is mostly based in Israel and Palestine, so near to where we suspect brewing was invented. In Proverbs 31 its nutritional value is implied: "Let beer be for those who are perishing," and that's certainly how some of it would have been used. The poor and sick were often given free beer at the monastery gates, as monks were required to help pilgrims and those in need.

For the next thousand years or so, monasteries were the biggest beer factories in Europe. In fact, there was hardly any commercial brewing outside of them until around the twelfth century. So it was housewives and monks who developed beer from Abydos's wild pomegranate wheat ales to what we might start to recognize as beer today. That's in part because the climate of Europe offered up better brewing ingredients—barley is far superior for brewing owing to the sugars being more easily extractable and the husk acting as a filter in the mash. Meanwhile hops, which add bitterness and help prevent bacterial infections, almost exclusively grow at more temperate latitudes. Their first recorded use in beer is found in the writings of Abbot Adalhard of the Benedictine monastery of Corbie in France around CE 822. According to beer historian Martyn Cornell, their preservative qualities were certainly known by CE 1150, when mystic and healer Abbess Hildegard of Bingen wrote that "as a result of [a hop's] own bitterness it keeps some putrefactions from drinks." She wasn't much of a fan though, saying the hop also "makes the soul of man sad, and weighs down his inner organs." We've all had that kind of hangover, to be fair.

Most monastic breweries remained small, in keeping with the needs of the monks and their local people, but as beer moved from a kitchen endeavor to a cottage industry to a commercial opportunity, some grew spectacularly and some are still household names—Belgium's Leffe (founded by the monks of Abbaye Notre-Dame de Leffe in Belgium in 1240) and Bavaria's Paulaner (founded by Munich's Paulaner Order of mendicant friars in 1634) are perhaps the best examples.

Eventually, however, almost all monastery breweries were closed or sold off as commercial businesses. This process was most stark in the UK, where they were closed and often destroyed swiftly during the Reformation—otherwise known as the most long-winded divorce litigation ever. As a result, beer professionalized pretty rapidly in England from the 1600s onward, giving it the jump on nations that took a little longer to secularize their brewing. We'll see the positive impact of that later in this book, but while the Reformation reinforced the connection between the English church and state, it utterly divorced church and beer. Strangely for an atheist, that makes me just a little sad.

It's a Trap(pist)

Sometimes I think if Henry VIII had sat down and really thought about the devastation he was about to wreak on Britain's brewing—and indeed cheesemaking industries because monks love making cheese, too—he might have tried harder to make it work with his first wife.

Despite his efforts, however, there are some monasteries still brewing in the UK today. In fact, around the world, dozens of them still brew and hundreds more contract out the work to lay breweries and take a little of the profit in return.

The most famous of those still brewing are the Trappist breweries, a club so exclusive they created a special badge in the late 1990s to stop people trading off its holy name. To qualify, a monastery must be a member of the Order of Cistercians of the Strict Observance—otherwise known as a Trappist monastery—of which there are more than 160 around the world. This order puts particular emphasis on the balance between manual work and worship, which means most of them still produce goods for sale like beer, cheese, bread and in one rather morbid case, coffins. For something to be considered an authentic Trappist product, it must be made within the monastery walls under the supervision of the monks, with all profits going to the upkeep of the monastery or good causes. That whittles the list of Trappist breweries down to thirteen—one each in the UK, Austria, France, Italy and Spain, with two in the Netherlands and six in Belgium (sadly America's only entry stopped brewing in 2022).

These thirteen breweries hold a remarkable sway over the beer geek psyche. For a start, they're the origin of a specific family of beers—the Belgian-style Single, Dubbel, Tripel and Quadrupel. They all have their intricate and much debated histories, but in modern times the Single is a nourishing, sensible-strength blond often drunk by the monks themselves; the Dubbel is a dark, raisiny beer at around 7% ABV; the Tripel is a dry, fruity and blond beer a few percent bigger; while the Quadrupel is the biggest of them all in flavor and alcohol, and is essentially a 10% or so version of the Dubbel.

Perhaps the most famous among these beers is Westmalle Tripel. Made at Westmalle Abbey near Antwerp, it's known as the Mother of Tripels because all strong Belgian blond ales that came after it are essentially an homage. It was first brewed in 1934 to celebrate an expansion of the brewery, and allegedly to capitalize on the rising popularity of pale 5% ABV lagers, making it both wildly inappropriate at 9.5% and about fifty years behind the curve. It is, however, one of Belgium's most-loved beers, with rich notes of brioche, banana, clove and pear, all of which bounce out of the traditional chalice glass thanks to champagnelike bubbles.

On top of these now much-copied traditional beers, some Trappist breweries make other styles—a few of which are unlike anything else in the world. England's Mount St. Bernard makes Tynt Meadow, which is somewhere between a strong British Bitter and a Belgian Dubbel—being dry, earthy, fruity and just a little boozy. It's Orval that receives the most reverence from beer geeks, however. Made at Abbaye d'Orval in the farthest southeast region of Belgium, it's an entirely unique beer that owes as much to England as it does to its home nation. It's a Pale Ale that gets a hefty dose of hops after fermentation, an old British technique that helps the beer avoid infection if it's stored for a long time. It was used particularly for the India Pale Ales that were sent to homesick officers and bureaucrats in India during the eighteenth and nineteenth centuries. Orval is reconditioned in the bottle with an unusual yeast called Brettanomyces, also common in historic British ales. This slow-acting yeast adds flavors of scrumpy cider to the beer, creating a complex combination of orange peel, caramel and autumn farmyards. It is perhaps the closest thing we have to a historic English IPA still being brewed today, but just happens to be made by some monks on the French-Belgian border.

Westmalle Tripel and Orval are considered among the greatest beers in the world, and their monasteries have become pilgrimages for both Christians and beer worshippers. I've been to both a few times, but the Trappist brewery I've visited most overshadows the reputation of Orval and Westmalle. Like all beer geeks its name gets my pulse quickening, not just because the beer is as hard to get hold of as it is delicious, but because it says so much about modern civilization.

The Best Beer in the World

If you've never been to Westvleteren, the brewery arm of Belgium's St. Sixtus Abbey, I should warn you that its location couldn't contrast more with its reputation. I'm sure the monastery and brewery itself are beautiful, but that's all walled off to normal people. Instead, we must make do with the rather nineties-looking café, In de Vrede, which is simultaneously a beer geek paradise and a refectory for West Flanders pensioners.

On my last visit in the summer of 2023, I took my YouTube cohost Brad Evans (or rather he took me, because he was the designated driver). When he saw not one but two people in wheelchairs headed for the café, he turned to me seriously and said, "Do you think they're here to be healed?" I had to explain that this just was the average clientele for a Trappist café, and all they wanted from God that day was a croque monsieur and an accessible toilet. While most of the customer base is past

sixty, it's peppered with overexcited nerds and American tourists who are less interested in glorified toasties and more in the
beer menu. One of the American tourists we walked past on
the way to our seat was receiving his first beer and saying to
his buddy, "I literally cannot believe we're here after all these
years." It was clearly a bucket list tick for him, and having been
in that thrilling position just a few years before, I made a note
to raise a glass to him.

Westvleteren makes three beers: a 5.8% Blond that's all banana, clove, pepper and white bread; an 8% Dubbel that's jet-
black with roasty coffee, date-y sweetness and a hoppy bite; and
a 10.8% Quad with caramel, licorice and herbal savoriness. My
personal favorite is the Dubbel, but the Quad is often touted as
the best beer in the world—wonderful news if you're a commercial brewer, but a real pain if you're a monk…as we'll see.

Considering where it ends up, the story of this monastery has
the most understated beginnings. I'm going to take you right
through its history because it shows how vital beer was to monastic and rural life, as well as the incredible role these brewer-
monasteries played throughout Europe.

First, though, the humble beginning. In 1610 a few hermits
settled in a run-down church that was being used as a timber
store. After five years they decided to form a monastery and
were granted permission by the owner of the church in 1630.
Between then and 1784 it was home to ninety-four monks, but
it was torn down that year as part of Holy Roman Emperor Joseph II's war against monasteries that did not educate, work the
land or tend to the sick. Only ruins of this place remain, around
a mile from the current abbey, but I mention it because on the
plans of the monastery there was a brewery.

Just over thirty years later, another hermit shows up. This time
it's a man called Joannes-Baptista Victoor, whose stepson had
come to own the land. Victoor had ambitions to set up a church
and school there, though it's unclear if he did anything about

it until 1831, when four monks fled to the area from a Trappist monastery just south of the French border, after the prior fell out with a bishop. These monks decided to set up a monastery there, but sadly Victoor died before it was constructed.

Despite donations from laypeople and Westmalle Abbey, St. Sixtus was constantly on the verge of bankruptcy. Construction was obviously the biggest cost, but as a religious entity they were traditionally required to supply beer to their laborers, too. Buying enough beer turned out to be so expensive that in 1838 they bought their own brew kit. Initially the monks made a table beer of scarcely 1% ABV, but a second brewery was installed in the 1870s to make full-strength ale, and shortly after it was decided to sell the beer externally to raise more funds.

The monastery, now upgraded to an abbey rather than a priory, continued to grow. As the only Belgian monastery not occupied by the Germans during the First World War, it housed refugees and Allied soldiers throughout, yet kept its function the same and even expanded the brewery a few years later. By the outbreak of the Second World War, there were twelve laypeople working in the brewery, making four different beers and delivering them throughout Belgium on a brand-new truck. They even grew their own hops.

All that came to an abrupt end, however. In 1945, Abbot Gerardus decreed that the success of the brewery had reduced the "zeal for manual work" among the monks, and brought them too close to the "pernicious" secular world. He shut down the commercial operation, leaving the brewery limited to serving the monks, other monasteries and those who visited. He then licensed out the recipes and name to a local cheesemaker, who brewed Westvleteren beers for forty years under a name Belgian beer lovers might recognize—St. Bernardus Brewery.

Even with the contract brewery serving the wider population, St. Sixtus kept running out of beer at its own gates. The tradition of buying beer from the monastery, and perhaps locals wanting to support a historic location, was clearly a powerful draw. It can't have been the beer itself, because the monastery batches were subject to many infections and issues—so much so that a brewer from Westmalle was sent to modernize the brewery and its processes in 1976. Despite some complaints from locals about the beer no longer being "real beer made the old way," a tech upgrade and automation followed a few years later. That was well-timed, because legal fights around the use of the term *Trappist* meant the Cistercian movement was looking to introduce the Trappist badge. The St. Sixtus monks therefore ended their contract with St. Bernardus—nearly taking that business down in the process—and took all production in-house, where it remains today.

In an interesting twist, the closest beer to Westvleteren's Quadrupel (known as the 12) of old is now actually the St. Bernardus version, called Abt 12. When the secular brewery lost its contract, it just kept brewing the same beers under its own name, using the same ingredients and most importantly the same yeast it always had. The monks at St. Sixtus, however, didn't have the facilities to look after their own house strain, so switched to using Westmalle's. I've tasted both side-by-side on several occasions, and Westvleteren is thinner, less fruity and more herbal. As it ages it takes on more caramel and licorice, while St. Bernardus's is rich and full, with a big sherry note coming out after a few years. My favorite is probably the latter, but it's the monks' version that, to everyone's surprise, went viral.

Dubbel Trouble

In 2005, a few hundred users of a niche beer review website called RateBeer voted Westvleteren 12 the best beer in the world. The result was posted online for all to see, and followed by a host of news reports around the world, invariably wondering why monks made beer and how this monastery outside a Belgian village with an unpronounceable name could possibly make the best one.

According to Belgian beer historian Jef Van den Steen, the queues to buy a case from the brewery were miles long on the following days, and the police struggled to cope with the chaos. The monks responded by installing an ordering hotline and insisting people call ahead to book collection, which freed up the roads but sent the local telephone exchange into meltdown. The government had to intervene and sort a national number for the brewery, which at its peak received 100,000 phone calls for just sixty collection slots per day.

These days you can book a slot online and pick it up by car, or grab a six-pack of whatever's available at the gift shop in the café. The beer's no longer considered the best in the world—the tastes of online beer raters have moved on from Belgian Quads to barrel-aged Imperial Stouts, and the title is currently owned by Toppling Goliath Brewery out of Iowa, of all places—but it's treated with hushed reverence by anyone who loves Belgian beer, and still funds the monks' way of life. In 2012, the abbey needed to renovate its buildings, so for one time only the monks decided to cash in on its fame and brew extra beer for export. Gift packs were sent across the Atlantic for sale, causing incredible excitement as people as far away as the west coast of the US had a chance to get their hands on it. Predictably, the gray market for these packs also flourished. Westvleteren's hype still echoes about the beer geek world like whispers in church.

Back at the café, we experienced as busy a lunch service as you'll ever see in a village café. Even though it was my fourth visit I was surprised by how nonchalant the staff are about the beers they serve. The bottles are cracked open before they arrive at the table (presumably to stop people taking them away) and plonked down unceremoniously for you to pour yourself. If that sounds like I'm being snobbish, this is in a country where the right glass, the right pour and the right ambience are so important that its beer café culture is UNESCO-protected. At Westvleteren there seems to be a conscious effort to ground the people and the beer; to remove the mystique. You can even get an ice cream sundae made with Westvleteren 12 and, as I tucked in, I wondered if the monks ever order one.

After trying all three beers I suggested walking them off with a stroll around the monastery walls. Ambling slowly as the alcohol and August heat took their toll, I noticed a small white brick in the run of red. I crossed the road to look closer and found it was mirrored, perhaps a two-way mirror allowing the monks to look out unseen. I like to think about how in 2005 they might have gathered to watch the storm of interest they'd accidentally created, through nothing more than brewing diligence and a hint of scarcity marketing.

A lot has changed for the monks of St. Sixtus. After centuries of using beer to welcome people to the Christian fold and feed the hungry, people now book slots on websites and roll up to parking bays controlled by traffic lights. Everyone who pulls up and puts a case in their car must be aware that they're yards from a historic monastery, but to most of them that fact will just be an anecdote for their friends. The spiritual link has long since broken—I bet most wouldn't even know the abbey itself isn't called Westvleteren.

Even so, Trappist breweries are effectively the last modern example of beer's close link to religion, a relationship that can be traced back to the Ice Age. I don't think it's an exaggeration to say that one helped build the other. If I could sum up beer's importance to the human world for their first 11,000 years together, it's as sustenance and a form of worship—arguably the two most important things in an ancient civilization.

That influence, of course, faded as technology and religion evolved. Despite their outsized reputation it's hard to claim that monastic brewing has had much impact beyond the eighteenth century, aside from giving names to the commercial breweries that took over. Still, they set the stage for the most important phase in both beer brewing and humanity, a story we'll start in a place that literally means *where the monks are*: Munich.

Chapter 2

Science

Or how beer spurred us on to new technological heights

What do the fridge, the pH scale, St. Pancras Station, the fan oven and antiseptics have in common? They were all conceived either by brewers, for brewers, because of brewers, or all three.

As we've seen, for the first few thousand years, humans thought beer-making was in the hands of the gods. It was considered beyond our mortal realm and to be honest, I've had similar thoughts while trying to brew my own. The implication for historic brewers, however, was that while humans could make a tweak here or there, success was down to a favor from a deity.

As we learned more about the world and the process, however, we came to realize just how much control we had. There's a strong argument for the idea that brewing was humanity's first engineering project, and it's absolutely one of the first examples of humans applying any kind of practical, scientific knowledge to a natural process—essentially bioengineering.

We saw several of these early feats of engineering at Abydos, with technology that would have impressed the Romans nearly 3,000 years later. Beer had its influence on all kinds of early, day-to-day inventions, from the tools and techniques used in farming to the shape of ancient pottery. But there is a particular era in human history where the scientific advances that came out of the beer world had a profound impact on how we live (and indeed whether we live) today. In this remarkable period from around 1840 to 1890, brewers essentially completed the work of their ancestors in wrestling control of fermentation away from nature, and in doing so changed modern life forever. Without spoiling too much, and trying to avoid hyperbole, the brewers and engineers in this period provided some of the biggest breakthroughs in biology, physics and chemistry. They were responsible for advancements in technology and food production, revolutions in large-scale construction, and ultimately laying the foundations of modern medicine.

Obviously that was the work of quite a few people, but it starts with the precocious son of a brewmaster who owned the smallest brewery in a town of just 40,000 people.

This Is Spaten

Munich is beer town, almost literally. Its history is rooted in monasticism, and as we've learned, where there are monks there is usually beer. Their influence has made Munich one of the best cities in the world to go drinking: there's even a brewery in the airport for God's sake.

On a bleak January afternoon in 2023, I didn't have time for a cheeky security-side pint, though. I'd ambitiously booked a tour of Spaten Brewing just a few hours after landing, and was hoping the fact that there was no on-site taproom didn't mean I'd wait hours for my first beer.

Things didn't look good on my arrival at the very industrial-looking entrance gate, around the back from Munich's main train station. Spaten is, tragically, something of a mothball brand. It doesn't have its own brewery, instead sharing it with another historic Munich brand, Löwenbräu, and wheat beer powerhouse Franziskaner. All three are owned by the world's biggest brewing company, AB InBev, and aren't really seen in the wild in Munich. In fact, outside of Oktoberfest you'll struggle

THE MEANING OF BEER

to find Spaten anywhere, which is an incredible shame because the beer's still pretty good and Spaten is arguably the most important brewery to have ever existed.

The front gate, however, is a little understated—in fact it's just a goods entrance. Unsurprisingly, the security guard didn't offer me a beer, but I had a feeling my guide Martin Wittal was going to. He had that twinkle in his eye; the look of a man who knows a cold lager isn't far away. We shook hands and he beckoned me into a tiny wood-paneled elevator. It took a few floors for me to realize that we were climbing the main tower, a former grain silo that looms over this part of central Munich. The rickety elevator shook to a halt and opened on a boardroom with glass windows on three walls. We were at the top, looking out across the city...and there was a bar in the corner. Martin poured me a crisp, pale beer with a healthy two-inch head, and we sat down.

"I've brought the book," he says, pointing to a biblical tome called *Die Spaten-Brauerei* that I'd skimmed numerous times, but struggled with due to the fact that it's in German. "I don't know how much you already know."

I'd translated enough by pestering friends, rinsing Google Translate and scratching together my twelfth-grade German to learn quite a lot about Spaten—but what I knew wasn't the issue, it was what I believed. The stories and the importance attached to them are so mind-bending that the fact it isn't the stuff of tired pub quizzes everywhere makes me doubt them entirely.

Just to add to the legend, the early history of Spaten is foggy. It can be traced back as far as 1397, but the story really begins in 1807, when the brewery was bought by a man called Gabriel Sedlmayr I. Back then, Spaten was the smallest of Munich's fifty-two breweries, though Sedlmayr was not a small name. He was a former brewmaster at Hofbräuhaus, owned by the Bavarian royal family and arguably the second-most important brewery ever (we'll get to that in the next chapter). He turned Spaten's fortunes around, brewing beautiful dark beers that were cold-stored (or *lagered*) to become as delicious as any in the city. Under his ownership the lager brewery became the third largest in barely a decade, yet the most important thing he did in that time was have a son, unhelpfully also named Gabriel Sedlmayr (II).

Gabriel Junior, as we'll call him, was as talented as his father, albeit one of those people who talks about their gap year a bit *too* much. To be fair to him his gap year was more productive than most: as part of his Master Diploma in brewing, he went on a European brewery tour, of which his father resignedly said, "Do what you like if you think you can derive something of commercial value from it." He visited countless countries in the early 1830s, but it was his trip to the UK with his best gap-year friend Anton Dreher (a brewer from Austria) that has resonated through history.

At that time, the UK was the world's brewing powerhouse. The incredible popularity of the dark, smoky Porter beer at home, strong (or *Stout*) Porters in the Baltic and Russian states, and demand from around the empire had created several of the world's biggest breweries, mostly focused in London and Burton-on-Trent. Gabriel Junior and Dreher were on a mission to find out how these beers were proving so popular, and would go to any lengths to find out. One of those lengths was a hollow walking stick, with which they secretly scooped up samples to analyze back at their hotel. Despite their beery espionage, they also made some great friends among the founders of the breweries they visited, many of whom were happy to share their expertise and even gifted them equipment.

What Gabriel Junior and Dreher saw must have been awe-inspiring; it was brewing on a scale they had never experienced, with technology to match.

One great invention they saw was actually made by an HMRC Excise officer called Benjamin Sikes, in a bid to tax these huge breweries effectively. While hydrometers, which measure the density of a liquid, had been around since the time of ancient Greece, Sikes perfected one to measure the sugar in beer. This was an important invention, because taking a measurement before and after fermentation allowed brewers to calculate exactly how much alcohol was in their beer.

Sikes used this to tax breweries according to that alcohol level, so while the brewer might not be too pleased to have a more accurate tax bill, he would have appreciated the ability to know how efficient his mashes and ferments were—and thus be able to experiment with different techniques and temperatures to get the most out of his malt. To do that, British brewers would have used a mercury thermometer, a gadget well known in Germany at the time, but not used by Munich breweries at all. Both these inventions amazed Gabriel Junior: brewing in Munich was still very much a qualitative endeavor—with brewers largely using *boiling* and *not boiling yet* as their temperature scale, and operating on an if-it-ain't-broke-don't-fix-it basis. Gabriel Junior brought both technologies back to his father, and suddenly Spaten was producing the most consistently delicious and efficient beer in Munich.

These two discoveries were overshadowed by another the pair made on their UK road trip, however. Until the mid-nineteenth century, pretty much all beer outside of the UK was a shade of dark brown, and by candlelight it was probably black. To get enough sugar from barley to brew, brewers needed to malt it, a process by which it is germinated and then dried—something that was traditionally done over an open fire. As anyone who's ever cooked a sausage on a barbecue will know, keeping the flames low and temperature even isn't easy, so much of the malt came out of Europe's kilns scorched and smoky. For better or worse, both the color and flavor of smoke were imparted into the final beer, making it smell like your clothes after a night around the campfire.

In the UK, however, brewers were doing it differently. As early as 1642 we know that some were using a refined coal called coke as fuel, which produced far less smoke and offered a more even heat. Around the same time, a series of patents were applied for by inventors of *indirect heat kilns*, in which the air was heated separately to the grain and then blown over it. The first was in 1635 by a Cornish lord called Sir Nicholas Halse, whose patent was "for the dryinge of mault and hops with seacole, turffe, or any other fewell, without touching of smoake."

Sir Halse seems a little eccentric, writing numerous letters to King James I and then Charles I advising them on their tax regime and foreign policy, despite having absolutely no experience in either field. He was, however, rather prescient about the impact of his invention. He claimed that his new kilning method would revolutionize several other industries and processes: "baking, boyling, roasting, starchinge, and dryinge of lynnen, all at one and the same tyme and with one fyre." Later versions of such indirect fire kilns did indeed go on to take over kitchens around the world—it's the principle behind the fan oven.

Now, these paler and less smoky malts were expensive to produce, so most breweries were still making (and selling millions of barrels of) Porter using cheaper grains when Sedlmayr and Dreher came to the UK. But some of the breweries they visited were making a name for themselves by making pale and remarkably clear beers with these new malts—breweries like Burton-on-Trent's Bass and Allsopp. These were the original India Pale Ales, a style we'll dig into later, and they opened Sedlmayr's and Dreher's eyes to the possibility of a paler, brighter and lighter style of beer on the continent.

On the return to their respective breweries, they began building what they called *British kilns* to produce their own pale malt. Both succeeded in creating a lighter, more consistent malt, which they put into use immediately. In Vienna, Dreher called his the um...Vienna lager, but in Munich, Spaten simply changed up the recipe for its Märzen, a style brewed in spring in huge quantities to ensure there was plenty of beer in the cellars over summer. The beer was such a hit at the 1841 Oktoberfest that it became a signature style mimicked by countless breweries around Bohemia.

Gabriel Senior sadly never saw the release of this beer. He died suddenly in 1839, leaving the brewery to his two sons. Gabriel Junior bought his brother Josef out and took the incredible modernization of his brewery to new heights—as he put it himself, he didn't want to leave any part of the brewing process to "chance." In 1844, Spaten became the first non-UK brewery to install a steam engine, and just under thirty years later he made his greatest contribution to the world by commissioning the world's first (viable compressed gas) fridge. You read that right. The first ever fridge was invented to keep beer cold—so next time someone asks why your food fridge is full of beer, ask them why their beer fridge is full of food.

It's Getting Cold in Here

The story is, inevitably, a little more complicated. Bavaria gets pretty warm in summer, but in a bizarre twist of nature, the local yeasts that fermented the region's beers were lager yeasts, a specific species that prefers to work at no more than 54°F.

This meant brewing stopped between April and September, because infections in the beer were too common. New beers still needed to be lagered, however, so those made in autumn, winter and spring were matured in cool, natural caves or man-made cellars beneath the breweries. Even this wasn't enough in summer though: laborers had to harvest ice from lakes, rivers and mountains during the winter and lug them down into the caves ready to maintain the cool temperatures. This was laborious and expensive work, with ever-growing demand and the hanging threat that if there was a warm winter, there might not be enough ice. Brewers had long looked for a solution, but while nature makes ice production look pretty easy, it was beyond human ingenuity. The idea of doing it on the scale that a commercial brewery would need was even more far-fetched.

That changed in the early nineteenth century, when scientists discovered how to liquefy gases, and found that evaporating them again cooled the air around them. Pretty quickly, entrepreneurial men began to play around with the idea. The problem was that these amateur fridges were incredibly dangerous, because they pressurized highly volatile gases: that is to say, liquids that boil and turn to gas at low temperatures. A clue to why you need to be careful with a volatile gas is in the name. Leaks were common in these machines, and if you breathed in some of the early gases used it might be the last thing you did. Imagine that, but in a machine cooling miles of cellars beneath a European capital, and you have the makings of an Age of Enlightenment Jerry Bruckheimer movie.

So the principle of refrigeration was established before Gabriel Junior came along, but no one had quite worked out how to make one not destined to kill someone. Gabriel Junior liked to think of himself as an engineer, but he needed a real one to solve this problem, and that's what he found in Professor Carl von Linde of the Munich Polytechnic. Linde had been publishing papers on refrigeration for a few years and was looking to solve the two key issues: the dangerous gas involved, and the fact that gases under pressure love to leak. He landed on methyl ether which, while flammable, wasn't as deadly, and designed unique mercury seals to keep the gas where it was supposed to be.

The next hurdle was to prove it worked in practice, which is where Gabriel Junior came in. In the early 1870s he approached Linde and offered to pay for the construction of Linde's system in the caves under Spaten. Linde agreed, and along with several of his students started experimenting on-site with systems capable of cooling the brewery cellar. By 1873, Linde had received a patent for a methyl ether refrigeration system, which he showed off at the Viennese Brewers Conference that year. In the meantime, a company in Augsburg started construction on the four-ton machine. It was installed that year…and promptly leaked.

Back at the drawing board, Linde replaced his mercury sealant with glycerin and the methyl ether with ammonia. He received a new patent in 1876 and installed a machine that year at Dreher's brewery. Amazingly, the drawings handed in with the application show that Sedlmayr himself had a hand in the design. This time the machine worked perfectly, and it was used at the Dreher brewery right up until 1908. Despite this success, Linde kept refining his machine and installed a third version back at Spaten, where it produced 480 tons of ice a day for the cellar, while also providing cold water to cool the wort to the chilly 54°F that the yeast liked.

Linde's system was a game changer, for Spaten, for brewing and for his own business endeavors. He gave up teaching in 1879 to focus on running a company that built them, and a decade later he'd sold 747 machines. Some of the names on his early customer list will be familiar—including Guinness, Heineken and Carlsberg. Not only did refrigeration remove the reliance on foraged ice, it allowed any brewery with a Linde system— or one of the many imitations—to brew year-round safely for the first time in history. It effectively meant the end of seasonal brewing, a doctrine brewers had followed for centuries.

It wasn't just brewers that adopted this new technology, either. Slaughterhouses, ice suppliers, dairies and chocolate factories all lined up for Linde machines. He even made bespoke designs for ice rinks and an air cooling system for a hotel in Kolkata, India. Linde continued to create new designs too, applying his technology to smaller fridges for ships and railroad cars, which went on to inspire the very fridges you use at home. The impact of those is, of course, inestimable. It changed the way we stored, cooked and consumed food at home, and it's hard to envisage a modern home without this incredible invention that can be traced directly back to Spaten.

Linde, however, was not done. He also liquefied CO_2 for the first time (to add bubbles to the beers of Guinness in Ireland, in fact), which led to him isolating oxygen and nitrogen from the air for the first time ever too. The former has a million uses, initially revolutionizing the welding used to build the supports for ships and skyscrapers in the early twentieth century, but now used for pain relief in hospitals. Meanwhile nitrogen is used in literally all commercial fertilizers, so Linde's invention is helping to feed the world. Linde's beer-inspired discoveries made his refrigeration and gas company one of Germany's greatest success stories. Now called Linde AG, it's the biggest chemical firm in the world, with 65,000 employees and an annual turn-over of $33 billion.

An interesting side note is that one of the earliest employees of Linde was Rudolf Diesel. He was taught by Linde at Munich Polytechnic and helped install and run an ice plant in Paris for him, before moving to Berlin where he started work on one of the most important advances in the nineteenth century—inventing and building the first diesel engine in 1897.

Back at the top of Spaten's old malting tower, I couldn't quite believe my luck. Everything I'd heard—the hollow walking stick, the creation of Vienna lager, the invention of the fridge—was all true. Beer's lineage is forever exaggerated and embellished like a great bar story, but here I was sipping a pint of history and being read quotes from the nineteenth century that proved this narrative is true. Wittal closed the book with the air of a teacher finishing story time, and we agreed to decamp to the Augustiner Keller beer hall next door.

The evening outside was misty and damp, with snow still icing the grassy areas. In the beer garden locals were playing bowls and drinking beer. It was a beautiful, idyllic scene, but we were hankering for the humid warmth of the beer hall. We sat down at the end of one long sharing table and ordered pork knuckles and Augustiner lager straight from oak barrels. We'd both done a lot of talking, so for a while we just enjoyed our beers, Wittal resting his voice while I processed the immeasurable impact that Sedlmayr's and Linde's work had had on the world.

As I supped on my second Helles, I mused that there was only one other brewery that could claim to rival Spaten's influence, and even that story starts with Sedlmayr—in fact, it was a gift he gave to the founder of Carlsberg Brewery in Copenhagen.

The Rise of Yeast

Before we explore one of the world's most important laboratories and its pivotal role in both brewing and modern biology, we need to rewind a little.

As we saw in the first chapter, the ingredients and methods of historic brewing varied wildly, inspired by and reliant on the local ingredients, climate and traditions. All manner of grains, herbs, spices and fruits were used but every one of them had something in common: yeast. This remarkable microbe has been humanity's invisible partner for millennia, and without it there would be no beer and no bread, two things that helped humanity survive, advance and civilize. It's not unthinkable to argue that without it, there would be no civilization at all.

Thankfully, there's lots of it. In fact, this microscopic fungus is found on pretty much every surface on earth. There are well over 1,000 species and in total they make up around one percent of all fungi, but in this book we'll focus on a small family you could crudely define as brewer's yeast, but is also behind the creation of bread, wine, whiskey, sake and other vital (delicious) things.

Considering it's a single-celled organism smaller than 1/3000th of a millimeter, yeast wields some incredible powers; powers that have made it one of the most successful living things on this planet. At its most basic, it's like all creatures (particularly drunk ones) desperately trying to survive and multiply. To succeed at either, you're going to need a lot of food. Yeast's technical name, Saccharomyces, literally translates as *sugar fungus*, which will give you an idea of what it likes to eat. Glucose is its favorite form, and in the presence of oxygen it will happily chomp through all the glucose you can give it, multiplying exponentially while peeing out carbon dioxide and water as a by-product.

Things get more interesting if all the oxygen has been used up. The lack of breathable air forces the yeast to change its chemical process, instead releasing carbon dioxide and...alcohol. This approach is less efficient than the first, but has one huge benefit. You see, few other microbes can thrive in alcoholic environments. Once the alcohol percentage reaches a certain level, everything else dies off and the yeast gets the pick of whatever it is consuming. It's such an important evolutionary advantage that yeasts have learned to kick out alcohol even before the oxygen is depleted, and this development is vital because it means that yeast usually produces enough alcohol to stop any nasty bacteria or viruses taking hold. That makes our beer taste a lot better, but more importantly it means it's very unlikely to poison us.

Despite brewing and baking since before the dawn of civilization, we've only known the intricate details of yeast for the last 150 years or so. Before then there were many theories about what caused fermentation. For the first few thousand years, religion and science butted up against each other. The religious argument would have been that god(s) had blessed certain pots and rituals, yet there was also an understanding that certain grains, specific pot shapes or particular temperatures were beneficial. We know this from the fact that Egyptian brewers (and all those who followed in the ancient world) applied intense heat, used pointed pots and slowly switched from wheat to barley.

By the seventeenth century we'd confirmed that the yeasty, tangy trub at the top and bottom of our fermenters was key to making good beer: we'd learned brewers could crop the trub from one healthy batch to another to kick off a reliable ferment, and even given it the name *yest*, derived over centuries from the Indo-European root *yes*, meaning *boil, foam* or *bubble*. This word made it into Dr. Johnson's famous first dictionary in 1755, and some enterprising folk started selling yeast for bread baking and brewing. Still, though, no one knew what it actually was or what it really did.

Yeast was one of the first things observed through a microscope by the world's first microbiologist, Antonie van Leeuwenhoek, but he didn't recognize it as a living organism. He thought it was a chemical by-product, so for nearly 200 years it was assumed that fermentation was a chemical transformation (rather than a biological process), with a cause that had yet to be determined.

It wasn't like people didn't want to know—brewers all over the world realized that understanding and properly harnessing fermentation could make them millions. They just didn't have the resources to figure it out. In 1779, the French Academy of Sciences offered two pounds of gold to the person who discovered the secret of fermentation, but the prize was withdrawn before an answer was found. In fact, it was nearly a century until the scientific community finally agreed on it.

Bubbling Away

Credit for the discovery of yeast's role in fermentation is often given to Louis Pasteur, but in reality he was just the first person the establishment believed. A lot of the theoretical work had already been done by less famous scientists. Perhaps the most important of those was Theodor Schwann, who in the 1830s was one of the first to consider yeast a living organism, and he went a step further than others by suggesting it was the key driver of fermentation.

To prove his theory that yeast was alive, present everywhere and responsible for fermentation, Schwann filled two jars with unfermented sugary liquid, blowing pure air (sanitized by extreme heating) into one and unpurified air into the other. Only the latter started fermenting, suggesting something had come in on the air to kick off the process. The idea that this *something* was yeast was backed by his microscopic observation that yeast had proliferated where there was no yeast before. It may seem a pretty innocuous hypothesis, but the idea that yeast causes fermentation (rather than being created by it) challenged the scientific establishment's fundamental view of the world, for reasons we'll get into. Suffice to say, old men rarely like their worldview being changed, and Schwann's work (along with others like Charles Cagniard-Latour's) was ignored by his colleagues for over a decade. Thankfully, in the mid-1850s, the kind of scientist you can't ignore backed up his findings.

Pasteur only properly delved into this realm of science when the father of one of his students at the University of Lille asked for help. Mr. Bigo owned a beetroot distillery—yeah, me neither—and was having issues with his fermentations turning sour. Perhaps partial to beetroot vodka, or out of kinship with his student, in 1856 Pasteur agreed to get to the root (sorry) of the problem. He started with some experiments that confirmed Schwann's conclusion that yeast was alive (causing a few small disagreements with other world-famous scientists), and moved on to working out what might be turning the liquid sour. What he found was the presence of lactic-acid-producing bacteria.

As his student, Bigo the younger, put it: "Pasteur had noticed through the microscope that the globules [of yeast] were round when fermentation was healthy, that they lengthened when alteration began, and were quite long when fermentation became lactic. This very simple method allowed us to watch the process and to avoid the failures in fermentation which we used so often to meet with."

This was obviously an important moment for the Bigo family, but the student noted that Pasteur was more excited than expected. No one can love beetroot vodka that much, and Pasteur was actually distracted by the notion that bacterial infection might not be unique to beetroot. It was a theory that not only changed the vodka, wine and beer worlds, but the field of medicine and indeed the theory of creation itself.

Pasteur is a fascinating character, seemingly capable of great arrogance and great humbleness. He needed both in the mission that followed, because he considered the study of fermentation to be "connected...with the impenetrable mystery of Life and Death." It was a connection that can only have been hardened by the loss of his eldest daughter to typhoid in 1859.

This might seem like a leap, so let me explain. If yeast was not created by fermentation but was its creator, then where did that yeast come from? For the 2,000 years leading up to Pasteur's experiments, it was widely accepted that life came out of nonliving matter—that mud could birth insects, dead flesh could create maggots, and beer wort could create yeast. Today this theory of "spontaneous generation" seems ludicrous, but until the microscope was invented we had no idea we were only witnessing a tiny percentage of life on earth. With the information we had, spontaneous generation offered a broad explanation for everything, from how maggots appeared in wounds to how life itself started. But from the moment Leeuwenhoek saw the thousands of microbes in his scope, that theory was put on notice. Schwann's jar experiment should have put the idea to bed: if spontaneous generation were true, both beers should have started fermenting. Pasteur knew it, so he took Schwann's theories and set out to prove them beyond a reasonable doubt.

To do so, he designed flasks with swan necks, and placed in those necks some asbestos (a mineral, nonliving) wool to trap any airborne flora. He filled the flasks with a sanitized, fermentable liquid and sealed the swan neck by heating and squeezing the neck. If the seal was broken (with hot scissors, so also sanitary) the flask would fill with wild air and the wool become saturated with whatever came with it. He could then tilt the flask and soak the wool, infecting the liquid once it was in a warm environment.

Most incredibly, he then took these flasks all over France, from the cellars of the Observatory of Paris, to Mer de Glace, a glacial valley near Mont Blanc. Proving his theory and backing Schwann's, without exception at least one flask in each location began to ferment. This led him to write "it can be affirmed that the dusts suspended in atmospheric air are the exclusive origin, the necessary condition of life in infusions." Essentially, for the first time in human history, science had shown that the air we breathe teems with life and, on occasion, with death.

Spontaneous End

In 1863, Pasteur was approached by Napoleon III to look into the blight of sour wine, which was affecting exports of this vital French product. As a wine lover and a famous patriot, Pasteur threw himself into the task enthusiastically, setting up a makeshift lab in an old railway workers' canteen in Arbois, home of Jura wine.

In his seminal work, *Études sur le vin*, he follows the full process of wine making, even noting the sunlight on barrels and the temperature of the rooms. He and his team recorded the flavors of both good and bad ferments so as to align them with what he saw under the microscope. All of this was done with one eye on his beetroot hypothesis, that bad ferments were caused by bacteria getting into the liquid—and everything he saw confirmed that. The suggestion he made to the industry, one that was not well received by traditionalists, was that they heat their wine to around 140°F once bottled to kill any microbes. He patented the idea, and by 1871 the process was being referred to the same way we refer to it today—*pasteurization*.

That same year, he next turned his attention to beer. Germany and England were the famous brewing nations of Europe, but Pasteur hoped France could become a brewing powerhouse. In 1871 he visited a brewery in Chamalières, near Clermont-Ferrand, which was having issues with sour beer. There he took the same approach as he had at the vineyards of Jura, but was amazed to only get generalized, outdated information back. Clearly, the French brewers had little idea of how their ferments were working. Undeterred and certain of his own beliefs and methods, Pasteur started searching for more evidence, and he found it on a trip to London.

There he visited Whitbread, one of the largest brewers in London at the time. The owners welcomed him and allowed him to look at some of their fermenting beer under his microscope. Pasteur immediately declared the beer infected, and asked if complaints had been made by any of the brewery's customers. Offended but amazed, the owners admitted they had just been forced to order fresh yeast after a quality issue. Pasteur examined the new pitch and declared it pure. On returning a week later, he found the brewery had bought itself a microscope.

Back in Paris he continued his experiments, collecting bottles from the world's most famous breweries, like an Untappd addict might today. He found that many of them would develop infections over a long enough period and suggested brewers adopt pasteurization as well as washing yeasts with acid to kill any bacteria. Finally, he said it should be standard practice to thoroughly clean all the brewing equipment—quite the reverse of the days when spontaneous generation implied that sediment was a good thing.

Together these processes changed the world of beer, giving breweries the tools to recognize infected yeast before it ruined a batch of beer. It also trashed the idea that organisms came from nowhere, fundamentally changing our understanding of how life begins and how it spreads. And yet Pasteur still had this feeling that there were more implications to his studies. His greatest discovery was still a decade away: one that both changed the world and proved his theories irrefutably correct. Before that though, we need to look at what he got wrong.

J-Day

It's a cold, wet Friday night in Copenhagen, and the bars are all rammed. Not just Friday-night rammed, but something-in-the-air rammed. The kind where *standing room only* is a gross exaggeration. I had to fight my way to the bar at Peders, a cozy cellar pub right in the heart of town, then carefully dodge my way back from it, my beer-wielding arm a gyro capable of any angle that stopped my beer spilling.

I took my pint outside and grabbed a table so recently vacated that a cigarette still glowed in the ashtray. From my rickety perch I could hear the revelry of Vestergade, a road I'd been told to both make sure I visit and avoid like the plague. You see, this Friday is the first Friday in November, otherwise known as J-Day: a forty-year-old tradition in Danish culture celebrating the release of that year's Christmas beers.

The Danes do Christmas beer differently from all other nations. Depending on where you live you might think of the Belgian family breweries; that regional brewery that's had the same Christmas label since the eighties; or cask ale pump clips with jokes about Santa's sack. But would you believe that one in four beers sold in Denmark is a Christmas beer—yet they're only on sale for a month of the year? Well, I didn't believe it, until I saw Vestergade.

I'd finished my pint, relinquished my seat to some grateful locals, and headed toward the melee. Vestergade is essentially a collection of bars that claim to have different themes—Irish pub, Belgian café, Tiki bar—but actually all have the same one: drunkenness. Tuborg's Christmas beer rules in Copenhagen, and the Vienna-style lager was due to be released at 8:55 p.m. By 8 p.m. the lines to get into the bars were spilling into the street, causing the taxi drivers dropping off yet more revelers to idle along, flashing their lights and questioning their career choices. Around half the people were wearing blue Tuborg Santa hats and looking like they'd had enough festive lagers for a lifetime. My plan had been to join the revelry, but looking at the queues I felt every one of my thirty-six years. Instead I walked north, over the bridge that separates the medieval town from the trendy Nørrebro district.

Things were a little quieter at the brewpub BRUS, but not much. I got a seat at the bar and, with my elbows tucked in tight, ordered a Czech amber lager called Crispy Christmas. It was sticky and sweet like the Quality Street gold penny, but also zippy and quick on the finish. Sensing this might be the last seat in any bar in Copenhagen, I ordered another, got out my laptop and started making sense of the last few days—days that had turned my beer world upside down.

The history of Carlsberg sounds sensationalist and exciting, but it's actually a rather sad tale. The brewery was founded in 1847 by Jacob Christian (JC) Jacobsen, who had previously run a traditional ale brewery he inherited from his father, Christen. The original brewery, located in a town house in the city center, had done well for itself and pulled the Jacobsen family up from peasantry to comfortable middle-class life. As such, Christen wanted more for his son. JC was to be a brewer, there was no doubt about that, but Christen was switched on enough to know that to survive the cliquey nature of the well-to-do, his son would need to be well-read. He also knew enough about brewing to predict that science had a huge role to play in how it would develop. So he took JC to scientific lectures, provided all the reading material he could ask for and got him involved in the business as soon as he was able.

JC proved himself curious, intellectual and even a little artistic, with his father's steady hand in brewing and finances. Christen died in 1835, and JC ran the ale brewery in his father's image...until the fateful day that he tried his first Bavarian lager at a wine merchant in town. Impressed by its color and bright, clean flavor, he decided to visit Germany to learn how it was made. I guess Bavaria seemed a little far at the time so he settled on a brewery called Langes in Hamburg. There he learned about lager yeasts and cold conditioning, and was inspired to try it at home, keeping his experiments secret by brewing with his mother's kitchen pots in the cellar of the family town house.

These lagers remained experiments for nearly a decade, but that changed when he visited our friend Gabriel Sedlmayr II at Spaten in 1845. There he learned about the British innovation of indirect kilning, but received an even greater gift in a vial of Spaten's house lager yeast. How he got this cold-loving organism home is the stuff of legend: he was traveling in a public stagecoach, so kept it in a tin at the bottom of his hat box. Every time the stagecoach stopped, the story goes that JC ran to the horse water pump to douse the tin in cold water.

Spaten's success must have made an impression on him, because on his return he decided that lager, not ale, was the future of brewing. His first move was to build storage cellars in the city's ramparts, where his new lager was conditioned and caused much excitement in the town—a bottle of his fresh Bavarian-style lager cost four times more than a loaf of bread. Quickly

JC needed a bigger production space, and he started sketching out a new brewery just west of the city, where the first railway line was being built and there was a source of good water. Most importantly it was on a hill, at an elevation that would allow him to dig lager cellars. Ground was broken on the new brewery in 1847 and JC called it Carlsberg, or *Carl's Mountain*, after his then five-year-old son.

It seems a sweet and heartfelt gesture, but in retrospect it's kind of devastating. JC and Carl fell out horrifically twenty years later, and reconciled only when JC was on his deathbed. The passage of time makes it all sound almost whimsical—the impressive new Carlsberg brewery tour uses the dispute as its main narrative—but the more you dig into the details the sadder it seems, even as you count the incredible breakthroughs they both made in their lifetimes, to some extent spurred on by their rivalry.

Carl was a bright young lad, but his father was extremely demanding. From reading about his approach to fatherhood, *not angry, just disappointed* is the best phrase I can come up with. For example, on Carl's thirteenth birthday, JC presented him with a beautiful watch and a letter that read "If you had been a really good, hardworking boy in the past year, this watch would have become yours today." To me this kind of parenting is unconscionable, but JC was so worried about Carl's nature that at the age of twenty-four he was effectively exiled to study brewing in Germany, France, England and Scotland. JC didn't see his son for four years, but still he sent admonishing letters in a bid to mold Carl as he saw fit.

When Carl returned home in 1870, his father was delighted with the change in him. He had become a much more technical brewer than his father, and was full of ideas of how to make Carlsberg's beer better and the brewhouse more efficient. He was given charge of production at a second brewhouse, built on the edge of the original Carlsberg to meet increasing demand.

But the creation of two breweries—and undoubtedly a little built-up resentment—started a rift between father and son. Carl wanted to grow the brewery by shortening lagering times, but JC saw that as a compromise on quality and was happy with the size the brewery was at.

In the end, the father offered to build a third brewery that would allow for expansion without making the supposed sacrifices to process. Carl agreed to the new construction, but continued brewing Carlsberg his quicker way anyway. The tension slowly ratcheted until, at some point, Carl made one shortcut too many and his father kicked him out of the business. JC gave his son one million kroner in return for Carl waiving his inheritance right. Instead the brewery was to pass into the Carlsberg Foundation, which already included a Carlsberg Laboratory and the Museum of Natural History, both founded by JC through his passion for science.

The resentment that must have grown for JC to make such a decision should not be underestimated: he disowned his only son over a business matter. Given the circumstances, you'd expect most sons to want to start again, in a new place and a new business. Carl, however, set up right next door: he built the brewery Carlsberg had been planning over the road under his own name, using his own funds. Not only that, he named his brewery Ny Carlsberg—*New Carlsberg*.

It was the start of an acrimonious and, let's face it, pathetic arms race. The breweries obviously competed for sales and reputation, but also engaged in a kind of childish corporate warfare. Most famously, a new road was built between the breweries that needed a name. JC wanted to call it Alliancevej, while Carl wanted to call it Pasteurvej. As described in Carlsberg Laboratory worker Emil Christian Hansen's diary, these "crazy people" kept placing bigger road signs to cover the other's as they fought to name it.

Thankfully for humanity, this particular lab worker had bigger worries. He was busy calling out French patriot Louis Pasteur for his erroneous conclusions on the sickness of beer...

The Nordic Pasteur

Emil had a hard upbringing. The kind of upbringing that would make the endless enlargement of road signs by feuding millionaires seem perverse and futile.

Born in 1842, the same year as Carl, Emil spent much of his childhood in destitution, following his vagabond father around northern Europe as he tried his hand at painter-decorator, artist and Prussian spy in a series of escalating and bleak moral tales. History records Emil's father as fascinating but cruel, on one occasion forcing his young son to defend his horse cart full of paints alone, overnight, on a dirt road, while he went in search of a spare wheel (or more likely, a drink). In another awful story, Emil feared his father enough to dive into frozen water at his command, despite never being taught to swim. After waiting far, far too long, his father had to dive in and rescue his drowning son.

Now, I'm no psychologist but I feel like this might have contributed to Emil's fierce work ethic, insatiable need to prove himself, and deep mistrust of everyone. After a few years of vagrancy in a bid to follow in his father's artistic footsteps, Emil decided he was destined for a more academic life. Eventually he got himself a tutoring job for a wealthy family, which inspired him to become a teacher. During his training he became obsessed with botany, which had been revolutionized by the works of people like Charles Darwin in the mid-1800s. While studying at Copenhagen University he was lucky enough to make a connection that got him a job at the Carlsberg Laboratory in 1877, where his attention to detail and microbiology experi-

ence was put to use checking the condition of the ferments and
bottled beers.

The work Emil was doing was, of course, inspired by Pasteur's work. JC was obsessed with the great scientists of the day
and followed their progress closely. How much he understood is
up for debate, but it was clearly enough to converse with them
because he frequently had esteemed guests to stay. When they
did, he needed a place that would impress them, as a brewery
lab, a research facility and a piece of architecture. That place
was the Carlsberg Laboratory, a building I have now walked
the echoey halls of and whose venerable benches I have leaned
on. It is grand but functional and reminded me a little of an old
boarding school.

Built in 1875, such a huge investment needed a greater purpose than beer quality assurance. On the main stairs, underneath
a five-yard landscape painting of the laboratory in full flow, are
the words *No result of the Laboratory's activities which is of theoretical or practical importance shall be kept secret*. This approach has put
the laboratory at the heart of world-changing research on several occasions.

JC was no scientist, but he wanted in his own way to be part
of that world. He was a man of great wealth, stature and intellect, but I think he was still that curious child too—swayed by
genius, curious of what he didn't know and desperate to impress.
There's a dichotomy in the historical writing on JC and Carl's
relationship, in that the father was so open to the scientific ideas
of the day but utterly unable to hear them from his son. It might
be that he saw Carl's approach as being driven by profit, but in
my view, his son also wasn't a good enough source for the information. He considered himself learned enough that he needed a
genius to tell him what to think. He closely followed the work
of Pasteur as he carried his jars around France, and marveled at
how he slowly pieced together the nature and significance of
microscopic life. In Emil, he found someone of arguably equal

intellect, but radically different nature. He brought a very particular energy to JC's lab—dogged, tireless, furious. And it was
these traits, learned as a child sitting in the dark on a horse cart,
that led him to take Pasteur head-on.

The story of the first ever isolation of beer yeast, a moment
that changed the production of all alcohol around the world,
starts with a plague. Not a human plague, but a beer one. In the
early 1880s, the beers of Copenhagen's breweries were all going
rancid and the processes adopted in light of Pasteur's research
weren't helping. No amount of pasteurization, cleaning, washing yeast pitches with acid, or bringing in new strains was fixing it. As the best funded and determinedly public laboratory,
countless samples were sent to Emil at Carlsberg and (perhaps
as a result) the worst soon happened: in the summer of 1883,
Carlsberg's beers got sick too.

It was all hands on deck, to the horror of the independent and
systematic Emil. Even JC got a microscope and started hunting for bacteria in their yeast pitches and beers. Emil suspected
they'd find nothing because he had another theory, one he'd
been working on ever since he read Pasteur's second seminal
work, *Études sur la bière*. Pasteur's acid washes killed any spoiling bacteria and left the yeast intact, but Emil wasn't sure that
Copenhagen's beer plague was caused by bacteria at all. From a
flavor perspective, he didn't witness the same sourness of Pasteur's beetroot distillations or wines. Nor could he find evidence
of Pasteur's elongated yeast cells or clouds of lactic cultures in
his beers. He did see differently shaped yeast cells, however,
and theorized that like in humans, there were different families, varying genes and distinct traits in yeast cells.

If his theory was right, isolating the different strains and
using just one of them to ferment the wort would result in a
clean beer. It wasn't some incredible new technology or process
that he used, but absurdly detailed and long-winded work. He
took a slide sample of Carlsberg's yeast and used a glass with a

grid which helped him estimate how many cells there were per cubic centimeter. Using this he attempted to put single cells into hundreds of bottles filled with sterilized wort, effectively isolating the strains to observe them. What he found were two very different-looking yeasts—one of which made good beer and another that did not. Emil was not done though. By putting the good yeast through a series of tests, such as fermenting at different temperatures, he found the good yeast was actually *two* good yeasts.

Emil preferred the results of one of these strains and used a flask he designed himself to grow it in an oxygen-rich environment, the phase where yeast makes constant copies of itself without creating much alcohol. The aim was to collect and breed enough to ferment a "pure" batch of Carlsberg. On September 7, JC wrote to his brewery director telling him of what Emil was attempting, and on November 12 it was done for the first time.

Historical accounts say the first batch was nothing to write home about, but it was the first time (perhaps in history) that a single strain of yeast had fermented a beer. Pretty quickly, though, it was seen as a radical success and that yeast, sometimes referred to as Carlsberg Bottom Yeast I or Saccharomyces Carlsbergensis (but officially named Saccharomyces Pastorianus) is the origin of pretty much every lager yeast still brewed with today. Within a decade, breweries all over the world were using the techniques and equipment that Emil developed for it—Pabst, Schlitz, Anheuser-Busch, Osaka, Foster and even Carlsberg's great local rival, Tuborg. This moment is perhaps the birth of the modern beer world, of beer as we know it. Lagers already existed, but this invention meant quality, consistency and (for better or for worse) uniformity was within easy reach. It spread so fast because, in keeping with the laboratory's original principle, JC gave samples away for free.

Emil's remarkable work went beyond that of brewing, and

even beyond that of bread baking, wine making and spirit production. His achievements made the Carlsberg Laboratory
world-famous, justifying the vision of JC. Pasteur himself visited not long after Emil's great triumph, and after a frosty start
as they sized each other up, the two scientists came to respect
each other. Emil visited Pasteur in France on more than one occasion, while Pasteur handed Emil the gold medal of the Society
for the Development of National Industry in France in 1886.

Emil's legacy encouraged some incredible scientists to join the
Carlsberg Laboratory, all working ostensibly to improve Carlsberg beer, but like Emil, changing the world at the same time.
If you've ever read the nutritional information of a food packet
then you've benefited from the work of Johan Kjeldahl, a colleague of Emil whose technique in measuring nitrogen (and
therefore protein) is still used today. Then there's Søren Peter
Lauritz Sørensen, who headed the lab from 1901 and invented
the pH scale. Measuring acidity in brewing is vital for efficient
mashing and fermenting, but its wider uses are countless, from
soil analysis in agriculture to wastewater treatment.

In the 1990s, Carlsberg's Christoph Dockter and his team took
part in the sequencing of the barley genome, a decade-long project done by a consortium all over the world. The project didn't
just help scientists create high-quality malting barley for sustain-
able brewing, but also high-quality baking wheat. Today it's vital
to the work of creating climate-resilient crops of all kinds. Most
recently, the laboratory announced the creation of FIND-IT, a
technology that allows scientists to quickly scan the genomes of
plants to identify those with the ideal genetic makeup for better yields, disease resistance and climate-suitable characteristics.
Usually such searches take years, but thanks to Carlsberg it now
takes weeks. The benefits in a world with a rapidly changing
climate and increase in crop diseases is incalculable.

How Beer Saved the World (Part One, I Hope)

I'm sure you're fascinated by all this yeast chat, but it's possible you might not yet see the overall importance of the work I've detailed here. Emil and Louis were at the forefront of the applied side of microbiology, a new field of science that was fundamentally reshaping everything humans knew about the world. In the case of Louis Pasteur, his interest in fermentation put to bed the idea of spontaneous generation—a convenient but flawed way to explain both nature and God's role in it. He didn't just trash the old theory, though. He helped develop a new one, an idea that still saves millions of lives every day.

I've dropped a few hints about it in this chapter: this nagging feeling Pasteur had about the wider implications of bacteria spoiling beer and wine: if microbes could cause sickness in beer, was it possible it could do the same in humans?

He was not alone in this regard. In 1850, Casimir-Joseph Davaine observed a microorganism in the blood of diseased sheep, and in 1863 showed it could be transferred to infect other animals. That organism turned out to be anthrax. In a similar experiment to Davaine's, in 1865 Jean-Antoine Villemin showed that tuberculosis was contagious by swabbing infected animals, and placing the swabs in the beds of others. Their experiments were mostly ignored though, because medical scientists still subscribed to spontaneous generation theory, which implied infections and diseases were born in the stricken organism and spread by impure or noxious air.

But these experiments were starting to question that, and suffice to say the answers were critical. If disease could be spread through touch, our breath and on surfaces, then we had a hand in the life and death of others, and a growing number of people in the medical world knew it.

Pasteur was not a medical scientist, but at some point enough of them decided his views might be important. Despite being invited to stand as an associate of the Académie Nationale de Médecine, he was only elected by a single vote: clearly his appointment was controversial, and he did not disappoint. He was shocked to find medical doctors still denying the work of Schwann, Villemin and Davaine, and how it could link to his own experiments. In his very first meeting, Davaine's work was attacked, and his conclusion that living microbes were being spread dismissed. With the matter decided, the newest member was asked his view. Pasteur started with reference to his studies in beer, noting that wherever sickness in beer was found, bacteria was present...before sticking in the scalpel:

"The correlation is certain, indisputable, between the disease and the presence of organisms."

According to a biography written about Pasteur by his son-in-law René Vallery-Radot in 1915, he spoke those last words with so much emphasis that the stenographer taking down the exchange underlined them. Still the Académie was unmoved, perhaps considering it beneath them to listen to a mere chemist. Pasteur later set up little experiments for them, using his jars to prove that fermentation could not happen without bacteria having access to the organic matter, but to no avail.

The situation was more desperate than the frustrations of a scientist and the fustiness of old doctors. The discovery of anesthesia in 1846 and its quick adoption across the medical world had quite literally opened people up to more ambitious, lifesaving surgeries. The problem was that the more invasive the surgery, the more likely an infection was. Spontaneous generation theory couldn't account for that, so little was done to address the issue. As such, while surgeries increasingly cured the original issues, resulting infections ended up killing the patient even quicker, to the point where one physician said surgeons should be "classed among the attributes of the executioner."

Thankfully there were those who were willing to listen to Pasteur and his forebears. The most important of those was a

British surgeon named Joseph Lister. His father was actually a wine merchant, which might make quick acceptance of Pasteur's beer-related experiments more understandable. Lister was not a famously talented surgeon, but he had a very keen scientific mind. He first read Pasteur on the recommendation of a friend in the mid-1860s, and quickly made the potential link between what was sickening beer and wine, and what was sickening people.

At the time, a compound fracture—that is to say a break where the bone goes through the skin—was pretty much a death sentence because of the risk of infection. Bad news for the patient, but an excellent injury on which to test a new theory. Inspired by Pasteur's acid washes for yeast, Lister washed the leg of a twenty-two-year-old patient, Neil Kelly, with carbolic acid. He then dressed the wound with acid-washed lint and covered it with metal to prevent evaporation. Sadly, Kelly's leg still got infected and he died. Undeterred, Lister tracked down a purer form of acid and applied it to the leg of an eleven-year-old boy who had been run over by a cart. This time, when he redressed the wound five days later, he found no infection. Six weeks later, the boy was walking again.

Of course, some people survived such fractures without an acid wash, so more evidence was needed. What better evidence than John Hainy, a twenty-one-year-old who had compound fractures in *both* his legs after a 600-pound pipe mold fell on him? Usually the treatment would have been amputation (incredibly, the risk was lower), but Lister decided to set the bones and wash the wounds with acid. He cleaned and dressed both legs, as well as the bed sores that Hainy developed as he convalesced. Hainy survived, backing Lister's recommendations to other surgeons, which included washing hands, cleaning equipment and even spraying the operating room air with carbolic acid.

Today, Lister is seen as the father of modern surgery, and alongside the likes of Alexander Fleming (who discovered penicillin) could make a claim to have saved the most lives in human history. Obviously the lion's share of the credit goes to him, but if you want an indication of how important Pasteur's flask and beer research was in Lister's work, you need look no further than a letter the surgeon sent to the Frenchman in 1875:

"Allow me to take this opportunity to tender you my most cordial thanks for having, by your brilliant researches demonstrated to me the truth of the germ theory... Should you at any time visit Edinburgh, it would, I believe, give you sincere gratification to see at our hospital how largely mankind is being benefited by your labours."

If you take one thing from this book, I hope it's this letter from Lister; this inconceivable story that our understanding of germs, and therefore modern medicine itself, started under the microscope of a man trying to work out why beer turned sour.

Changing Track

Through writing this book I've found that beer's influence on the world is easy to imply, but rather hard to prove. On one level, literally everyone walking around today owes something to Gabriel Sedlmayr's madcap refrigeration scheme with Linde, Emil Christian Hansen's unrelenting work ethic, and Pasteur's patriotic decision to study beer. But on the other hand, tracing those stories and decades-long developments takes several thousand (thrilling) words.

There are some quite literally concrete examples of beer's historic influence on the world, however. Take a walk around downtown Milwaukee and you'll note hotels, bars, shops and even part of the university are old Pabst buildings; half of Dublin south of the river is given over to Guinness's campus; and the chimney of Truman Brewery, now one of London's largest events venues, still looms over the curry houses of Brick Lane.

My favorite example of the English capital's beer heritage, however, is one of its most iconic pieces of architecture—a literal
gateway to the UK for 140 million people every year.

There are worse ways to spend an afternoon than nursing
pints of London Pride while watching the trains roll into King's
Cross Station. From my seat at the Parcel Yard, I could see train
after train headed to my hometown and revel in the fact I had
a few more hours before I had to jump on one.

This Fuller's pub is on the first floor of one of the world's
busiest railway stations, and plays an important role in the world
of British beer because it's the closest pub for people using the
Eurostar to mainland Europe. That means it might well serve
them their first (and/or last) ever pint of real ale.

Cask beer is one of those bucket list things people want to try
when they visit the UK, but it also has a reputation for being
warm and flat. Ensuring it is neither of those things at the Parcel Yard is our first line of defense. Luckily my pint of Pride
was, if anything, a little too cold and was topped with a glorious rich foam—so the hundreds of millions of people that pass
through each year should know they'll likely be well served.
Whether they'll know the incredible beer history that flows
through King's Cross and St. Pancras Stations in particular,
however, is less certain.

I'd just spent a rather revelatory hour with Dr. David Turner,
whom I can best describe by saying he has a PhD in trains. During the long, late-night Google odysseys that mark the start of
any book idea, I'd come across a blog of his. Off the back of
it, I took a self-guided tour of St. Pancras, confusing tourists,
Londoners and station staff by taking close up pictures of pillars, arches, ceilings and floors. I was gathering evidence in a
bid to prove that what he'd written could be true—because I
lived ten minutes away from the station for a decade, and always assumed St. Pancras's beautiful architecture was simply
the whim of its designer, William Henry Barlow. Dr. Turner's

blog, however, claims that its two-level layout and archway design is entirely down to the amount of beer that was expected to come through it.

First we need to tell a bit of beer history, specifically the history of India Pale Ale. There are books and books about this, but the short story is that back when Britain thought that pillaging countries for their natural and cultural resources was its God-given right, it had a lot of soldiers and civil servants abroad. Brewing beer in these mostly tropical climes was tricky before refrigeration, so instead the East India Company would ship beer on the empty boats headed out. Unfortunately, with the long journey and flips in temperature as the boats went below South Africa and back up, the beer was spoiling before it arrived. So breweries started adding extra hops to preserve the beer, even going so far as to add hops to the cask—which we know for certain because of a diary kept by a shipwrecked sailor, who wrote about chewing on the flowers to survive.

Initially most of the beer came from Bow Brewery, which was conveniently situated right by the East India docks across the water from Greenwich. Unfortunately, the owner got greedy and started shipping his beer out direct, which caused the powerful East India Company to switch its custom to the brewers of Burton-on-Trent in the Midlands. It wasn't just out of spite— these breweries had found their local sulfurous water accentuated the hop character and helped the beer look sparkling clear. As a result, huge amounts of Burton beer was suddenly coming into the capital.

At the time, Burton-on-Trent's operator Midland Railway had no direct route to London, so it was coming by canal barges or rather aimless train routes. Dr. Turner says that while there's nothing in the board minutes that "explicitly" says it, it's pretty obvious that the beer-based opportunity was so great that Midland Railway general manager James Allport decided to build a brand-new station in London—one specifically designed to han-

dle beer. That station, finished in 1868, was St. Pancras and now
if anyone wonders out loud (as I have many times before) why
two major stations are literally a road apart, the answer is *Beer*.

Allport had exclusive agreements in place with Burton's Bass
Brewery, which had a warehouse just north of Regent's Canal.
The site for St. Pancras was chosen partly because of this, but
as a result the track had to be raised to get over Regent's Canal
at the last minute. Given the amount of beer that was going to
be coming through, the designers embraced this quirk, leaving
the tracks high to create room for a barrel store underneath. To
maximize floor space, the platforms were suspended by metal
columns and girders rather than brick and—in a move that blows
my mind—literally distanced to mirror Bass's beer warehouse
just down the road. To achieve this feat, the layout of St. Pancras's downstairs—where you'll now find Starbucks, Marks &
Spencer and last-minute-gifts-for-people-you-don't-really-know
specialist Oliver Bonas—was measured not in feet and inches,
but in beer barrels.

"So what would happen is," says Dr. Turner, moving his
second pint out of the way to demonstrate, "a train would pull
in, a carriage would be uncoupled and brought down on a hy-
draulic lift, where there was another small network of rails.
These carriages would be pulled to the corresponding place in
the warehouse, unloaded and refilled with empty barrels, then
taken back up."

From there, the breweries would distribute the beer via horse
and cart, exiting the station via the pointed arches that were
specifically high enough to allow for drays. You can still see
these arches because they make up the entire western flank of
the station, where you might catch a cab today. It's a remarkable system, so remarkable that we're still not up on all the details: if you look at the surviving pillars between the rows of
shops, you'll see a ledge about halfway up, jutting out a few
inches in all directions. Turner has no idea what the purpose of

this ledge was, nor do any other historians because they're not mentioned anywhere.

Whatever their use, we can say that the layout and ground-level architecture of St. Pancras was, in fact, designed exclusively for beer. As you can still see, absolutely no expense was spared in making it look beautiful, which reflects the amount of money that Midland Railway expected to make through their new terminus. Even if it is over the road from King's Cross.

The East India Company was actually dissolved just six years later, but the trade of Burton beer into London continued apace thanks to its reputation and the fact that London's Porter fad was coming to an end, with Pale Ale and Mild on the rise. In 1877, Bass became the biggest brewery in the world, making more than a million barrels a year with huge swathes of it going to the capital. It was so famous that it was forever encountering imitators trying to trade off its name. When trademark law was enacted in 1875, Bass's iconic red triangle was granted the first one. A clerk from the brewery allegedly slept on the steps outside the government office to ensure he was first in line.

Bass's impact outside beer doesn't end there, either. The Bass family may have been millionaires in a time when being a millionaire was borderline unthinkable, but they all had great interest in the working class. Michael Thomas Bass, who took over the brewery in 1827 and grew it to become the world's largest, was also a Liberal MP who seems to have cared deeply about his employees and those in related industries. After investing heavily in and (to be very cynical) becoming heavily reliant on the railways, he recognized the exploitation of its workers and founded the Amalgamated Society of Railway Servants (ASRS), a trade union looking after the rights of all those who worked on the railway. The union was not only one of the precursors of the modern National Union of Rail Maritime and Transport Workers, but even influential in the foundation of the Labour Party. In 1899, an ASRS union representative called Thomas

R. Steels proposed that the Trade Union Congress form a body to sponsor new parliamentary candidates sympathetic with its cause. The motion was passed in February 1900, and is considered the origin of Labour.

Incredible as this link is, it's not the first time that the ambitions and actions of a brewery have gone on to change a country's political landscape. Because when you have a mildly intoxicating but important foodstuff produced and controlled by the wealthy, try as you might, you occasionally have to swallow a dose of politics too.

Chapter 3

Politics

Or how beer has influenced the way the world is run

Really, beer should be about as apolitical as life gets. Going for a pint is pretty much code for *let's forget about the state of the world for a few hours.* Sure we sometimes drink and set the world to rights, but for most people that means complaining about traffic on the school drop-off or lineups at the post office…though as I write that I realize I am a very dull drinking partner.

Anyway, this is my way of saying that I have sympathy for the army of people I've met who, confronted with the notion that beer might have a political element, retort with something along the lines of "It's just beer."

I have sympathy, but they couldn't be more wrong.

I used to have a carefully plotted, highly intellectual riposte to this statement (in fact this whole book is kind of a riposte). But hit with "It's just beer" while a little worse for wear at a beer event a few years back, I came up with a better one; one that neither I nor the other person had an answer to.

"If beer has nothing to do with politics," I slurred, "why are there so many bars in the Houses of Parliament?"

The silence that followed was long. I remember my adversary kind of blinking at me, as we both struggled to comprehend my point. I couldn't actually remember how many there were (only that there were "many"), and over the coming days the question started to burn itself into my brain. How many other workplaces have a bar—let alone multiple bars—and who could possibly think it's a good idea for the people who run the United Kingdom to do so under the influence? That was the question I set out to answer, as I got off the Tube at Westminster on a hot July afternoon. I was so deep in my thoughts as I emerged from the Underground that I missed the last step, stumbling and taking a huge EU flag directly to the face.

Confused, I apologized to the flag, much to the amusement of the demonstrator who was holding it. I crossed to the middle of Parliament Square and saw the rest of the protesters, holding their *Fuck the Tories* banner high and singing along to Billy Bragg coming out of a cheap, bassy stereo. On the political spectrum you'd find me pretty close to the protesters, and yet today I avoided their eyes, because I was going for a beer with a Conservative MP.

The Estate

I'm a good twenty minutes early and feel like an impostor as I go through the airport-style security—a feeling compounded by the fact that no one seems to know where to send me. I'm left to sweat in a strange purgatory: a baking hot side room with peeling paint and those ubiquitous stackable chairs that cheap wedding venues have. In the corner, on a tiny flat-screen TV that makes the cheapest Blackpool B and B look decadent, BBC News 24 plays silently.

As official-looking people walk by, I stammer that I'm here to see Alun Cairns at The Strangers' Bar, and several people suggest I call him…while standing under signs that say *No Mobile Phone Use*.

As the minutes tick by, the heat seems to rise. Thankfully I'm rescued by his special adviser, who arrives as cool as you like at the precise time he said he would. I pretend I wasn't on the verge of a nervous breakdown, and even manage a smile when he jokes about how *Star Trek* it is to get in here. I glance at the old wedding chairs and wonder what series he watched.

To be fair, the actual entrance to the "estate" as everyone I meet calls it, is pretty *Star Trek*—a circular glass airlock barely big enough for one person, that stays sealed just long enough to get my heart racing again. We head through more hotel wedding venue–style decor and out into what I can only describe as an airport lounge, with a huge glass ceiling, lots of tables and chairs, and food kiosks all around. I'm told there are over 10,000 people working on the estate, so they need an informal place to gather for meetings, food and breaks. I can't even begin to work out where I am in the complex of buildings, and only get more confused when we head downstairs and outside. Next we're on a subterranean one-way service road, and above us I'm told is Big Ben. We take a right through a small, ancient door and finally enter the Palace of Westminster.

It's not my first time, but it's still disorientating to be in a place that looks so familiar yet feels so alien. I have seen these corridors hundreds of times on TV, and they smell identical to the church I was forced to go to as a child, and yet I've never felt quite so out of my depth. We reach another door with a very relaxed and comfortable-looking security guard, who ushers us through to the terrace. It's the one you look down on as you cross Westminster Bridge, wondering what underhand deals are going on over glasses of French wine and cigars. The truth is more prosaic—most people sit alone tapping away on iPhones, drinking Diet Cokes, and placing their cans neatly in the large recycling bins. One of those people is Alun Cairns, MP for the Vale of Glamorgan in Wales.

Alun isn't a typical Tory, or indeed MP. His manners are warm but he always sounds serious, even when he's talking about his love of pubs and the excesses of his youth. Memories like this, plus an encounter in this very bar, are why he's now chair of the

All Parliamentary Pub Group. This club is essentially a cohort of MPs from all parties who can put their differences aside long enough to agree that pubs, the people in them, and the drinks served there are important to the fabric of British society. He's a beer lover, and is only on the Diet Coke because he's driving back to Wales later, but he kindly offers to buy me a taxpayer-funded pint at the bar (if you're a Brit, thanks!). To do so we head to the place I've come to see—the famous Strangers' Bar.

There are several places to get a drink in the Palace of Westminster—some are fully-fledged pubs, some are restaurants, some are extensions of others, and a few are little more than a room with a fridge. From my best count, at its peak in the early 2000s, there was The Lord's Bar, The Bishop's Bar, The Peers' Dining Room, The Peers' Guest Room, The Pugin Room, The Terrace Pavilion, The Strangers' Bar, The Terrace Cafeteria, The Thames Pavilion, The Speaker's State Rooms, The River Restaurant, Bellamy's, The Debate, The Jubilee Room, The Adjournment, The Members' Dining Room, The Strangers' Dining Room, The Sports and Social Bar, The Inter-Parliamentary Union Room, The Churchill Room, The Cholmondeley Room, The Barry Room, The Home Room, The Jubilee Cafe, The Attlee Room, Millbank House Cafeteria, The River Dining Rooms and Moncrieff's (a clubhouse for journalists).

Even with 10,000 people on site, it feels excessive, and seems to have an equally excessive historical justification. The Houses were partially rebuilt in the early nineteenth century when London's men's clubs were in their heyday. MPs of the time demanded similar comforts to the men's clubs they were inevitably members of, which is where the bars came from and also how my clichéd view of The Strangers' Bar was formed.

Alun tells me that there are now just five drink-focused bars, and four restaurants serving alcohol. To me that's still a lot, and it's not only the principle of it either—a lot has happened in them, some of which made the news and some did not. The police have been called to break up fights in the past, and arrests have even been made. There are also infamous live TV interviews from Parliament where MPs have seemed a little worse for wear. I won't name and shame, I'll let you google them. As recently as 2022, the House Speaker Lindsay Hoyle admitted The Strangers' Bar has "a bad reputation," but Alun is keen to explain that the licensed premises play a vital role in our democracy, and of course reflect it.

"The different parties used to congregate in different ones," says Alun. "The Conservatives used to go to the smoking room, which is more like a private club, while the Strangers' was referred to as 'the Kremlin' because it's where the Labour MPs went."

The Strangers' Bar is just off the terrace. I expected some kind of large, wood-paneled hall with green leather seats, notary lamps, newspapers, thick carpet and curiosities hung on the walls. A classy Wetherspoons, I guess.

I got the wood paneling right, at least. Really, The Strangers' Bar is a short hallway with a small bar at the end. It has a distinct rugby club bar vibe, but without any seating or atmosphere. When I visited, the Ashes were on, and a few MPs were hovering by the one TV, pint in hand. Alun ordered me a pint of Noble, a lager supposedly only served at the Houses of Parliament. The beer insider inside me knew it was just a relabeled beer that's sold in countless other places under different names, which is more common than you'd like it to be. The beer was also flawed, with huge notes of diacetyl, a chemical that makes the beer smell like Werther's Originals and is caused by either rushing the fermentation or the pub not cleaning its lines properly. Perhaps sensing my disappointment, Alun took us back outside onto the terrace and started to explain the role of Strangers' and the other bars.

MPs are typically at the Palace of Westminster from Monday to Wednesday. During the day, they work with their staff and meet colleagues, and later in the day attend relevant debates and votes. These debates and votes can go late into the night, and it's these long hours that justify having food and water within such easy reach: popping out to Tesco isn't really an option when you're the home secretary.

"On evening votes you'd grab something to eat, and while you waited for the vote you'd think, 'Well, I might as well go for a drink,'" he says. "Once you're there you meet colleagues and talk about this or that business."

That business might be the wording of policies and the phrasing of a Commons question, or networking when an MP wants support for a bill or a chairship they're running for. People are more amenable with a pint in their hands, whether it's The Strangers' Bar or a 'Spoons in Manchester.

But as I learned, the bars have become much more than that. The House of Commons itself (that's the room with the green benches) is too small to accommodate all 650 MPs—about 200 short in fact. That means that even if they all wanted to be part of a debate, they literally can't fit into the hall. As a result, many MPs have to wait elsewhere for the debate to finish and the vote to be called. Sadly for democracy, MPs vote almost exclusively the way they are told to by their superiors, so the debate is mostly posturing. Still, they have to physically vote and being the closest to the Commons means they often wait in The Strangers' Bar. This is because once the division bell is rung to announce a vote, MPs have just eight minutes to get into one of the two halls that run down the side of the Commons—the "Aye lobby" (voting yes) or "No lobby" to be counted.

So unlike most bars, The Strangers' Bar is busiest on Mondays, Tuesdays and Wednesdays, when the votes happen. During emotionally charged debates you can see why disagreements might occur, especially as whips (those charged with ensuring the MPs vote the way their party wants) go about their business of persuasion. Those whips could be whipping up a frenzy, or simply ensuring everyone is present, calm and ready to vote.

THE MEANING OF BEER

Alun says that while it's unlikely that someone might switch lobby off the back of what was said in Strangers', it was pretty common for information to be shared—sometimes even across party lines—that might highlight issues with policy, or people.

"You might get a bit of this in the bars: if you wanted the government to do something and you've exhausted your processes, you might have tipped off colleagues to ask questions about this or that," he says.

Alun frequently talks in the past tense, because while The Stranger's Bar still has a huge impact on the day-to-day life and rhythm of UK politics, its central role has been diminished by the early debates (now finishing at 7 p.m. on Tuesdays and Wednesdays unless it's a vote on finances or constitution) and the adoption of WhatsApp, which allows whips to contact all their MPs in a heartbeat without prying ears. Nevertheless, Alun says it's still vital to his day-to-day work, even if he's just having a Diet Coke.

"Strangers' is sort of the oil that kept the place running."

In a predigital world, though, the pub and its main product (that's beer, obviously) were central to political decision-making. As I leave and take one last look at The Strangers' Bar, I imagine the centuries' worth of people who have drunk diacetyl-riddled pints here, making deals and arguing over history-making policies. And that's just one bar, in a world with millions.

Drowning in Politics

So the truth is that while we desperately scrub any wider meaning from beer, it drips with it like condensation on a cold pint. It's simply too important to exist in a political vacuum. There's a reason every British prime minister to have ever held office has poured a pint in a pub for a photo shoot, and it's not because they like beer. In fact, if you look at the pint itself you might wonder if they have ever seen a beer before in their lives.

Politicians may not all be beer lovers, but they understand the power of being seen to like it. Breweries understand it too, which is why so much beer advertising and branding is about identity politics—social groups, class, gender, nationality. People don't just love the liquid, they love the idea of drinking a premium beer from Italy, the beer their mom or dad drank, or that brand that used to sponsor the League Cup.

Beer writers make this argument a lot, and are invariably piled upon for their efforts. The response of *stick to beer* is so common in our social media feeds and comments sections that there's even merchandise out there with that very phrase emblazoned. What people mean by *stick to beer* is *I disagree with your view, so please stop sharing it*, a sentiment that underpins pretty much every online argument. This theory is backed by the 2023 boycott of Bud Light in response to trans influencer Dylan Mulvaney appearing on a can—directly causing AB InBev's operating profit in the US to fall by 30 percent.

The decision to work with Mulvaney was not strictly political: aside from a passing reference to her "365 days of womanhood," she talks exclusively about beer and sport in the promo video. It was simply a bid to appeal to a broader and younger demographic than Bud Light's usual clientele—a bid that caused Kid Rock to attack several cases with an assault rifle. The boycotters were clearly unaware that by reacting to the simple appearance of a trans woman on a beer can, they were actually highlighting beer's inherent politics rather than stamping them out.

You see, all elements of production, marketing and sales include an element of politics. Whether @SnowflakeSmasher69 likes it or not, they are furiously commenting on a phone that was made by workers with rights, imported by a company paying tariffs, and powered by electricity that's regulated. The road @SnowflakeSmasher69 walks along was laid by the local authority; the bar they're headed to is licensed by the same people; and the beer they will drink there is taxed by a central government. The alcohol is produced to definitions and guidelines laid out by law, using ingredients grown by farmers who can only use certain approved chemicals and processes; and brewed and sold by people with their own freedom of thought and expression.

In short, if you're breathing, you're surrounded by politics; if you're drinking, you're drowning in it. And throughout history, beer has been used to influence, encourage, distract and even save people's lives.

Under the Influence

George Orwell famously wrote that "Who controls the past controls the future: who controls the present controls the past." I'd add that "Who controls the beer controls the present." That might sound faintly ridiculous, but rulers have known it for millennia.

As we've discussed, beer has been at the very heart of civilization since it was conceived. It was safer than water, bigger than Jesus, and definitely here first. This is because it was vital to our survival, with huge quantities being made and demand often outstripping supply. This created an opportunity for leaders to flex their muscles and earn some money: some took charge of its production, some controlled its pricing, others taxed it. Many did all three.

In 1697, the UK Parliament decided to tax the use of malt in brewing, effectively raising the bills of all breweries. To reduce costs, some enterprising London breweries started using cheaper malt that had been dried directly over fire (rather than in the modern kilns of Chapter 2) leaving parts of it dark and charred. This gnarly, smoky flavor took months to round out in the beer, forcing breweries to age it for longer at the brew-

ery. The increased risk of infection during this time meant
they had to up the amount of hops they put in. The result was
a cheap, dark, hoppy and still-slightly-smoky beer that breweries sold to the working classes, especially London's street porters (effectively nineteenth-century courier drivers). The style
of Porter was born.

Today, Porter has mostly given way to its Irish twin, Dry
Stout, but for more than a century it was the most popular beer
in the UK. London's Truman's and Barclay Perkins were both
at one point the biggest breweries in the world, based mostly
off their Porter production. As it became universally popular,
Porter started influencing politics in return. Endless barrels of
it were shipped around the world, including to Russia where
the politicians and royalty of the imperial court drank the stuff
day in, day out. It greased the wheels, or rather halyards, of the
East India Company too. IPA got the headlines as the beer that
went to India, but that was only because the ruling classes drank
it. The lower-class civil servants and soldiers all drank Porter,
and way more dark beer was sent to India than IPA. So it was
the profits from Porter that kept these sailors taking the huge
risks that the Indian passage presented, and helped the East India
Company grow into the brutal, global power it became.

I enjoy this story because it shows how long the fingers of
beer can be, reaching into events most people never consider.
But the interplay of beer and politics doesn't stop at creating
beer styles and inflating the pockets of already-rich colonialists.
I mean, it continued to do both those things for centuries, but
it also directly altered the course of entire nation-states, and in
one example saved thousands of lives...all the while propping
up the longest dynasty in the history of humanity.

This amazing story starts in Bavaria in 1516, when a law was
written that literally defined what you could and couldn't call
beer. The law, which is still in effect today, is perhaps the most
important document ever written about beer, not just because

of its application back then but because of how it went on to define the biggest selling style of beer today—Pilsner. All the more odd then that very few people seem to know its history, its impact…or the fact that if you're in Bavaria and ask the right person, you can see an original copy.

Castle Kaltenberg

The prince of Bavaria is sitting below six portraits of his ancestors, on the first floor of his seventeenth-century castle. In a rather unlikely twist, I'm sitting opposite him.

I'm a little hungover from my exploits at the Augustiner Keller after visiting Spaten, but I've just taken an hour-long train from central Munich to Geltendorf, the last Metro stop west of the city. My destination is the home of Prince Luitpold, of the House of Wittelsbach. To say I had no idea what to expect still gives my imagination too much credit. As I looked out of the window I saw the reflection of a man utterly out of his depth.

The weather is bleak. The passing scenery is covered in week-old snow that's turning gray and slushy, and dense fog obscures the horizon in every direction. I'm forcibly reminded of Jonathan Harker's journey to Dracula's castle, an image brought into sharper focus by the stark, wrought-iron sign that announces my arrival at Schloss (*Castle*) Kaltenberg. I cross the moat, head up the icy stairs and through a heavy oak door.

Prince Luitpold isn't smiling, but he's not as serious-looking as, say, Ludwig III, who stares disapprovingly at me from his painting. In fact, none of the men on the wall seem particularly pleased to see me. *Say cheese* was clearly not invented until the twentieth century. Together these dukes account for more than a century of the Wittelsbachs' 900-year reign of Bavaria—the longest tenure of any royal family in history, according to the prince.

His left hand rests on a mottled gray book. Despite the grandeur of the room, and the fact that this is my first scrape with royalty, it's this that I can't take my eyes off. It's why I'm here. Or at least I think it is. I can't quite believe that the most famous brewing document ever produced is not only on this table, but coated in the same cardboard as a WH Smith binder I had at school. Surely one of the original copies of this 500-year-old book should be leather-bound, kept in a glass case that's only opened in perfectly humid conditions and handled with gloves and hushed tones. I'm also a little confused, because a quick Google of this remarkable piece of history yields endless pages of beautifully designed, large-format posters with wax seals and hand-drawn borders. Perhaps this is a copy, or a draft, or something else entirely. Rather bravely I say as much, which finally causes the prince to smile.

"The image most people have seen, the big poster, was a fake so brewers could put it in their breweries," he explains. "The Reinheitsgebot is just one part of this law book, and the part about beer is actually very small."

So in some ways the book *is* something else entirely. It is, in fact, a very dry set of regulations put together after the unification of northern and southern Bavaria in the sixteenth century. It covers all manner of topics, but mostly how much tax people were going to be paying the Wittelsbach family from now on.

Prince Luitpold picks up the book and flicks through its pages. Even for a law book it looks daunting and dense: blocks of justified paragraphs in Gothic font, broken up by drawn-out titles in bold. Its condition is incredible considering the prince says he found it in a church archive, and that it was printed in 1520 (printing and distribution took a while in those days). At this point I'd love to tell you that the printing press was modeled on some piece of brewing equipment, but some stories claim it was a wine press that inspired goldsmith Johannes Gutenberg's original design, barely a century before.

The prince keeps on flicking through, the pages stiff with age and thick ink. Finally it falls open on one marked by a torn strip of paper. He traces an index finger along the lines as he translates, struggling a little with the archaic font and the fact that Germans like to put their verbs at the end of sentences. The section on beer is barely a page, and the most famous part is just one line.

"...we wish to emphasize that in future in all cities, market-towns and in the country, the only ingredients used for the brewing of beer must be Barley, Hops and Water."

The prince keeps reading, but I've tuned out. So much fuss, so much history, for such a small and simple law—one written more like a passive-aggressive note in an office kitchen than a piece of legislation. But this one sentence would echo for centuries to come, and is still debated today.

"That's the beauty of writing law," says the prince. "With the EU you'd have pages and pages of notes for such a thing. But it's amazing that this simple law has lasted 500 years, and defined a product."

Now, anyone who has done a brewery tour is probably scratching their heads. Hops, barley and water are the three main ingredients of beer...what else were the Germans making it with? The obvious answer is yeast, but this law was written 350 years before yeast's role was discovered. It actually refers to the fact that you can make beer with lots of different grains, herbs and spices. In fact, with modern breweries obsessed with oat-heavy hazy IPA and most multinational lagers made with maize or rice, a minority of beer these days is actually just made with barley, hops and water. That was true in the sixteenth century as well, though for very different reasons. Back then, beer was made with whatever you had available to you. If you couldn't get your hands on enough barley you might use wheat, or rye, or spelt. If you had no access to hops you'd use bog myrtle, yarrow, Myrica gale, henbane or wild rosemary. And that had its risks, risks that the prince says needed to be regulated:

"The Wittelsbachs are the longest ruling royal family in the world," repeats the prince. "How do you achieve that? You have to keep people safe and happy."

The Reinheitsgebot translates as *Purity order*, and the prince says it was enacted to protect consumers. The simplest thing it did was set the price of beer at an affordable rate, so no brewery could extort their customers. Beer was still a vital source of nutrition and hydration, and any fluctuation in price could see people resort to drinking water. Obviously we'd all rather drink beer than water, but that's especially true when the local water supply was occasionally frozen solid or riddled with disease—between 1348 (the first Black Plague) and 1680, Munich had no fewer than twenty-five major epidemics. That's nearly one every decade.

With the price fixed, the law went on to solve another major issue. Beer may be free of disease, but that didn't ensure it was safe. The purity law prevented brewers from improvising with things that were a bit (and sometimes a lot) poisonous. Before 1516 it wasn't uncommon for less scrupulous brewers to make weak beer, then use psychoactive herbs to create the sense of inebriation. Unfortunately some of these herbs, when consumed in large quantities, were poisonous. Wild rosemary is toxic and even hallucinogenic in large quantities, while yarrow could induce menstruation, making it dangerous for pregnant women. Henbane was extremely common in beer (its German alias Bilsenkraut is even credited as the origin of the name for the Czech town, Pilsen), but it too was hallucinogenic and could cause a fever, vomiting and unconsciousness, essentially an instant hangover.

It wasn't just intentional stuff that the Reinheitsgebot looked to protect consumers from. In 1893, a brewery was charged with "spoiling its beer" when the brewer accidentally "dropped" a cat in the mash tun—killing and partially dissolving it. Incredibly, a local Nürnberg court acquitted the brewery on the grounds that occasional animal contamination was unavoidable. Thankfully the appeal was successful.

Now, it's hard to see Bavarian beer drinkers begrudging the removal of slightly deadly herbs or slightly dead mammals from their beer, but the purity law also precluded one nutritious and delicious ingredient: the tight definition meant that breweries were no longer allowed to brew with wheat, a common grain in Bavarian brewing at the time. The aim was to lower its price and ensure there was plenty of wheat for bread baking, which was as vital as beer for feeding the population. One bad harvest and suddenly bread might become too expensive for the average person, which would cause famine and, more important to the Wittelsbachs, civil unrest.

The result was one of the earliest recorded food safety laws, and anyone who has run a food business or farm can tell you that there are a few of those around today. In fact, the law was so important to Bavarian lawmakers that when they were negotiating joining the German Empire in 1871 (and later again the Weimar Republic in 1919) they insisted the whole of Germany adopt it.

But its impact is even wider than that—or rather a loophole in it is. You see, the Wittelsbachs allowed a select group of people to keep using wheat in their beers, and that decision went on to save Bavaria from political chaos and potentially genocide.

Where the Jousting Happens

We've finished our formal interview and the prince suggests we tour his brewery. The Wittelsbachs have owned breweries as far back as the twelfth century, and Prince Luitpold owns three, one of which has been under our feet the whole time. Here he brews several different brands of beer, from the mass market Kaltenberg Lager to the specialist König Ludwig Dunkel, Hell and Weissbier.

We step out through the heavy oak door and I breathe in the cold air, glad to be away from the unblinking stares of the Wittelsbach family portraits. We head down the stone steps to the courtyard, where a huge chrome tanker is delivering malt. I look around for the trade entrance and realize the truck had come through the same small arch we did—the clearance must have been millimeters. We step through a door right by the funnel where the malt is being dropped and into the brewery.

The tiles are Bavarian sky blue, reminding me more of a seventies swimming pool than a brewery. The copper-coated tanks radiate heat, and there's clearly a beer going through the system right now. I ask the prince what's brewing: "Probably Dunkel," he shrugs. Dunkel is his flagship beer—a beautiful dry, cocoa-tinged beer that has become Bavaria's best-selling dark lager. With the competition for pale lagers heating up between the big six Munich breweries—Spaten, Augustiner, Löwenbräu, Hofbräu, Hacker-Pschorr and Paulaner—Prince Luitpold decided to stay well out of it, instead focusing on a style none of them really paid any attention to. As a result, it's his dark lager that fills the huge vertical tanks of the cellar and forced him to stop using the less efficient but beautifully carved oak barrels that still sit next to them.

The kit is a jumble of postwar and modern equipment, and littered around the brewery are endless machines no longer in use, including (to my genuine excitement) a mid-twentieth-century Linde cooler. Prince Luitpold says they are hanging on to everything they can in the hope that they can create a historic brewing tour, and I wonder who he expects to come this far out of Munich. My answer comes pretty quickly.

We head back out to the courtyard and through the entrance arch. The thick fog has lifted and buildings I had no idea were just a few feet from the road loom out of the gloom. There's a stand-alone pub that could easily fit 500 people, and a beer garden that could triple that number. During the interview the prince had said something about hosting an annual medieval event, which I'd filed at the back of my brain as *interesting but not relevant*. As we stumble down a grassy embankment, however, I have to reevaluate that opinion. Out of the mist, a mock medieval stadium comes into view, one I write in my notes would *render a midtier English soccer field tiny in comparison*. I later learn it can fit 13,000 people, and forms the center of the world's largest medieval event.

"This is where the jousting happens," the prince says simply. I decide it's probably beer time.

Back in the room with the portraits, Prince Luitpold reaches for the wheat beer first, and I notice the glass he's holding. It's a classic Bavarian Weissbier glass—an elegant, thin vase with lines twisting their way up to the rim—but this one is the size of a cigarette lighter. I look at the table, where he's lined up about ten beers, each with their own bespoke, traditional glass rendered in two-inch perfection. There's a tiny Mass for the lager, a handled jug for his Dunkel. I wrench my mind away from the idea of adding checked luggage to my return flight so I can take a few home, and taste the beer. It's beautiful—rich foam banana, soft vanilla, a little floral note and lots of tiny bubbles that make it feel lighter and brighter than the aroma suggests. Impressed, I take a look at the Weissbier bottle, and do a double take. The text that runs around the circumference of the label reads *Brewed to the Bavarian Reinheitsgebot*.

The thing is, Weissbier has wheat in it.

The Loophole

You won't find it written in the law book, but in the aftermath of the Reinheitsgebot, one brewery was still allowed to brew with wheat.

Not a huge amount is known about the Degenberg dynasty for reasons we'll get into, but they were one of the few Bavarian families important enough to be invited to meetings with the Holy Roman Emperor. We know this because their coat of arms appears in what amounts to a 500-year-old roll call document of one such gathering.

The Degenbergs lived in a castle in Schwarzach, near what's now the border of Bavaria and Czech Republic. We believe that Weissbier originated in Bohemia—western Czech Republic today—so it was likely the most popular beer style in the Degenbergs' hometown. Since the Degenbergs brewed the beer for the region, they must have been shocked to see the Reinheitsgebot enacted. There were, in fact, lots of breweries still brewing wheat beer illicitly and hedging their bets on some kind of customary right should court officials come knocking (for those wondering, customary rights can be neatly summed up as *Well, it was legal when I started doing it*).

The Degenbergs, however, had the social clout to make their business legitimate and obtained an official right to brew with wheat in 1548. With the little detail we have, we can be fairly sure they obtained it in a *Game of Thrones* kind of way—by pledging allegiance and paying a ton of money to the Wittelsbachs. Both families must have thought they'd won the negotiations, but it was the Degenbergs who got the better deal. The Wittelsbachs had the loyalty of one of the few families that could threaten their rule, but in doing so they had given their great rival the license to print money. You see, the Degenberg family now had a monopoly on Bavarian wheat beer, which had a big advantage over the other beers of the era: you could brew it in summer.

As we've discussed, brewing of lager beers had to stop from April to September because the summer heat was so likely to spoil the fermentations. Wheat beer is an ale, which means it's fermented with a much more temperate strain of yeast that will happily ferment more than ten degrees warmer. It's not clear whether the Degenbergs saw the full potential of their situation, but they did kick up a fuss when another family was granted the right to brew wheat beer. The Schwarzenberg family were granted permission in 1586, which caused a bitter dispute only ended by a border being drawn equidistant between the breweries to dictate who could sell where. We do know that the Degenbergs were making plenty of money, though. They opened five breweries to keep up with demand and bought themselves a large property in central Munich. Their good fortune would have been painful for the Wittelsbachs to see because, quietly, the extravagance of the royal family had taken them to the brink of bankruptcy.

Now, I'm not one to speak ill of the dead or initiate spurious rumors of murder and intrigue, but if I had been around in 1602 I'd have been stroking my pointy beard at the fact that Hans IV, Duke of Degenberg, died middle-aged and without an heir. A seventeenth-century Columbo might point to the fact that his death meant the right to brew wheat beer reverted to the Wittelsbachs, and that this happened just five years into the reign of a young and ambitious duke of Bavaria who had inherited an empty state coffer. Just one more thing: documents from the time show that this new Duke Maximilian had the Degenbergs' head brewer, Peter Wolf, do a test batch of Weissbier at his Munich brewery just months before Hans died. But like I say, I'm not going to spread any rumors.

Now, it's here that beer starts to dictate this part of the world in a way that no one could have expected. Faced with ruin, Maximilian needed to make money quickly. He was only twenty-four when he came to power, but he proved to be something of an economic prodigy. On receiving the rights to brew wheat beer he set off on a fact-finding mission, determining the best locations for wheat beer breweries around Bavaria—ones that would have plenty of local demand and good transport links. Over the next few years he opened breweries in Munich, Kelheim, Traunstein, Vilshofen, Weilheim, Möring, Haag, Miesbach, Hals and Mattighofen, and had plans for another eleven that never materialized. These beer factories were not just there to produce beer for the locals and money for the state: beer was a staple and controlling its production meant controlling the people. These breweries were symbols of the duke's political power and supposed wealth, designed and built to impose themselves upon the citizens.

Given the Wittelsbachs' financial situation, the time and money spent was a huge risk. In a move that was well ahead of his time, Maximilian did precise calculations to ensure that he could recoup the costs of every brewery he built within four years of founding them. He is remembered as one of the early adopters of mercantilism, the dominant economic theory for the next few centuries and essentially the approach of countries hoarding money by producing as much resource as possible to reduce imports and ramp up exports.

Being an economic freethinker is all well and good, but it also helps to have supreme power over the laws of a dukedom, and Maximilian ensured the success of his breweries by making it mandatory for all inns and taverns to serve his royal wheat beer. The combination of his prowess and power told, and money started flowing into the Wittelsbach coffers. Within thirty years, Maximilian had to keep his immense wealth secret, storing the gold Scrooge McDuck–style in a remote castle.

In this way, wheat beer saved Bavaria from financial collapse and potentially civil war, but its importance was far from over.

In 1618, a territorial game of cat and mouse between the central European Protestants and Catholics boiled over into the Thirty Years' War, a brutal conflict that saw at least 4.5 million people die. Caught physically in between the main warring factions, Maximilian had to act quickly to avoid a huge tragedy for his people. When the Holy Roman Emperor Ferdinand I was deposed as king of Bohemia, Maximilian used his great wealth to help the empire strike back, despite the emperor's deposer being Maximilian's cousin, Frederick V. Spurning the chance to be cousin of the king rather than a mere duke, the astute Maximilian's money helped defeat Frederick, and in return Maximilian was given his cousin's land, adding to the wealth and power of Bavaria.

Maximilian's good fortunes did not last, however. The Thirty Years' War was, in many ways, World War 0.5, with few countries remaining neutral and any that tried eventually being invaded...which is how the Swedes of all people ended up knocking on the gates of Munich with some rather large weapons. Sweden, which was allied with the Protestant French, was led by King Gustav Adolf, a man referred to today as the Father of Modern Warfare. His army had conquered and laid waste to around half of the Holy Roman Empire since the start of the war. Luckily for Bavaria, however, he had one rather convenient weakness. Despite promising to "turn Bavaria entirely to waste and ashes," Gustav rather took a fancy to Munich, calling it "a golden saddle on a very scrawny horse." More precisely it seems he liked the beer and offered to spare the city in return for 300,000 thalers (large silver coins) and 195,000 pints. Maximilian, who had fled to Salzburg, gratefully accepted the offer and *stick to beer* took on an entirely new, life-and-death meaning.

As I drained the last milliliters from my tiny Weissbier glass back at Castle Kaltenberg, I suggest my line of thinking for this chapter to Prince Luitpold.

"So could you say," I ask leadingly, "that beer saved Bavaria?"

There is no hesitation.

"Absolutely. In many ways."

The Hofbräuhaus

When I arrive back in Munich, everything feels subtly different. Wandering through the streets in search of a beer, I'm no longer just admiring the patchwork of Romanesque, Baroque and Gothic architecture I did before. Instead, I'm wondering which of these buildings were breweries and beer halls, which were owned or built by the Wittelsbachs as they brewed up their legacy.

Perhaps I've simply been naive to the incredible power that monarchies had in Europe historically, but it feels like you see the Wittelsbachs on every street. The Neues Rathaus (*New Town Hall*) is a nineteenth-century Gothic cathedral to power and bureaucracy on the main town square. Its facade along Marien-platz is an epic 100 yards long, featuring statues of the entire line of Wittelsbachs up to that point in time. They peer down at selfie-taking tourists and rushing commuters, most of whom won't give a second's thought to the people who funded and saved the beautiful city by brewing the beer styles they'll likely drink tonight.

Walking from the station, my feet take me past the Neues Rathaus and through the arch of the old one—which bears the Wittelsbach coat of arms—then round to the left and up Sparkassenstrasse. I'm headed for perhaps the most famous pub in the world, a place so instilled in Bavarian and beer culture that it's the subject of countless books and folk songs. It is also the perfect place to show how beer and politics can never, ever be divorced from each other: it was founded by royalty, is now owned by the state, and has served as the backdrop for some of the darkest times in German history.

Jarringly, the main entrance to Hofbräuhaus feels like a hotel lobby. Glass doors, polished floors and signs everywhere. The only clue you're headed to a beer hall is the hum of hundreds of voices, the muted sound of horns and percussion, and the heady mix of old oak and freshly spilled beer. Opening the main doors is like surfacing from underwater: the noise and sheer enthusiasm rush at you like cold air. Everywhere you look, benches are filled with revelers shouting over the music, tearing into pretzels and taking gulps from liter jugs. I'm meeting friends, so find a table around the corner from the music to give us at least a chance of hearing ourselves. I order three small Helles in my schoolboy German, but big ones turn up anyway...as tourist exploitation goes, it's a trick I can forgive. The beer is what every Helles should be: cold, lightly carbed and frothy, with notes of brioche, lemon and honey. It's not the best Helles made in Munich (for that look to Augustiner), but it's close. We order three more, quicker than any of us were expecting, and I mentally apologize to the waiter. Clearly you don't need to have worked for Hofbräuhaus's full 500-year history to know that a British tourist's first beer always goes down quickly.

The Hofbräuhaus was founded in 1589 by Duke Wilhelm V (Maximilian's father) as part of his pretty ineffective cutbacks as their finances tightened. I don't know about you, but when I have money worries, the last thing I think is *I must open a brewery*.

Until that point there were two main sources of beer for the royal household and its staff. One was the myriad monastery breweries that had given Munich its name, but the higher ranks drank the famous beers of northern Germany, most notably the bock beers of Einbeck. These strong, sweet Braunbiers (*brown beers*) were very well regarded in central Europe, but the Wittelsbachs were getting suspicious that they didn't conform to their Reinheitsgebot law. It also happened to be eye-wateringly expensive to import enough beer to slake the thirst of the 600 or so courtiers, who downed their way through over 200,000 pints a year.

Both would be valid reasons to stop drinking bock, but as always, politics played a large part too.

In 1510, Dr. Martin Luther came through Munich on his way to Rome, and according to his writing happened to agree with me that Augustiner were the best brewers (though he was an Augustinian friar, to be fair). In 1517, however, he began the Protestant Reformation with his "95 Theses against the Sale of Indulgences," and as we know, by the 1580s, relations between central European Protestants and Catholics were boiling over all around Europe. Most of Northern Germany had decided to follow Luther, but Duke Wilhelm was loyal to the Holy Roman Empire and wasn't called Wilhelm the Pious for nothing. He decided that filling his stein with Protestant beer every day was intolerable and started looking for a solution to his purity, financial and Protestant swill issues.

His noblemen came up with the idea of a court brewery and clearly started making preparations before they even told him, because the pitch included the ingredient costs and even a brewmaster named Heimeran Pongratz. All they needed was permission to dig up the old court bathhouse to build the beer cellar. Within four days of showing Wilhelm the plans, construction for the Hofbräuhaus was approved.

For the first few years, Hofbräuhaus made beer exclusively for the royal court, and only Braunbier—the dark lager that dominated Bavarian brewing thanks to the Reinheitsgebot. But when Wilhelm abdicated to live out his remaining days as a monk (I told you he was pious), the ambitious-but-definitely-not-a-murderer Maximilian began to expand the brewery's remit. That started with brewing Weissbier under the stewardship of Peter Wolf and expanding the output of the brewery until it outstripped consumption at the court. This meant the brewery could start selling to other wealthy families and generate revenue for the Wittelsbachs. Since they had a monopoly, this proved a success and Maximilian moved production of the Weissbier to a second brewery around the corner on the Platzl, or *square*, where I have just ordered a third liter of beer.

Here the Hofbräuhaus was part of Maximilian's Weissbier empire for over 200 years, but aside from selling some beer direct to the locals—some of whom decided to drink it right there and then—it wasn't the epic beer hall we know it as now. Even so, it was a vital part of Munich for both the rulers and the workers. When King Gustav Adolf invaded, the Munich brickworks delivered its last 2,000 bricks in case repairs were needed after the fight. Even I can think of a few places where those bricks might have been put to better use (the ramparts, or Adolf's face). Thankfully, all Gustav was after was some Hofbräuhaus beer, which a relieved city provided in abundance. It wasn't the only time that the brewery saved the city: in January 1823, Munich's National Theater went ablaze and the water set aside for fighting fires had been frozen solid by a brutal winter. Faced with the risk of the fire spreading, desperate Münchners went to Hofbräuhaus and grabbed barrels of beer to extinguish the flames—presumably on a *one for me, one for the fire* basis.

By this time the Hofbräuhaus had actually become a pub of sorts, in that it had rooms where employees and special guests could enjoy a beer. But the demand to drink at this special place, which was already a symbol of Bavarian identity, was overwhelming. And so in 1828, Ludwig I, whose wedding in 1810 was such a wild party that it spawned Oktoberfest, licensed the brewery to serve beer and food on-site, opening it up to the people who had loved its beer for centuries. On the first day, thousands of citizens turned up and were blown away to find the king himself among them, drinking in the same beer, sights and sounds that I was doing 200 years later. When the crowd realized he was there, an eyewitness remembers that a call of "God save the king" went up so loud that it made "the barrels in the cellar shake." This remarkable event realized the intangible thing that had made Hofbräuhaus so special—you could be the poorest person in Munich, but when you had a glass of Hofbräuhaus beer you were drinking like a king.

If this all makes Hofbräuhaus sound like some kind of utopia, beer's influence over Bavarians had a dark side. Populist politicians have long understood the power of being seen among the people, pretending to know and love the things they love. As a symbol of identity, freedom and camaraderie across Bavaria, the Hofbräuhaus was constantly visited and exploited by people with ulterior motives. In fact, the Nazi Party was born there.

Dark Times, Dark Beer

Had Hitler been a slightly better painter, none of it might have happened. He first visited the Hofbräuhaus around 1913, when he fled Vienna after being roundly ignored by the artistic community there. He rented an apartment on Schleissheimerstrasse, where he told the landlady he was an "architectural artist from Vienna." She later said that he rarely left his apartment, only doing so to sell his paintings of Munich and Vienna landmarks around town.

Young Hitler's home was just a few blocks away from the Löwenbräukeller, but he spent more time in the garden of Hofbräuhaus, where he'd try to offload his paintings to tourists and the odd sympathetic local. One of those locals was a Dr. Hans Schirmer, who spent a summer night in the garden watching Hitler fail to sell any paintings at all, despite them costing just 5 marks—about $30 in today's money. Schirmer eventually took pity on the man, but found he only had 3 marks left. He offered the money to Hitler and said if he came by his house with the painting the next day he'd pay the rest. Hitler gave Schirmer the painting and went straight to the buffet with the money, ordering "Vienna sausage and bread, but no beer."

Despite being a very average painter by the standards of such an artistic city—one that spawned several movements during its golden age in the early twentieth century—Hitler did start to make a living through commissions. That, of course, stopped when he volunteered for the war effort in 1914. In theory he shouldn't have been allowed to serve in the Bavarian army—he was, after all, Austrian. But either desperation or clerical error made it possible, and he was involved in several battles before being temporarily blinded by mustard gas and spending the last months of the war in hospital.

By that time, the *Gemütlichkeit* (*good feeling*) for which Munich and the Hofbräuhaus had become famous was drained. Like all of Germany, the city suffered greatly for four years, with food shortages getting so bad that the city opened soup kitchens and children were sent to the countryside where they might be better fed. As the war drew to a close, Bavarians were existing on watered-down beer, and powdered milk and eggs. As you can imagine, that was a far cry from the king's diet they were used to, and the city descended into riots and political protest.

That came to a head on November 7, 1918, just four days before the war ended. Munich's beer halls acted as a lightning rod for rioting and, presumably emboldened by drink, a gathering of soldiers and workers at the Mathäser beer hall decided that the king of Bavaria, Ludwig III (Prince Luitpold's great-grandfather), had to go. They declared themselves a Workers' and Soldiers' Soviet on the same day that the leader of the Bavarian Independent Socialists party, Kurt Eisner, demanded that King Ludwig abdicate. That very night, the king fled to Austria, and Eisner declared himself prime minister.

Eisner's time was short and chaotic. With fears of a communist revolution and destitution a real risk for thousands of Bavarians, the city was volatile. Eisner was shot dead within three months and the arrival of Russian-backed Bolsheviks meant all hell broke loose. They started by forming a Red Army, which went out and closed the banks, schools and theaters, then (most

egregious of all) enforced curfews on the beer halls. The Hofbräuhaus became the headquarters for the regime, holding daily
meetings that included the Bavarian and Russian revolutionaries, who spent most of their time arguing over pints of beer.
When the Bolshevik regime was indiscriminately put down by
the German army, the Hofbräuhaus witnessed one of the most
brutal moments: twelve alleged communists were murdered in
cold blood in the beer garden.

As a symbol of Bavaria and its people, you can see how read-
ily beer and blood mixed at the Hofbräuhaus. It was owned and
loved by the people, a place where anyone could come and feel
like a king. But that had been desecrated by the elite: stripped
to fund a war that was lost, used by foreign communist politicians, and ultimately turned into a murder scene. Once-proud
Münchners were hungry, thirsty and broken, and their brewery, the beating heart of Munich, had become the perfect place
for someone to exploit them.

Hitler, at this point, was still a nobody, but he'd impressed
his superiors in the army with his eloquence. With the German army limited by the Treaty of Versailles, the army enrolled
Hitler in a politics "course" at Munich University and then sent
him out to talk to the troops about the dangers of Marxists and
"Jewish revolutionaries" (the same thing in their eyes). Hitler
was far from the first to preach this kind of hate—anti-Semitism
was already rife among politicians and voters in the postwar re-
cession. As part of that job, he was also asked to observe small
and revolutionary political groups in Munich, pretty much all
of whom met in the city's beer halls. It was a task that set him,
and the world, on the terrible course it took.

One of the meetings Hitler attended was a German Workers'
Party gathering at the Sterneckerbräu beer hall. There he listened
to what he called the "insignificant" speakers, and was about to
leave when one suggested that Bavaria renounce Germany and
form a new state with Austria. The suggestion triggered Hit-

ler, who loathed his home country and city of Vienna. He took to the stage to spout his views and, pleased with the response he received, ended up joining the party he was sent to spy on.

He quickly became a popular speaker at their meetings and his infamous angry staccato drew bigger and bigger crowds. Gatherings were eventually moved to the larger Hofbräuhaus, where in February 1920 over 2,000 people turned up. Munich was still in political turmoil, its working class furious at the indignity of surrender. They didn't know the horror of what lay ahead, only of what they were trying to leave behind. With Hofbräu, their beloved national beer in hand, they listened to this militant nationalist.

A large bulk of the crowd were actually left-wing revolutionaries who had come to throw beer at him. That played into Hitler's hands though—violence brought more people, more newspaper coverage, more infamy, and more hearts to win. He knew plenty of undecided-but-angry drinkers would witness it. Once his loyalists had (violently) cleared the hall of anyone who might disagree, he gave a short speech detailing the "twenty-five points" of a new party, before declaring the formation of the National Socialist German Worker's Party—or the Nazi Party.

The Hofbräuhaus, and indeed all the beer halls of Munich, became his home turf. Hitler was a lifelong teetotaler, but he understood how malleable crowds of drinkers were and how quickly they could be whipped up. Meetings like this were happening in pubs all over Europe, but it spread like wildfire in Munich, where the pubs could fit thousands. In the beer halls he preached the kind of hate we've seen throughout history, but also things that people might complain about over a beer, when only their friends were listening and they'd had one too many. In Munich's revolutionary and insular atmosphere it was intoxicating, and unlike many right-wing movements it was mostly the young who were swept up in it. In August 1921 he gave a speech called Why We Are Anti-Semites, and was interrupted by applause no fewer than fifty-eight times—once every two minutes.

On November 8, 1923, he used that swell of hateful emotion to make his first bid for power—instigating a coup directly from Munich's beer halls. Frustrated at Germany's weakened state after the war, the Bavarian local government arranged an emergency public meeting at the Bürgerbräukeller. Hitler saw an opportunity to seize power, filling the other beer halls in town with Nazis and sympathizers, then plying them with drink and nationalistic speeches. At 8:30 p.m. he and a small militia entered the Bürgerbräukeller, where he shot his pistol into the air and declared a new Nazi government with the support of the police and army. In truth he had the backing of neither, which the government quickly found out. They violently put down the revolution, now known as the Beer Hall Putsch, and Hitler was arrested.

By any right he should have been deported, but the judge presiding over the trial sympathized with Hitler's views, and refused to do so. Instead, he spent less than a year in jail, where his infamy and reputation grew. It was during those months in Landsberg Prison—about 40 miles west of Munich—that he wrote *Mein Kampf* (*My Struggle*) before resurfacing as a martyr during the unrest of the Great Depression for his final, tragic rise to power.

It would be easy to overstate the roles that beer halls and beer itself played in the rise of Hitler and Nazism. It was not the Treaty of Versailles by any means, but it would also be naive to ignore it. The Hofbräuhaus among others was the setting, and beer was a magnet, an intoxicant and a social leveler that made Hitler's job much easier. It literally brought his target demographic together, bonded them, loosened their lips and impaired their judgment.

It's also interesting to wonder whether the Nazi revolution could have happened in any other city. His Beer Hall Putsch failed, but it created the legend and recruitment tools upon which his second attempt was built. Its fifteenth anniversary even served as the backdrop—and part of the inspiration—for Kristallnacht, a night of horrific violence against Jewish people in 1938. Could Hitler's rise to national political symbol have happened in a city with a less ingrained beer drinking culture, or without the vast beer halls in which he made his name? Where else in Germany offered him the same access to his desired audience, at such scale, in such a febrile state?

People the world over ask what would have happened if Hitler had been stopped from joining the army, or had been killed by that mustard gas attack, or deported after the Beer Hall Putsch—but I think there are also interesting questions around whether his voice would ever have been heard had Munich's beer hall culture been less pervasive. Maybe Bavarians wanted to stick to beer, but in 1920s Munich it was impossible.

Chapter 4

Identity

Or how beer defines who we are as individuals and nations

"We can die now."

It was said in a whisper, but the sound carried on the frozen air. For a few moments it echoed off the concrete walls and nothing moved but our icy breath. Then the laughter broke.

We were in the lager cellars of Budvar in south Czechia, taking illicit tasters from the giant tanks that lined the walls. Standing on the lowest level, there was about 30,000,000 liters of Pilsner lager maturing above our heads, and we'd just reached tank 372-220, on which a hurried hand had written *16%, ŽtC, 16/9* in chalk. It was brewers' code for the fact that this tank contained around 22,000 liters of 7.5% Budvar Reserve, brewed with fresh Saaz hops from the Žatec region, that had been maturing since mid-September—more than six months.

The Budvar cellars are kept at 36°F all year round, and we'd come in from a March blizzard with a wind chill of 14°F. Maybe it was the cold, but my permafrosted brain was only just starting to comprehend our tour guide's joke: that we could die happy having tasted this beer. For me, though, a Pilsner this delicious is a reason to keep living. Hell, it might even be the elixir of life. Think about it, my slushy brain was telling me, a lager would make sense: a historic liquid that saved millions of lives and only improves with age. Yes, this Budvar Reserve tasted life-affirming—it dripped with moussey foam from my clumsy tank pour, and swam with floral, strawberry jam hop oils and croissant malt aromas, all chased down by soft, moreish bitterness.

It may sound like hyperbole, but our tour guide knows what he's talking about. Honza Krátký has worked at Budvar for fifty-five years, joining in the late sixties as the head of quality control when the brewery was under the control of the Soviet government. Although he retired from production a few years ago, he still gives tours, which I'm told often include allusions to death. At eighty years old I guess you might have a different perspective on life; you might actually be picking your spot. Not many of us want to die at work, but Honza hopes he'll meet his end beneath the tap of tank 372–220.

To be fair, this life is all he's known. He went straight from university and into his role at Budvar, where he's worked for nearly half of the brewery's 130-year history. He will have tasted pretty much every beer that has been through that tank since it was installed in 1968. Walking around he knows every step to watch out for, and every person he sees. He is the embodiment of this brewery, one so closely linked to the Czech nation that separating the two is impossible, literally: Budvar is Czechia's brewery, and Czechia is the Republic of Beer.

The Republic of Beer

The Czech people have drunk more beer per capita per year than any other nation on earth—most recently an average of 227 pints—since 1993. What happened in 1993, you may ask? Well, the country was founded.

This beautiful, hilly and resolutely landlocked country has been caught in the crosswinds of European politics for centuries. It's been part of the Holy Roman Empire; the larger Duchy of Bohemia; a united State of Czechoslovakia; Nazi Germany;

the Soviet Eastern Bloc; once again the independent state of Czechoslovakia, and finally the Czech Republic—which they then rebranded as Czechia.

Such a complicated history should make for a complicated national identity, but the Czechs have such a strong sense of self that it has endured everything. Much of it is the language, developed from the early Slav peoples who settled there after the collapse of the first Roman Empire. As the country's boundaries shifted and blurred, the language remained a constant in the region, even when invading nations tried to extinguish it. Most recently, it set the Czechs apart from the Slovakian-speaking citizens of Czechoslovakia, and ultimately it was practical differences like this—as well as differing economic fortunes—that led to a peaceful split of the countries in 1993. What I find fascinating about this split is how the Czech Republic got beer in the divorce. While the average Czech still puts away 227 pints a year and tops all the leagues in that regard, the Slovaks consume roughly half that. Clearly beer is an intrinsic part of Czech identity—in fact, I'd argue it's as much a defining feature as the language they speak.

We've already discussed how Weissbier, that great symbol of German politics and culture, might actually have originated within Bohemia (what is now western Czechia), but this is by no means the nation's most important contribution to humanity (no, it's not Skoda either). The nation is, in fact, the originator of the most popular form of alcohol on earth—Pilsner. It's hard to overstate the incredible impact that this style of beer has had. Gold in color, vivid in its fizziness, and bittersweet in flavor, it has come to define what most people visualize when they think of beer, and as we'll see, it's spread to become the heart of many cultural identities around the world.

It starts, though, in a small town in Bohemia in the late 1830s, decades before Pasteur cleaned up our beer or Linde started chilling our cellars. Producing clean, fresh and delicious beer back then was much harder, and the people of Pilsen seemed to struggle more than most. The town's beer was brewed by some of the wealthier residents, whose properties on the town square came with the right to brew commercial beer. By historical accounts, their smoky brown ales were dreadful. In 1467, the head of the Bohemian Catholic church wrote that Pilsen beer was "venomous and acrid," and around a hundred years later a writer called Ondrej Bakalar Klatofškvy said if you poured the beer up a pig's ass it "wouldn't stop squealing for a fortnight." To be fair to Pilsen I think that might be true of any beer, but the point is the ale was so bad that the few people who could write back then felt compelled to use valuable paper warning others.

To the citizens' relief, brewing on the town square was nipped in the bud due to the inherent risk of amateur brewers lighting giant fires in a wooden terrace. From the 1700s, the citizens' beers were brewed at four communal breweries, which competed with three more private breweries that had sprung up. While health and safety improved, it seems the beer did not, and by 1838 the other townsfolk had had enough. That winter, the local council tipped thirty-six barrels of beer down the drain, having deemed it unfit for human consumption (and decided against pouring it up a pig's behind). It was done in a rather mocking ceremony in the town square, and it's said that the townsfolk who witnessed it cheered sarcastically, like when someone drops a glass at a beer festival. They then went to the pub to drink some of the delicious lager beer that had recently made it to the region from Bavaria: perhaps it was even Spaten. Feeling hard done by, some of the brewing-rights residents complained about the imports to the mayor, who quite rightly told them to either brew better beer or lower the price…ideally both. And so a few of these well-to-do but terrible brewers decided the best option was to pool their resources, build a state-of-the-art brewery, and find a Bavarian brewmaster to lead it.

Construction began on the banks of the Radbuza River, tak-

ing advantage of the boat transport and soft sandstone for digging lager cellars. The whole concept was heavily inspired by
the breweries of Munich, and in 1842 the citizens hired a German brewer, Josef Groll. Rumor has it they also "borrowed"
a German yeast from the Hacker Brewery in Munich, cun-
ningly disguising its origin by calling it the *H yeast*. The other
ingredients were all Czech, however. Observing the German
law of never brewing in summer, they waited until September
and took advantage of fresh hops from the Saaz region about 50
miles north, as well as that season's barley from Moravia to the
east. A few days before the first brew, they scattered the grain
on the huge malting floors of the brewery to germinate, then
lit the fires that would kiln it.

There are three possible explanations for the miracle that happened next: one is that Groll made a mistake, another is that
he was a genius, and the last is that the history of beer has been
written wrong.

To dry their barley for brewing, the owners used the British method of indirect fire kilning. The Germans and Austri-
ans had been using this technique for a couple of years by now,
making amber lagers that were blowing the minds of those used
to dark brown beer. But the malt that came out of Groll's kiln
was even paler, resulting in a beer that was, to go all Benjamin
Moore on you, more Summer Straw than Autumn Leaf. Rather
than be blocked by it, light would have shone straight through,
making the beer glow like a gas lamp. Flavorwise it would have
been lighter, brighter and even less roasty. In short, it was like
no other beer before it.

So how did they do it? It's possible that Groll dared to dream—
that he aimed to make an even paler, fresher beer by kilning it
for the shortest time or at the lowest temperature he could risk.
Another is that he'd seen it successfully done at some small, un-
known brewery already and we'll never know who did it first.
Or...he accidentally underkilned the malt but brewed with it

anyway to avoid getting fired. In Mark Dredge's excellent book *A Brief History of Lager,* he finds numerous sources that imply Groll—who is considered the inventor of pale lager—was not half as bright as history implies. Even his father is on record calling him a bit dense, so it could well be the latter.

Whatever the truth, the first lager to leave the brewery's cellars was as pale as anyone had seen, and was delicious enough to wash away the muddy reputation that Pilsen had gained for itself. At its first tapping a few months later, a chronicler of the brewery said there were "exclamations of awe" at the color and "snowcap" of white froth, and that drinkers cheered its "crispy, delicious taste." Taking its name from the town, Pilsner was born and brewing changed forever.

I changed forever too when I tasted the beer that's closest to the original Pilsner. You can try it as well if you brave the deep, damp cellars of Pilsner Urquell. The brewery, the name of which literally means *original source of Pilsner,* has kept just a few giant oak vats to ferment the beer as it was done two centuries ago. The official story is that it allows the brewers to ensure that the now-steel-fermented beer tastes the same as the original oak-fermented one, but let's be honest, the real reason is it makes one hell of a closer for the public tour. After seeing the brushed copper, glass-fronted modern brewery, walking down the steps to the cellar feels like stepping back in time. The air gets colder and somehow older, like it hasn't left the caves since they were dug. As I wandered down the gently sloping corridors, I couldn't help but feel sympathy for those that once worked here. Each damp, freezing walkway would have been lined with vats kicking out choking layers of carbon dioxide. If your light failed you'd have been left alone in a darkness I can hardly comprehend, potentially miles from the warmth of the surface.

I was on a tour with a bunch of American and Chinese tourists, however, waiting in line for a taste of the beer straight from the barrel. An efficient but slightly grumpy white-haired man was taking glasses from a metal trolley, and filling them in seconds with great skill. The beer's color didn't inspire much awe in people well used to pale lager, but each one had a two-inch head of wet, dense foam. This vatted beer, which adds a dry oakiness and prickle to the soft caramel, butter and lemon of the modern version, is as close as we can get to a flavor of what the people of Pilsner tasted in 1842. Within a few decades, imitations of this beer were being brewed all over the world, with industries, cities and whole cultures being built around it.

Beer of Kings

Pilsen may have taken centuries to finally make a beer worth drinking, but other parts of Bohemia already had a great reputation for their beers.

The first surviving record of actual brewing in České Budějovice, home of Budvar, is in 1300. Just like in Pilsen, the breweries in České Budějovice were owned by citizens, who gained the rights to brew by living inside the walls and paying enough taxes. That year a local brewer and maltster called simply Zacharius found himself so successful he was able to give a huge endowment to found the town's first hospital—apparently beer doesn't just put people in hospital, it sometimes builds them first.

When Zach's success was noted by the town council in 1495, it decided it wanted a go at brewing too. The council built its own Civic Brewery that focused on brewing wheat beer, so as to not compete with the brown beer made by most of the citizens. The new brewery was a huge success—just fifty years later, Ferdinand I, the Holy Roman Emperor and king of Bohemia no less, complimented the brewery on its wheat beer— eventually asking (probably telling) the brewmaster and his laborers to travel to his court in Augsburg, Germany, to brew a batch and teach the staff their secrets.

But with wheat beer on the rise in both Bohemia and Bavaria, the citizens started to feel like they'd been a bit shafted by the council. By 1703, all the citizen breweries put together were selling less than half the amount of the civic one, and the resulting dispute—which lasted the best part of a hundred years—ended in the citizen brewers being given control of it. By this time (1795) it was the fourth biggest brewery in Bohemia, so this was quite the coup for the 387 already wealthy inhabitants.

It's worth pointing out here that for most of its history, Germans made up a huge portion of the population of České Budějovice—or Budweis as they called it. Even in the nineteenth century, when the industrial revolution started sucking in rural workers to their nearest cities, their numbers were only just below half. The Germans were also typically the wealthier citizens, making up most of the council, owning most of the businesses in the town and possessing the majority of the brewing licenses.

This was a source of frustration to the Czechs, and disagreements frequently spilled into the streets. Tensions came to a head during the 1890 census when German business owners leaned hard on their Czech employees to put German as their main language. Back then, the census counted the *customary language* as the only identifier of nationality—so it was effectively an attempt at erasure. When the Czech employees pushed back they were told that if they didn't like working for Germans, they should set up their own businesses. Which is exactly what they did.

Czech citizens threw caution to the wind and started founding all sorts of new companies in the town—a fertilizer farm, a cask factory, a matchstick maker, even a pencil manufacturer. If the sudden entrepreneurship made the German elite nervous, they must have at least thought their brewery was safe from competition—after all, only a handful of Czechs had the rights to make a profit from beer. Surely they didn't have the money to rival the 400-year-old Civic Brewery?

And so we come to the moment that a brewery was founded directly out of a sense of national pride. You see, the wealthy Czech citizens within the walls did found a brewery—and the cocky Germans panicked, threatening to stop paying them profits from their brewing rights. It was an unclassy, probably illegal, move and if anything just poured petrol on the flames. Some Czechs invested anyway while the more cautious just invested in their wives' and children's names. It didn't stop there, either: two enterprising Czechs called August Zátka and František Hromada set up a stockholding company that allowed *anyone* to invest. All of a sudden, thousands of České Budějovice Czechs, who had never been allowed to profit from the town's brewing reputation, had the chance to own a part of it. Rich and poor signed up and the word spread. Proud Czechs from as far away as Prague chipped in, with hundreds of investors putting in a total of 85,000 gulden (about $1.77 million today).

Even with this incredible national support, the Czech brewery's success was far from assured. The Civic Brewery was huge and powerful, as were several other mostly German-owned breweries in the region. Some of the original backers stepped away when the scale of the task really hit home, but at the first meeting of the new company, some sixty-one major stockholders elected a founding team, with Zátka at the head of the table. Many of this team had worked at the Civic Brewery, and between them they had all the technical and administrative skills needed to realize this Bohemian dream. They set their sights at a modest 8 million pints a year—around half the Civic Brewery's output—and found a site right by the train station and on the main road to Prague. Most importantly though, it was close to a source of pure groundwater, and the founders had waited on chemical analysis of it before buying the land. When it came to fighting the bigger breweries, they intended to do it on quality, rather than nationalist feeling. With that mission in mind, they also employed a brewer from what had become Czechia's best brewing town, Pilsen. Mr. Antonín Holeček was a junior brewmaster at what's now known as Gambrinus brewery, whose beers are still brewed today at Pilsner Urquell.

Construction started in August 1895, and even before it was finished, the offices were overwhelmed by beer orders from just about everyone, including members of the Bohemian royalty. An apparently nervous Holeček kept his notes from the first brew short and to the point: *God willing*, he wrote, before simply listing his target volumes.

Battle of the Breweries

The German population of České Budějovice, who were not short of national or brewing pride either, were shocked at the hype around this new upstart. Some of them began a propaganda campaign via its German language newspaper, the *Budweis Zeitung*. Before the first batch was released, it declared that "the Germans won't drink Bohemian beer brewed from river filtered water, so as not to spoil their stomach!" It was a desperate ploy, and when it had little effect they followed up with a fake recipe: "This is how the glorious Bohemian beer is brewed—a cauldron is filled with straw from barley, chuck in waste from hops." The irony is that the Civic Brewery was the one with quality issues, driven by financial woes and a membership at war over how to remedy them. In fact, they were the ones using river water. Not above a war of words, the Czech language paper retorted that the German pubs were emptying as people went in search of the Czech beer.

The popularity of the new brewery didn't just shock the Germans—it surprised the Czechs too. Within two years they were sending beer by their own fleet of railway cars to Prague, Bratislava, Linz, Vienna, Budapest, Trieste and eleven locations in Serbia. For a people more used to being invaded than doing the invading, it was a source of great pride that their beer was loved so far away, and they did everything they could to encourage it, such as building warehouses near their biggest markets, including Vienna. These new markets meant the brewery outgrew the German one within a decade. Most notably of all, however, the brewery became a direct supplier of the Habsburgs, who had ruled the Holy Roman Empire for centuries. Its beer was being consumed by the most powerful people in Europe, chosen over thousands of other breweries in the Austro-Hungarian Empire. Long before the Czechs had their own nation, they had a national brewery to be proud of.

It wasn't just the beer doing the talking, however. The savvy board of directors didn't miss a trick. They inserted ads into every Czech language newspaper that had space, and paid papers for positive press in the news columns. The brewery was also a huge supporter of education, arts and sport in Bohemia, especially if it promoted Czech culture. The brewery held annual Czech food and drink festivals, funded the national gymnastics program, supported local cultural preservation societies and donated to Czech language schools. It kept up nearly all of those commitments when the First World War broke out, and in the face of declining sales and the seizure of its equipment for the war effort, still found money to donate to servicemen of its territorial army and the Red Cross.

The brewery made it through the war relatively unscathed, and its international reputation helped it rebuild its export markets quicker than most. It was for this purpose that they looked to create a new beer and brand—one that was a little easier for foreigners to pronounce than its trading name of Akc. Pivovar Budějovice. Budvar was a portmanteau of the town's name and the Czech for *brewery* (Pivovar) and it was first applied to its 5% pale lager. The name proved so catchy that it eventually came to be the brewery's alias, with the addition of *Budějovické pivo* or *Budweiser Pivo* to ensure people understood its famous origin.

Unfortunately it wasn't long before war broke out a second time. When Germany annexed large parts of Czechoslovakia in 1938, Budvar once again stepped up for its people, providing financial support to the Czech refugees who flooded toward the central parts of the country until the brewery was brought under the control of the Nazi General Directorate of State Forests and Farms in March 1942. For the rest of the war, drinkers and workers quietly sought to limit the Fascist influence on their beloved brewery. When the new Nazi-imposed CEO Wilhelm Bäcker changed its name from Budvar to the catchy Protectorate of Bohemia and Moravia, České Budějovice Brewery Management, drinkers boycotted the brewery so effectively that the change lasted just six months.

Undoing the physical damage caused by the war was less easy. While the brewery was never hit by a bomb or caught in cross fire, most of the equipment was stripped, its transport derailed and even its horses dispersed in the name of Nazism—one lonely stallion remained for beer deliveries (even in a one-horse town, beer takes precedence). When the Nazi regime fell and Bäcker handed back the keys to the board in 1945, it was left to the workers to decide what came next. True to Budvar's form, their main concern was that Budvar became a fully Czech brewery once again. They invited back the board of directors but insisted that two members—J. Pařízek and the board's vice chairman V. Žák—were prevented from ever entering the brewery again for collaborating with the occupiers.

The Czech people's nationalistic—and increasingly socialist— ideals went a step further in 1946. The new government decreed that all Czechoslovakian breweries that made more than 150,000 hectoliters of beer before Nazi annexation were to be nationalized. Budvar just about fell into that category (they made 158,000 in 1937) and against the wishes of the board, the workers insisted that the brewery be nationalized for the common good. As part of this process, Budvar was merged with several breweries to become the South Bohemian Breweries. Remarkably, this included all the assets and brands from Budvar's former competitor, the Civic Brewery, which was seized for being run by traitors to the Czech people.

Budvar had become not just a symbol of the Czech state, but part of it. To the workers who pushed for it, it saw the unification of their political, national and social beliefs...but Budvar under communism didn't live up to expectations.

First there was another political purge of anyone not seen as left-wing enough—many of the top brass resigned, were booted out, or demoted. While believers in the system enthusiastically worked all hours of the day for the great cause of slaking their comrades' thirst, those promoted to management roles were either entirely underqualified to run such a large operation, or hampered by those that were. By 1949, the highlight of Budvar's export was to send a case of six beers to Stalin for his birthday.

While the Western world evolved at lightning speed, things moved slower in the Eastern Bloc. Corruption, fear and political inflexibility caused betrayal after betrayal of the workers' hard labor throughout the region. Budvar did its best in this strange new world, and its export within the Soviet nations eventually started to blossom, helping the Czechs retain their national identity as world-class brewers. However, this brought its own issues. With demand growing, the brewery needed new equipment, and funding for any such expansion now lay with the politicians—ultimately the Ministry of Food Industry in Russia. Approval was granted in 1967, but delays in getting any funds to the brewery (as well as holdups in stainless steel manufacturing) meant that by the time all the works were under way, communism had fallen and Budvar's place in the world was once again under threat.

Beer of the People

It's strange to think that our tour guide lived and worked through all this—a long and complicated history that feels like it happened centuries ago. To Honza, an eighty-year-old bundle of energy and morbid wisecracks necking beer despite having five more tours this afternoon, it's not history: it's his career.

Just as it feels like my brain has defrosted and a million questions start to form for him, I'm told he needs to prepare for his next tour (which I assume is code for *more beer*). I'm pulled away like a drunk teenager from a fight and up to the brewery's "training center"—which of course is a bar. We're here, I'm told, to learn how to pour beer properly. It's not said unkindly, but the meaning is clear: Brits don't know how to pour beer. They're right.

The phrase *top that up* is all too common in British pubs. Perhaps it's because our beer is increasingly expensive and we want our money's worth (ideally more), or perhaps it's because no one's ever really explained to our average drinker just how important the foam on your beer is. As far as I'm concerned, the best way to explain it would be to give them a pint of perfectly poured Czech lager.

Our fixer for the brewery visit is Radim, a six-foot barrel of a guy who has just been promoted to global brand ambassador. He's a trained *tapster,* the Czech word for a barkeep and a role given huge respect in Czech culture. While pouring a glass of half foam, half liquid and handing it over, he explains that to a Czech brewer there are three things that make a great beer: the ingredients, the brewing process and the pour. The first two are a team effort, with many people all working together to grow the best barley and hops, before combining them at the right times and temperatures in a brewery. But only one person pours your beer, and in the Czech Republic that makes them the single most important person in the process. The reason that tapsters are so revered in Czechia is that pouring a Pilsner beer properly is far from simple, as I was about to learn to my cost.

It starts easily enough. A clean glass, dipped in cold water to match the temperature of the beer and remove any dust or soap. The glass is then brought up to an unusual kind of tap—rather than the handle pulling down, the tapster twists it to the side, first to 45 degrees then, after a beat, the full 90. The result is about two inches of smooth, dense foam, under which the rest of the beer is poured. This method protects the beer from oxidation (which kills aroma) and kicks out about half the carbonation to stop you getting too bloated. Most importantly though, the resulting silky foam transforms the texture of the beer, from spiky, fizzy water to Guinnesslike smoothness. This foam is so delicious, so creamy, that the Czechs even sometimes enjoy a *mliko* pour—a pint of pure foam (don't worry Brits, they're charged half for it). My favorite pour is a special one for those who want a quick one for the road—the Snyt. It's a half pour that's two-thirds foam, making each of the few sips it takes to finish feel like pure silk.

Radim rattles all the pours off, making it look as easy as flicking a switch. Then it's my turn, with the added pressure that the author of Budvar's official history book has arrived for me to interview. Rather cockily, I offer him the pint I'm about to pour, safe in the knowledge that Radim can save me if I don't get it right. Just as I open the tap, however, Radim's phone rings and he disappears through a door with a key card lock—leaving me with a Czech beer historian who speaks no English, and a glass that's rapidly filling up—no wait, now overflowing—with foam.

It takes me three attempts to pour a beer I feel is acceptable to give to a Czech. Ivo Hajn accepts it with grace, which is the best I could hope for, and we sit at a table with Veronika, Budvar's head of PR and semiwilling translator. Over the next hour he gives me the full story of the brewery, the one I've just given you, complete with sketches of the town and diagrams of the ownership of the two breweries. Every now and then he refers back to his own book, but it's clear he knows pretty much all of the 130 years of history off the top of his head.

I've only done a few interviews via translator, and it's a fascinating experience. You get the live emotion long before you get the facts, as the interviewee's face gives spoiler after spoiler. You know you've asked the right question when, rather than speak to the translator, they turn directly to you, imploring you to understand their point even when you have no way of doing so. That's what happened when, after an hour of digging deep into Budvar's history, I ask why Budvar is still so important to the Czechs.

"Even in communist times, after bread, beer was our second food," he says. "I'm not sure young people understand how much this brewery has influenced our society and culture throughout history. It's part of our national identity."

The Baptism

That night we head out to the local craft brewery in town, Solnice, where we're well and truly initiated into the culture we've been discussing. The building itself is unlike any beer bar I've ever been to—a centuries-old salt store with nothing to indicate it isn't still full of salt aside from an understated sandwich board out front. As we approach it, Radim turns to me and points out an oak beam jutting out from the third floor.

"That's where we hang the people who ask us to top up a pint," he deadpans.

I'm used to Czech humor by now—it's always beer or death with these people. Solnice, however, is full of life for 7 p.m. on a cold Tuesday. A band is playing covers of classic indie tunes right by the door, and a drunken cohort of women are dancing enthusiastically. One beckons us to dance as we walk in. Radim smiles; I keep it British by pretending I haven't seen them. We walk past the stack of horizontal lager tanks, a few of which drip with the telltale condensation of a vessel deep into its cold conditioning phase. Toward the back of the restaurant things are a little more restrained, but only just. There's a large party in the corner, chattering away under a solitary, silver balloon zero. Looking at the group, I surmise that an inflatable three or four has already been sacrificed.

Craft breweries are different beasts in Czechia. Where British ones will mostly focus on cask Bitters or hazy IPAs, here the heart of every brewery's taplist is lager. Pretty much without exception you'll find a 10 and a 12—that is to say a 4% and a 5% pale lager on tap. It's the former that Radim and Veronika urge me to order. It arrives topped with two inches of foam and again I get all those sustaining aromas of brioche, strawberries and freshly cut grass.

As I sip I wonder what the people drinking here, at a small brewpub in the shadow of the government's own brewery, think about Budvar. In the UK, craft beer drinkers tend to dismiss or even boycott large breweries, let alone ones owned and run by the state. Perhaps that's part of our island identity: a deep mistrust of anything politicized or influenced by elsewhere. According to Radim, the pride in owning a brewery coveted and loved all over the world is still there. Sure, it's partly a hangover from communism, but that sense of shared ownership in something ungovernmentlike makes Czechia unique. In the UK we've privatized most of what made our nation great (the railways and the NHS come to mind) because there's too much profit to be had. Here, however, there's too much national pride to let anyone else own Budvar.

That's not to say that state ownership is uncontroversial. For a start, it creates a sense of entitlement among those who pay taxes toward it. Radim regales me with the time a guy in a bar showed

him his Budvar tattoo, then asked for a free pint—Radim had
to point out to the guy that he was drinking a Pilsner Urquell
at the time. Anecdotes aside, that entitlement creates all sorts
of issues for the brewery. Every rebrand is bemoaned, each new
beer treated with suspicion, and its annual accounts pored over
and criticized. Radim says that every election, one party suggests they should sell Budvar off. Presumably it's a bid to appeal to those who want a smaller state and can think of a lot of
things they'd do with the billions that the brewery's sale could
raise, but the suggestion always backfires.

"This is Czech identity in a nutshell," says Radim. "We complain and complain about it, but if politicians actually tried to
sell off our national brewery there would be riots."

Right on cue, another beer arrives, and I look down the menu
in search of something heavy to soak it up. We talk about food
matching a lot in beer, but the Czechs seem to have it the other
way around—they get the beer then see what food will go with
it. Everything is dense and designed to absorb alcohol—heavy
bread, dumplings, rich sauces. Food and drink also seems to
take a long time in this country: the entire menu is either lagered, stewed, roasted or pickled. I order a traditional pickled
cheese dish, served with crunchy (pickled) veg and sourdough,
followed by the goulash. I'm on my third pint by the time the
food arrives and starting to tap along with the band: one more
and I'll be dancing with the welcoming party. Just as I make a
conscious decision to slow down and spare everyone a drunk
Brit screaming "Sex on Fire," the shots arrive.

We don't initially know where the shots come from: they're
placed on the tables of everyone in the bar without explanation. The spirit looks like dark rum, and smells a little like it
too. Radim and Veronika hail a tapster, and after a conversation
that sounds like a hail of bullets, Radim smiles and Veronika
rolls her eyes. The shots, it turns out, are from the party with
the zero balloon. The slightly ruddy, smiling man in the corner

had become a dad that day (inflatable mystery solved), and is following the custom of taking the extended family out for dinner.
Part of that custom is also buying everyone in the place a drink.

I turn to Veronika and ask where the mother will be at this
point. "Still at the hospital," she sighs.

Radim suggests we go and congratulate the man before drinking our shot, and as we do he looks as out of his depth as we feel.
As a new dad myself, I wonder what the Czech for *get used to it*
is. We leave his table as more shots come his way, and I hope
visiting hours aren't first thing in the morning.

As we head to another bar for a nightcap, I express my surprise at such a gendered approach to the arrival of a baby, but
it's shrugged off by both our Czech guides. Beer is how they
celebrate these things. If someone can't be there for the beer—
mother or child—you raise a glass and you drink in their name.
This baby just didn't make it to its baptism. Births or funerals,
life or death: both are greeted with beer and a smile in Czech
culture.

Back to the Future

When the Iron Curtain fell in 1989, there was a lot of sweep-
ing up to do in Czechoslovakia. I think it's fair to say that a lot
went under the rug, but not everything that happened at Budvar during Communism was bad. Progress had been slow but
steady, mostly thanks to its power as an export brewery. By the
end of the 1980s, Budvar was pretty hard to find locally, but
sent all around the world.

That left it in an interesting position as Communism crum-
bled. Did the new government hold on to its nationalized
breweries or find buyers? In the case of Budvar, that would
mean relinquishing one of the nation's most iconic businesses—
potentially overseas. Clearly Budvar was worth a huge amount

of money, and part of the reason for the Velvet Revolution was the dire state of the nation's finances. In addition, Budvar's brewery and buildings were in need of extensive modernization: its latest updates were still uncompleted over twenty years after they were approved, and the bits that had been finished needed replacing again. The situation was further muddied by the fact that Budvar was still part of a conglomerate of breweries that totaled eight different sites. Extracting the good parts from the bad was a legal and logistical nightmare for a brand-new government, and it would have been much easier to sell the lot. It was heart versus head, but when it comes to Czech beer there's only going to be one victor.

Budvar's director at the time was pushing for Budvar to be sold off independently of the rest of the company, but all his efforts achieved was to get him fired. Communism was gone, but the workers at the brewery were campaigning for Budvar to remain a civic asset. With the winds of change blowing directly at them, they took the only measure they knew worked: they went on strike. That action forced the minister for agriculture to sit down with the employees and management, and a deal was struck for the brewery to be publicly funded. The official beer of Czechia was to remain in the hands of the people, a reminder of their heritage and indestructible identity.

As Ivo told me this protracted story back in the training room over a pint of foam, I started to feel like I was missing something. Why did the government decide to keep Budvar, with all the legal baggage and much-needed investment, when the other national brewing icon, Pilsner Urquell, was sold to the highest bidder (America's SAB Miller)? Ivo hesitated and puffed out his cheeks. I wasn't sure whether he didn't know, or we were getting into something he wasn't supposed to talk about. I suspect it was a bit of both.

"I think," he shrugged at Veronika, "it has something to do with copyright."

Coming to America

The dubious award for Longest-Running Copyright Dispute in the World goes to a joint effort between Budvar and America's Anheuser-Busch, the brewer of Budweiser. If you're reading this thinking *I've never heard of Budvar*, you're probably from the US where the beer is currently called Czechvar. If you're reading this in the Czech Republic and wondering what Budweiser is, that's because in much of Europe it's simply branded *Bud*.

Despite being named after the town of Budweis, there's no actual evidence anyone significant from Budweiser (other than, more recently, a lot of lawyers) have been there. Budvar and Anheuser-Busch (now AB InBev) have more in common than they'd like to think, though. Budweiser is, in fact, an American equivalent of Budvar—a beer so tied up in the identity of its home nation that they are almost inseparable. It's not so much the king of beers as the president.

As always, however, history isn't that simple. Budweiser wasn't even created by an American—it was two German immigrants. In fact, if you look at the biggest beer brands in the US past and present, they were all founded by German immigrants—Budweiser, Pabst, Coors, Miller, Schlitz, Yuengling, Hamm's, Narragansett and Shiner. It's Germans for Alle Zeit, and these breweries built American national identity in ways most Americans might not even be aware of.

So how did German immigrants come to dominate the New World's brewing industry? Well, it starts with political unrest in their homeland in the mid-1800s. Central Europe was in a deep state of flux after the Napoleonic Wars. At the time, Germany was a confederation of thirty-nine independent states, but their independence only went so far. The confederation's laws took precedence over local ones, and left them little power to make decisions for themselves. Inspired by the working-class revolutions and liberal advancements in France, uprisings happened in almost all German states, and at risk of being removed from office, in 1848 the rulers allowed the formation of the Frankfurt National Assembly, with the aim of uniting Germany and creating an elected parliament.

It did not go well, however. With personal and local interests of one state conflicting endlessly with another's, if anything it made the situation worse. The assembly was dissolved within months and the revolutionaries were left ostracized and scared enough that many of them fled. While the resulting diaspora included working-class Germans, many of them were middle-class liberals, with university degrees and plenty of money. They ended up all over the world, including, as we'll see, Brazil, China and the UK, but they came in their millions to America. Most stuck to the coast, settling in New York, Philadelphia and the Deep South, but some headed for the wilder middle of the country, in search of land to farm or employment in less densely populated cities. That took them to newer settlements like Cincinnati, St. Louis, Milwaukee and Chicago.

These were formative times for such cities, and German immigrants (as well as large numbers of Irishmen and later Italians) had an outsized impact on their development. Today in Cincinnati you can still see the German influence on life and architecture in areas like Over-the-Rhine. Most of Chicago's architecture burned down in the epic fire of 1871, which a German by the name of Louis M. Cohn admitted to causing, on his deathbed in 1942. Despite Cohn's efforts, records of Germany's cultural influence remain and there are some incredible tales of these people's public lives, which were often at odds with the previous generation of immigrants.

Before we get to them though, it's worth noting that, for the first half of the 1800s at least, Americans didn't really drink beer. Don't get me wrong, they drank far (far) too much, but it was mostly rum made with sugarcane from the West Indies, and whiskey made from the corn that drove the farming industry at the time (and still does). In fact, on average, around one in ten Americans drank more than a pint of whiskey a day. By contrast they drank less than a spoonful of beer a day, and all of it would have been British-style ale brewed by the pitiful 130 or so breweries that existed.

It's going to come as no surprise that this began to change when the Germans arrived. Few of them actually wanted to leave their home, and to them beer was a way to cling on to their national identity. By the end of the 1850s there were around 1.4 million Germans in the US. I'm only half-joking when I say many must have doubted their decision to leave when they arrived in the New World and found virtually no beer at all, but some saw the opportunity. According to Mark Dredge, the revolution seems to have started in 1840 in Philadelphia, where John Wagner brewed the country's first lager in a "miserable shanty" using yeast he'd muled over from Bavaria. Some historians say that the first could have been in 1838 in St. Louis, however, right over the road from Anheuser-Busch at Adam Lemp's brewery. Either way, wherever Germans settled, breweries started popping up. Between 1840 and 1860, beer consumption in the USA tripled, and almost all of it was lager brewed by the Germans themselves.

Chicago got its first lager brewery in 1847, founded by two German immigrants called John Huck and Johan Schneider. Together they rented a large spot on the city's North Side and built a brewery that left plenty of green space and trees. It was a common feature of German breweries, where grass and leafy plants were used to shade the ground above the cellars to help keep them cool. This was the origin of the Bavarian beer garden, and there was now one in Chicago for expats to enjoy with their families on weekends. The joy of drinking lager started to spread to bars too, with beer halls springing up around the city where anyone could enjoy a delicious cold beer alongside German cuisine.

The idea that such idyllic scenes could create any negative feeling seems laughable, but they did. In the 1850s there were 675 licenses in the city, with all but fifty of them owned by immigrants. Some longer-standing Americans were beginning to resent the number of Germans coming to Chicago. Indeed there was a burgeoning nativism movement, and enough skirmishes occurred that new immigrants were forced to create small gangs for physical protection. Some attacks were more subtle and insidious, however. With so much change happening, wealthy people who had time for hand-wringing started to worry about the moral compass of the nation. Part of that angst came out in the form of temperance, which was perhaps understandable given America's whiskey habit. But it put them more at odds with Irish and German immigrants, for whom beer was a daily fact of life.

As the fledgling temperance movement struggled for impact, it decided to ally itself with the nativist movement. Together they attempted to paint all immigrants as beer-swilling Germans, but while that created division between longer-standing Americans and new immigrants, it united the latter in a way they hadn't been before. This outright xenophobic approach created a sense of us versus them, with *them* being any new arrivals "with drink acting as a marker of ethnic identity," as historian Sabine Meyer puts it.

Given that their goal was to reduce the amount of alcohol consumed in Chicago and limit the immigrant population's cultural impact, their mistake backfired spectacularly.

The Beer Riots

By 1853 there was enough anti-immigrant and antialcohol feeling for the temperance-nativist alliance to get their own mayor, city collector, attorney, treasurer, surveyor and six councillors elected. The terms were only a year, but the goal was clear—to claw back influence from the Germans and Irish.

The new Mayor Levi Boone immediately brought back an old law prohibiting the opening of pubs on Sundays—the day that most Germans and Irish preferred to drink. Meanwhile, the council raised the cost of buying or renewing a liquor license from $50 to $300 (around $12,000 today).

Worst of all, the law was quietly changed on a Saturday, meaning most bar owners were unaware of it when they opened their doors the following morning. Boone was counting on that, and had expanded the law enforcement in the city with "sober" and "powerful" men, all of whom had to prove they had been born in America. Many licensees were arrested, tried and found guilty in barely a week.

According to historian Brian Alberts, the German community considered the council's new stance on alcohol as an "assault on their rights and livelihoods, akin to slavery," but initially the response was peaceful. Innkeepers, wholesalers and brewers founded and funded a newspaper called the *Anti-Prohibitionist*, calling out the protemperance *Chicago Tribune* and appealing for reason. Other tavern owners and saloon owners petitioned the council, explaining that the new rate would ruin them. The council ignored the German and Irish appeals, but the rules weren't the same for everyone. While the immigrant-owned bars and shops were kept under close watch, a blind eye was turned to the few American-owned ones. Beer became not just a marker of immigrant identity but a battle line. John Huck organized a society to lobby against the new law, and among others gave rousing speeches at meetings attended by hundreds of Germans.

Still, the protests were nonviolent, with many licensees simply refusing to pay. Just eighty new licenses were bought at $300, while more than a hundred people were arrested for continuing to operate without one, with their fellow immigrants

happy to pay their bond to get them out of jail. The court was
unrelenting in its approach, and it was eventually agreed that
a single test case should be the precedent for all further fines.
For the council it made a lot of sense—a single case that would
act as a huge deterrent to anyone considering serving without a
license. However, it also created a flash point for immigrants,
whether they owned a beer hall or simply relied on them. On
April 20 when the judge was due to deliver his verdict, hundreds started to gather at the courthouse on the corner of Randolph and Clark.

Unfortunately the judge was delayed out of town, so according to the *Chicago Tribune*, the Germans went for a few
drinks in the beer halls—resulting in more fines for the owners. Hangovers be damned, they turned up for the rescheduled
hearing the next day. But this time with muskets, revolvers,
pitchforks and clubs. They claimed they simply wanted to make
their presence felt and to free their "beer martyrs" in jail, but
the *Tribune* called it sedition. Either way, they marched up the
steps and swarmed the courthouse. The security managed to
eject the protesters without incident, but violence broke out as
the police and nativist bystanders tried to disperse them. There
were injuries on both sides as the Germans were forced to retreat north. One of the organizers, a city councilman called
Stephen D. La Rue, was arrested as he tried to make a speech
from atop a wagon—all he managed to say was "My friends!"
before he was dragged down.

The Germans didn't give up, as (clearly untrue) whispers
went around the crowd that the nativists meant to burn down
immigrant houses and murder their families in revenge. They
regrouped and marched once again on the courthouse. The
mayor bought himself time to swear in more police officers—
presumably some of those bystanders who had helped with the
first skirmish—by raising the bridge on Clark Street, but eventually the two sides squared up again. This time, the violence

was deadly. A German called Peter Martin shot a policeman in the arm, and the returning fire killed him as he fled. The Germans retreated once again, many hiding in beer hall cellars where they were hunted down and arrested.

In the short term, the riot achieved nothing. Boone and his council continued to hand out fines, but he and his temperance-nativist allies were on borrowed time. While the demonstrators had been overpowered, the Lager Beer Riots as they became known galvanized the entire German and Irish population politically. A referendum on Prohibition later that year failed, and Boone was kicked out of office at the next election, even losing the support of some nativists who were worried about the city's finances after so many beer halls stopped paying for their licenses. Under the new mayor, the cost of an alcohol license dropped back to $50. German immigrants had made a huge mark on their new home, and around the country their votes against Prohibition set the stage for the rise of lager.

Living It Lager

More than 170 years later, I stood at the corner of Clark and Randolph—the exact spot that these brave Germans, fighting to retain their social hubs, their jobs and their culture, squared up to a bigoted regime. Very few buildings from the time survive because they burned down in 1872, but the road's width still hits you. To block the street there must have been thousands and thousands of them. Looking out of the courthouse window, Boone must have wondered whether he'd survive the day, let alone whether his laws would be upheld.

He's not alone in underestimating the incredible power that beer holds as a cultural force; how it embodies the kind of rights people are willing to die for—freedom, expression, employment. As a nondrinker he'd have forgotten or never known how beer connects families, communities and nations. For those immigrants it was one of the few things they could bring from their homeland, a homeland they had been willing to die for during the revolution of 1848. Now, they had shown they were willing to die for this homeland too.

With a head full of thoughts, I walked a few blocks south down Clark and took a left on Adams Street. I was looking for the oldest known Chicagoan German business still around today. Technically it's a restaurant, but I wasn't going for the food. The Berghoff was founded in 1898, and its history is one of the greatest examples of American storytelling I've come across. It's the tale of a down-and-out immigrant, in a foreign land, finding the American dream against all the odds, thanks to his roots.

Herman Berghoff was born in 1852 in Dortmund. He received a basic education but was precocious enough at seventeen to believe his future lay in America...despite speaking no English. The Berghoff cookbook, which includes a history of the family, says it might have been due to the fact he was the third son (so unlikely to inherit) and because military service was compulsory in Germany at the time. They also mention that young Herman was fascinated by tales of the American Wild West, a fact that will come up again.

Things did not start well for Herman in the US. He was fleeced for all his possessions by a con man right off the boat in Brooklyn, worked on a sugar plantation where he was cheated out of his pay, and ended up a pastry chef on a freighter...until it was found out he couldn't bake. Remarkably he landed on his feet working for a year in Buffalo Bill's Wild West Show (told you it would come up again), and then moved to Fort Wayne, Indiana, to unite with his younger brother Henry. The pair jobbed around as they got married and had kids, but were hardly living the American dream. That changed in 1882 when Herman secured funding from Henry's employer to start a brewery. His dream was to brew lager like he'd experienced at home in Dortmund—pale, frothy and hoppy. To achieve that he did what few other breweries were doing: he imported his ingredients from Germany.

Lager was now America's favorite beer, and the brewery did well enough that Herman was able to expand quickly. He barely stopped even when a fire ripped through his brewery in 1888. According to the newspapers, Herman sat in his office while the fire raged around him, ordering new equipment and writing to manufacturers to ask for skilled hands to install it. He was quoted in the local paper on the night saying, "Tell your readers…we will be brewing again in a month at the latest."

He was true to his word, and that determination went on to serve him well. In 1893 the World's Fair came to Chicago and Herman saw the chance to make a name for himself. Unfortunately, he couldn't get a license to serve inside the event, so he simply set himself up right outside the entrance. Either Chicago loved his beer or he loved Chicago, because when his wife died in 1896 he moved there. The plan was to be the local salesman of Berghoff beer, but he was denied a wholesale license, with city officials seemingly keen to back local breweries. Herman had to think laterally and opened his own bar just a few doors down from where the restaurant is today.

There he served his brewery's two beers—a light Dort-munder like the style of his home, and a dark lager modeled after the Braunbiers of Munich—alongside free sandwiches. The Berghoff café flourished and he opened two more in the city before Prohibition brought beer sales to a halt in 1921. The ever-resourceful Herman closed his two newer cafés and turned the original into a full-service German restaurant, with classic dishes like schnitzel and apple strudel. The brewery, meanwhile, switched to making low-alcohol beer (which was legal if it was below 0.5%) and soft drinks like root beer, which the restaurant still serves today. The Berghoff became known for its delicious food, but when Prohibition was repealed in 1933, he jumped at the chance to serve alcohol again. In fact, he was the very first Chicago business to get a license, and the certificate with its *Number 1* is still above the bar. There is an incredible photo of that first night, where it's about twenty deep at the bar, with frothy mugs of beer being passed over-head and beaming faces look up at the camera. Such was the Berghoff's reputation and goodwill that it's now tradition that every year, when Chicago's alcohol licenses are renewed, the Berghoff is always granted the first one. Given Chicago's his-tory, that's quite the turnaround.

Herman died in 1934, living just long enough to see his res-taurant flourish once again. It's still open on Adams Street and takes over most of a city block these days, with the original bar far left and the dining rooms spanning out west toward the Wil-lis (formerly Sears) Tower. The epic sign is three stories high, and looks straight out of a scene from Chicago's gangster era. The dining room is closed when I arrive, but they know I'm coming and let me in through the bar. We go through a staff-only door at the back, and I'm instantly lost, not just within the building but within space and time too. We go up three steps, then down five, left, then right, then down twenty steps before going up a few again. The restaurant takes great pride in mak-ing everything from scratch and doing everything in-house, so we pass the kitchens, an in-house bakery and even a launder-ette. A few more turns and we end up going down a short slope and into the brewery cellars. A sweaty, hop-soaked brewer in-troduced as Jim greets me, apologizes for his appearance, then confusingly says, "Jim's on his way." I wonder if the CO_2 from the tanks is getting to him, but then another brewer enters and introduces himself as Jim as well.

The two Jims are what's left of the old Berghoff brewing em-pire. The original brewery in Fort Worth closed in 1954 when it was bought out by Falstaff Brewing—whose roots are in the

Lemp Brewery of St. Louis we mentioned earlier. The family retained the rights to brew under the Berghoff brand in Illinois and did so via contract for the restaurant for decades, but when the Berghoff family decided to revive its brewing tradition properly they couldn't get the rights outside of the state. And so they changed the name to the Adams Street Brewery—not a bad idea given that it's the only brewery within Chicago's famous Loop. The branding isn't the only thing that's new. Both Jims cut their teeth at the height of American craft brewing in the late 2000s and early 2010s, working for small breweries that were mostly trying to make the hoppiest beer they could. Adams Street's taplist inevitably has plenty of those beers, but many are still taken up with classic central European styles, served in everything from flights to liter steins—which creates some excitement among the less savvy drinkers, who pick the strongest and richest beers in rather ambitious sizes.

"I watch these younger guys ordering liter steins of Hazy IPA and I wonder how the hell they're going to get through that," says the first Jim.

Like most brewers who have been in the industry more than a few years, Jim is heavily into his lagers. A lifetime of massively bitter IPAs leaves you gasping for clean, easy-drinking beer and thankfully that suits the history and vibe of the Berghoff perfectly. While we chat I sample a honeyed, dry Helles and a delicious raisiny Dunkel. Excited by my enthusiasm, Jim explains that they have a great Oktoberfest beer every year, and even brew traditional Doppelbocks—8% dark lagers drunk in volume every March by Münchners—in spring.

There couldn't be a better location for these beers. The food menu is huge but still largely authentic—"still no currywurst though!" cries the first Jim—which means the beer is born to match. The brewery itself, which sits in pride of place in the middle of the room, is new, but the room's original wood paneling survives and so do the hand-painted scenes of Bohemia behind the bar. Remove the big beer taps and change the language everyone is speaking and you could be in one of the touristy beer halls of Munich itself—it reminds me of the Augustinerbräu Keller where I did my best to forget everything I'd learned about Sedlmayr after visiting Spaten.

Adams Street is perhaps the most authentic location, but it's far from the only lager-focused brewery in Chicago. In fact, the entire Midwest is littered with brilliant lager breweries, modern and historic, so when we think of American lager, really we're thinking of Midwest lager. Of those German brewery names I listed earlier, Pabst, Miller, Schlitz and Hamm's all come from the Midwest, and the most famous of them all comes from another city that saw a huge influx of German immigrants in the mid-1800s.

The Gold Rush

Rolling over the Mississippi and into St. Louis by train you don't know where to look. The river is as wide as most lakes in the UK and the 238-yard-tall arch that frames downtown is like something from an alien civilization. But my eyes were drawn by something much older on the opposite side of the tracks—a distant redbrick industrial complex that looms above everything around it and clearly covers tens of city blocks. It's home to a company older than twelve US states, and atop one giant, flat-roofed building is a name as American as apple pie, but German-Czech in origin: BUDWEISER.

Such success would have been beyond the wildest dreams of founder Eberhard Anheuser when he acquired St. Louis's tiny, struggling Bavarian Brewery in 1860. He'd emigrated from the Rhineland area of Germany about twenty years before and started a highly successful soap and candle manufacturing business. When the owners of the Bavarian Brewery defaulted on a loan he gave them, he and two others bought shares in the brewery at a huge discount.

It was a low-risk venture, and not one Eberhard spent a lot of time working on. Instead, he entrusted it to his other shareholders and an enterprising young brewing supply salesman he'd recently met called Adolphus Busch. Adolphus's first ambition was to marry Eberhard's daughter, which he did in 1861. A cynical person might think the marriage was a calculated move, but the brewery business was still small and, according to a quote in old American brewing magazine *The Western Brewer*, the beer was so bad that first-time customers "were known to project mouthfuls of it back over the bar." Anyway, Eberhard had two sons much more likely to take over the brewery than Adolphus.

Despite that, Adolphus wound down his own business and joined Anheuser. By 1875, Eberhard was so impressed with his son-in-law he made him treasurer and changed the name of the brewery to Anheuser-Busch. Neither of his own sons got a look-in. One, it seems, was too ill to ever work properly and was given a nominal job at the brewery. The elder son, William, had convinced his father to invest in his own soap business that went belly-up, costing Eberhard so much he never trusted his son again, even putting his inheritance in a trust run by Adolphus.

Eberhard must have been relieved to have such a reliable in-law to be a custodian of the brewery, but Adolphus was a lot more than that. He was a big character, a keen modernizer and pretty tech-savvy. Until the 1870s, Anheuser made the same dark brown, slightly sweet lagers brought over by German immigrants who arrived before Spaten introduced British-style kilning. But Adolphus had come over in 1857 and was keen to modernize the beers in the vein of those from Bavaria and Bohemia. After some trial and error he did so to historic effect in 1876 with his friend Carl Conrad.

Conrad was an importer of wines and liqueurs from Europe who was keen to take his own brand of beer to market. While traveling through Bohemia, he's supposed to have dined at a monastery where he was served the best beer "he'd ever tasted." On his return he approached Adolphus and asked him to brew a version for him, and together they attempted to make a beer that echoed the brilliant golden color and crisp flavor of Czech Pilsner. Doing so with American malt was tricky, though. Getting the pale color was challenging enough, but American barley was too heavy in protein, which resulted in hazy beer. They weren't the first to have encountered this problem, and it's what led to the invention of American-style lager, with breweries all over the country replacing up to forty percent of their barley with corn to get their beer as clear as possible. Conrad and Adolphus were two of the few who opted for rice instead, which was more awkward and expensive to brew with but resulted in a much cleaner (or rather less corny) flavor. Conrad named it after one of the towns associated with excellent pale beer—a word that would be familiar to German immigrants and perhaps even other nationalities. Budweiser was unveiled in 1876, and Conrad sold 250,000 bottles in the first year. By 1882 he'd sold an incredible 20 million, but somehow his business went under the following January (most historians blame a shortage of bottles and the surge in price that followed). The result was that Anheuser-Busch acquired the now incredibly lucrative rights. Sadly Eberhard didn't quite live to see that, though when he died in 1880 he must have at least been certain his family was set for life—another immigrant who made it in the land of opportunity.

Adolphus wasn't done, however. Buoyed by the success of Budweiser, he started to invest even more ambitiously. Over the previous years he had made regular trips to Germany, where he learned about the advances being made in beer production and distribution. In 1882 he invested heavily in not one, not two, but three Linde-inspired ice machines. He used these American-made models to keep his cellars cool, as well as to produce ice that he packed into insulated train cars to keep his beer cold all across the US. He then built railside icehouses that stored the beer and sold the remaining ice to locals. He bought shares in several railway companies in a bid to influence where lines were built and who could run on them, as well as building his own railways to carry brewing supplies in and out of his fast-growing brewery. On one trip to Europe he learned of the work of Louis Pasteur, which inspired him to invest in a pasteurizer to help his bottles keep longer and travel farther without spoiling. Even though the technology was expensive, it was an inspired decision at a time when home drinking was on the rise. He also bought the US patent to the diesel engine, installing the first one to be built in America at his brewery in 1898. Initially he just licensed out the patent for money or machines, but in 1915 a company he part-owned started building diesel engines for U-boats. Such achievements could easily have gone into Chapter 2, but in my opinion Busch and Budweiser had a greater impact on American identity than technology...

Bow to the King

In barely twenty-five years, Budweiser went from a local brewery mocked for the quality of its beer to one known throughout the world for its incredible quality and consistency. When Adolphus joined the brewery in the 1860s, it made 8,000 barrels of beer; by 1890 it was making over 700,000. The brewery hit 1,000,000 barrels in 1901, and most of that was thanks to his investment in technology, which meant Budweiser traveled better than any other beer.

Its omnipotence and quality led to its tagline as *The King of Beers*, a moniker with an interesting background. Some claim it is an inversion of *The Beer of Kings*, which was allegedly applied to the beers made in Budweis because they were drunk by the Habsburgs. The chance of Adolphus knowing this is pretty slim, however, and having never drunk that beer himself it would be a daring comparison to make. Another story is that the nickname originally applied to Adolphus himself, who was known to be larger than life and incredibly generous with buying rounds in St. Louis and when traveling. At some point either the drinking public or the brewery transferred that nickname to the beer itself.

Today Budweiser is still known throughout the world for its consistency and quality. It might not be the kind of beer you like to drink, but you have to respect the incredible attention to detail that goes into making consistent beer at these volumes—especially back in the 1800s.

The scale of the original Budweiser brewery, which is just one of a network around the world, is beyond any brewery I have witnessed. There were seven floors of canning, bottling and kegging lines all working at once. As we wandered around the freezing finishing rooms, where beer is held and sampled for quality by employees and tours, I couldn't comprehend the amount of beer in each of the hundreds of tanks. Our tour guide Dave wasn't much help, either. As we stood waiting to pour our free pint directly from one, he said that if you drank a pint every hour it would take you over twenty years to empty it. Predictably one guy in the tour party said he'd give it a shot, before pouring himself a pint foamier than the one I'd given my Czech historian.

What impressed me most, though, was the beauty of the campus. Immaculately kept in shiny cobble and redbrick, the outside is like a Hollywood studio complex, and inside it's even more ornate. The multimezzanine brewhouse was all wrought ironwork banisters, hop-entwined chandeliers, mosaic tiles and gold-leaf pillars. At one end is a 10-foot Renaissance-style painting called *Germania*, featuring a warriorlike lady surrounded by iconic landmarks of Germany. Above her is the Latin *suum cuique*

or *to each what he deserves*. Its German translation was a common
motto in Germany until it was written on the main gate of the
Buchenwald concentration camp. On the stairs on the way out
is another lady, called *America*. She too is surrounded by interesting locations: the Capitol and Brooklyn Bridge, which would
have been one of the first sites German immigrants saw on their
arrival in America. At Lady America's feet is a scroll with *Aboli-
tion of Slavery* written on it, and another saying *Declaration of Independence*. It's a clear, performative statement of pride in their
new homeland. Both are epic, genuine works of art; the kind
of thing you see in the historic cathedrals of Europe.

Comparing such places to Disneyland is overdone, but as I
lined up for my tank pint, I wondered whether it was truly fresh
beer in there or a fake tank with a keg behind it. To be fair, it
was the best pint of Bud I've ever had: its crispy, toasted white
bread flavor fresh enough to make me believe. Budweiser will
never be my favorite beer, but it has quickly become one of my
favorite brewhouses, and that was a very conscious choice of
Adolphus. It wouldn't have just been about selling beer. It was
a projection of his and his employees' German identity. In one
way it was an attempt at assimilation: to be part of the landscape and the growing city of St. Louis, but it also must have
been born partly out of national pride—a statement saying that
the Germans were here to stay. Chicago's beer riots were still
recent history, and millions more Germans had arrived since.
Many of those people still felt like foreigners, and were treated
like them by people who hadn't even been in America that long
themselves.

German beer and brewing culture went a long way to bringing
the disparate immigrant nations of America together, and thanks
to its scale, Budweiser has perhaps done more than any other
brewery to enable that. In a nation without its own clear identity, Germans built it in their own image. At some point, the so-
called natives stopped considering Budweiser immigrant-brewed

lager and started thinking of it as American beer. Nothing about the liquid changed, but the people did. Their acceptance, and indeed love, of Germanic-American lager is everywhere in US culture today, from its breweries to its bars; from its architecture to its art; from its TV to its sport. German lager had helped America form a cohesive identity, and now it was going to help build its culture.

Chapter 5

Culture

Or how beer is a key part of everything from TV to sport

Even the absence of beer can be a cultural force and there are few better examples of its power than the fact that large portions of American society wanted beer banned.

German immigrants may have been instrumental in blocking Prohibition in the mid-1800s, but they could do nothing to stop it in the early twentieth century. Picking apart the collective madness that led to the criminalization of all nonmedicinal alcohol would take another 10 chapters, but it may never have happened if it weren't for the First World War. The outbreak of war simultaneously created the argument that grains were better used for the war effort, while sidelining the opinions of German Americans—many of whom suffered persecution and violence because of their heritage. It was these elements that finally resulted in the constitutional amendment to enact Prohibition in December 1917, but laughably it only came into force in 1920. The government put in interim measures to limit the strength of beer to 1.28%, but that also failed to help the war effort because it was signed into law the week after it ended.

The phased approach did little to help breweries prepare and Prohibition went on to ruin them indiscriminately, but that doesn't mean people weren't drinking. Most brewers pivoted to making low-alcohol beer—anything under 0.5% ABV was still legal—but the process involved making full-strength beer first, and there's plenty of anecdotal evidence that employees, their families and friends were helping themselves before it was watered down. Even August Anheuser Busch Senior, who took over the brewery after his father Adolphus's death in 1913, was known to take a few jugs home. People also turned to their new alcohol dealers, doctors, who were legally allowed to prescribe alcohol to patients. Winston Churchill even got a prescription after being hit by a car while in New York in 1931 and suffering chest pains. Quantities were limited to a pint of spirit per ten days, however, and from 1921, even doctors were stopped from prescribing beer. So it was the black market that really filled in the gaps, making the names of gangsters like Al Capone, who was a local hero in Chicago until the bodies piled too high.

In 1920, due to an economic depression and the fact people didn't yet know what they could get away with, consumption dropped to about one-third of the year before. But according to academics, within two years it was back to about 70 percent. So Prohibition wasn't just a terrible idea, it was a terrible failure.

That didn't stop the celebrations when Prohibition ended in 1933. The policy was a disaster from the start—gangsters made millions, people died from consuming illicit and dangerous liquor, state income dropped as alcohol taxes dwindled, and employment across breweries, pubs and restaurants fell as businesses closed. Several states, including New York, stopped enforcing the laws, and the Great Depression was the last straw. America's people, its businesses and its politicians needed beer.

On the day Prohibition was repealed, 25,000 people gathered at the gates of Anheuser-Busch to get their hands on a case of beer. Perhaps a few jugs deep himself, August gave a rip-roaring speech to the press about how important beer was to the American nation. He talked of farming coming back to life after the Great Depression, and of millions getting their jobs back after fourteen years of self-inflicted misery. He talked as if the railways were veins and beer the blood of America.

"More than beer is back," he declared. "There is a song in our hearts and happy days are here again."

It wasn't quite as simple as that, though. The ten or so years of self-enforced sobriety (or rather underground drunkenness) had leveled the playing field among America's biggest breweries. Technology meant that quality and consistency was now the same across the board, and the proliferation of corn and rice lager meant they all pretty much tasted the same. Where the beer barons had once fought over how good their beer was, there was now little to choose between them. It was no longer a battle for drinkers' taste buds, but for their hearts. The knock-on effect was astounding, setting the trajectory not just for the breweries but for the country as a whole.

This Bud's for You

The archives at Budweiser are small and windowless; the kind of box-and-pipe-filled basement office forced upon a down-and-out detective because he just can't let his last unsolved case go.

But within these four walls are some of America's most important relics, collected over decades and carefully organized. Some artifacts were held by Adolphus himself, and the history of the nation can be traced right through to today. You can see the formation of American identity as Budweiser's heavily Germanic and Romanesque origins give way to neons and sports memorabilia. To me, a Brit, the Budweiser script font and lopsided bow tie are as powerful a national symbol as the Stars and Stripes.

I'm getting a tour from archivist Mike Thompson, who is enthusiastically opening drawers and dusty boxes like a kid showing off his bedroom. There are hundreds of iconic glasses, pull-out screens of paintings and photos of the brewery through the years, and perhaps Mike's favorite—a collection of penknives.

"Adolphus used these as business cards," he says, handing me one and telling me to put my eye to a small peephole in the middle. Staring back at me, illuminated by the strip lights of the archive room, is a portrait of Adolphus himself.

It may be tucked away, and access is only granted to those with a genuine need to see certain things, but the role of the archive at the brewery is big. It was actually started as evidence for a copyright dispute against Pennsylvania's Dubois Brewing Company in the 1940s, but its role now goes well beyond litigation. As well as showing jet-lagged beer writers around, the curation team advises marketers and designers by providing historic inspiration for brand revamps and campaigns.

And there are a lot of new products. The Budweiser bottles have only shifted subtly from decade to decade, but everything around them is in a constant state of evolution. With its German roots in mind, my eye is caught by a wall of liter and half-liter steins (stone tankards) that seem to have filled some very niche purposes. One shows a skier up a mountain and next to them, impossibly, a sunny boating lake. The writing says *Utah…naturally!* Another is the shape of a short, rotund man in a Lycra superhero suit with the words *BUD MAN* emblazoned on it. But we'll come to him later.

The room is so full of ephemera because of the cultural and economic shift that happened in the early- and mid-twentieth century. Much of that stemmed from Fordism, the economic model that encouraged mass production to drive down the cost of goods. Fordism wanted every household to have a fridge, a dishwasher, a car, a certain beer. But first they needed to persuade consumers that they needed those things. The goal was expansion, but winning market share from other breweries when your product was essentially the same would require significant spending on something only a few breweries had ever really tried—advertising.

There were about 750 breweries left in the USA after Prohibition, around half the amount there were in 1919, and even though the amount of beer being made and consumed rose steeply, the number of breweries kept declining. Much of this was down to the success of the so-called shipping breweries— those that had invested in the infrastructure and technologies to get outside their local market. Pabst and Anheuser grew spectacularly in between the wars and even during the second one, so by the end of the 1950s, thirty percent of the market was controlled by just five breweries. They were helped by the work of Gabriel Sedlmayr and Carl von Linde, whose invention had been condensed down to residential refrigerators that meant beer lovers could stock their homes with whatever they pleased, rather than relying on their local saloon. But for them to choose a Budweiser or a Pabst, they had to be sold to. That required a totally new technology.

Like so many revolutions, political or cultural, it all started in the pubs. In the forties, the best chance to watch television for your average American was still at the bar, and in 1945, Narragansett Brewing in Rhode Island (still German, still making lager) first saw the potential of pitching to customers as they chose their beer. According to historian Carl Miller, Narragansett got the advertising placement rights for all Boston Red Sox games for free because, as a Red Sox exec put it, "You don't know what you're doing and nor do we."

Clearly the chance to reach the beer drinker on their barstool proved too good to miss, however. In 1947, half the TVs sold went to saloons and beer halls, and the breweries came flocking. St. Louis's Hyde Park Brewery placed the first prerecorded beer ad that year, featuring an animated stick man called Albert who got into scrapes that he recovered from by drinking Hyde Park beer. Miller says it was standing room only in New York bars with TV sets for the Dodgers versus Yankees World Series the same year, and by 1950, beer was all over TV programming. Many of those ads wormed their way into the national American consciousness and remain there to this day: phrases like Budweiser's *King of Beers*, Miller's *Champagne of Beers*, and Carling's *Black Label, Mabel*.

Most of these ads involved well-dressed people drinking crystal-clear lager from flutes, with huge frothy heads that would send an Englishman speeding to the bar for a top-up. Generally people are in their beautifully kept homes and dressed up for a dinner party whether they're having one or not, with the women indulging as much as the men. Some of these ads are so disarmingly wholesome that it's hard to know what is being advertised for the first few seconds—it could be anything from beer, to washing powder, to cereal. The key element was that aspirational setting and never-faltering, keeping-up-with-the-Joneses smile.

Such homely wholesomeness and equality would not last. They had helped establish a tone for TV advertising, jingles and testimonials, but a new advertising paradigm was starting. Tobacco giant Philip Morris had noted the huge success of a handful of American breweries, and in 1970 bought Miller. It immediately started investing in sports sponsorship, perhaps aware that being on the shirts, billboards and banners of sporting events killed two birds with one stone—it got you on TV and in the high-volume stadiums.

Thus began a new arms race for the domination of that mostly male world. The upshot is that America's biggest breweries ended up funding some very niche American sports, giving those pursuits budgets and exposure way beyond what they could have achieved without such sponsors. The impact of that investment on the small teams, towns and lives within them is incalculable, and on a scale that's hard to comprehend. I'm going to throw a statistic at you that I'm not sure I believe, but comes direct from Budweiser: at one point in the late twentieth century, the brewery sponsored ninety percent of all the nation's professional sports brands. That's thousands of teams across all sports, whether it was the National Hot Rod Association (that's drag racing to most of us) or the New England Patriots. There's a fantastic story in Mark Dredge's *A Brief History of Lager* where a Budweiser exec swears he was flicking through channels and accidentally tuned into a televised duck race, only to see the Bud logo. In 1990, Anheuser-Busch sponsored twenty-three of the twenty-four domestic Major League Baseball teams, eighteen of the twenty-four National Football League teams, twenty-two of the twenty-seven National Basketball Association teams, and thirteen of the fourteen domestic National Hockey League teams.

This doesn't include the fact that Anheuser-Busch outright owned its historic, local baseball team, the St. Louis Cardinals. CEO Gussie Busch was made team president, and under his stewardship and continued investment, the Cardinals won the National League six times and the World Series three times. Gussie only relinquished the role when he died in 1989—despite being ousted as brewery president by his son in 1975. Finally, until 2022, Anheuser-Busch was the sole alcohol sponsor of the Super Bowl and invested over $40 million in its advertising for the event in that final year.

It's not just the US where beer advertising has had a significant effect on the landscape of sport. Globally in 2022, beer was the eighth biggest spender on sports advertising, and in terms of companies, AB InBev was seventh, beaten only by sports companies themselves and PepsiCo.

Sport and beer sponsorships don't always go to plan, though. In 1974, the then-named Cleveland Indians (now the Cleveland Guardians) attempted to increase attendance at a grudge match with the Texas Rangers by selling pints of Stroh Brewery Company beer for just ten cents. The offer is a study in both cynical marketing and toxic masculinity. It came in the wake of an on-field brawl between the players at the last game, after which the Rangers coach was asked by a journalist if he'd bring armor to Cleveland. His reply of "Nah, they won't have enough fans there to worry about" incensed Cleveland supporters, especially once they were five or six ten-cent beers in. Just weeks later he found himself on the field surrounded by intoxicated Cleveland fans—some armed with clubs fashioned from portions of stadium seats.

More recently, Budweiser themselves were left red-faced after Qatar decided to ban the sale of alcohol in and around the stadiums of the 2022 World Cup, just two days before the first game. Budweiser's first response was a hastily deleted tweet saying *Well, this is awkward.* The brewery was left selling Bud Zero instead, and wondering if it would ever see a return on the $75 million it had invested in sponsorship.

Sports advertising may be the most obvious thing we think of when we consider beer's impact on popular culture, but it has seeped its way into all elements of society. If you asked for my most defining beer moment in popular culture growing up, it would be a poignant scene in Jim Carrey's best ever film, *The Truman Show*, that left me bereft.

Truman's best friend (played brilliantly by Noah Emmerich) takes him to the river with a six-pack of beer to hash out the fact that Truman is either having a mental breakdown, or is in fact the lead character of the world's most exploitative reality TV show. Spoiler alert: it's the latter, and everyone Truman has ever known has been playing a role scripted in-ear by the producer.

The thing that gets me most in that scene is the device of the sixer. A sixer between friends is a simple but meaningful expression of love, respect and given time. It says we've got more than enough beer here, so this conversation, this moment, takes as long as it takes. The fact that this sixer was not that, that it was in fact another prop designed to trick Truman back into believing in this fictional world and his fake best friend, makes my blood boil in a way that only really great fiction can. The deeper genius of it from a filmic point of view is that the beer, that damned exploitative sixer, was a fictional product placement—a sponsor of *The Truman Show*. As is always the case in the world of

Hollywood, that prop can of Penn Pavel's (*Naturally brewed!*) was later reused in many other films and TV shows including *Donnie Darko*, *The Dark Knight Rises*, *Cougar Town*, *Fargo* (the TV version), *That '70s Show* and even *24*.

When it comes to fictional beer brands though, there's one that has actually been made in real life (not that I'd recommend drinking it). It's not Schraderbräu from *Breaking Bad*, though that is the beer I'd most like to try, it's actually from a cartoon.

That Wonderful Duff

Like most British kids who grew up in the 1990s, my understanding of American culture mostly comes from *The Simpsons*. Six o'clock on a weeknight was sacrosanct to me, and my mom even started giving my brother and me dinner at 5:30 to ensure we didn't miss it.

I don't need to patronize you by introducing the show, nor really its iconic beer. Duff was designed to be a generic lager that could be from any of America's big breweries, but as a symbol of the US there's one brewery that it resembles most. The joke is enhanced by the fact that pretty much the only other beer shown in the entire show is Fudd (consumed in Shelbyville, obviously) which is close to both Duff...and Bud.

As a caricature of the average American man, Homer is loyal to his chosen beer brand to a fault. *The Simpsons* did a great job of displaying all the sides of alcohol, especially that blurry line between enjoyment and dependence. Along with my dad's penchant for French stubbies, Homer showed me that beer was a natural, fun and comforting part of modern life. The *Simpsons* quote I most associate with comes from an overexcited Homer, running off through a parking lot shouting, "Beer beer beer, bed bed bed!" But Homer's interactions with the barflies of Moe's Tavern taught me that alcohol could have a dark side. It does this best in an episode called "Duffless," aired in 1993, during which I did my first ever brewery tour...with Homer and Barney. To my delight, the episode was written by David Stern, the brother of Daniel Stern, who played the taller Wet Bandit (Marv) in *Home Alone*. This makes the Stern brothers responsible for most of my childhood and teen misbehavior.

For me it's one of the finest episodes of *The Simpsons*, and in about eight minutes of screen time it manages to lampoon the entirety of American beer culture. The most famous scene is, of course, the tour group standing by the beer tanks watching as the same liquid is dumped in tanks labeled Duff, Duff Light and Duff Dry. This is paired with a conversation in which the tour guide admits they have no "ideas up their sleeve" about where to take the brand. The best bits of the tour for me, though, are the pokes that Stern has at beer marketing.

We're taken through most of the twentieth century's marketing approaches as the camera pans down a corridor: there's the poster that says *Prohibition getting you down? Drink Dr. Duff's Health Tonic*, a reference to the fact that the best way to get alcohol during this time was to be (or pretend to be) ill. The tour guide walks determinedly past one that says *I knew he was a COMMIE 'cause he didn't drink Duff Beer*, but stops to proudly show a TV ad with a doctor saying that Duff was the only beer to "fill your Q zone with beer goodness"—which echoes all kinds of spurious claims about beer's health effects. The ad ends with *Proud sponsors of the Amos 'N' Andy Show*, a radio show in which two white men played African Americans. It was a national phenomenon, but fiercely criticized for its lower-class characterizations and racial stereotyping.

The last one we see is a presidential debate between Nixon and Kennedy, in which the two men leave their podiums to promote Duff—with Kennedy getting cheers and Nixon getting boos. Homer mutters, "The man never drank a Duff in this life." It's this phrase that sums up the entire goal of beer advertising during the twentieth century. I can't think of another product that engenders such loyalty in people, where something you consume becomes a key part of your identity. Kennedy could be a Duff drinker, Nixon couldn't. It's clear from who they are, and yet it's not clear how we know that. Your beer brand is like your sports team, unchangeable and probably decided for you by your family, your friends, your location or your politics.

Later in the episode, after Homer is arrested for drunk driving, Marge asks him to give up drinking for thirty days. During that time, Homer comes to realize how inescapable beer advertising is, and how intrinsic it is to his understanding of the world. It's on road signs he drives past, the side of a train he waits for (which goes *chugalug-chugalug* as it goes by). At a Duff-sponsored baseball game, sober for the first time, he says, "I never realized how boring this game is," as an excited Barney double-fists red cups next to him. Finally, when a Duff ad comes on-screen he says, "TV, have you turned on me too?"

He doesn't make his debut until 1997, but one of my favorite bit-part characters in the whole series is Duffman—or as barfly Lenny excitedly describes him, "That guy in a costume who creates awareness of Duff!"

We met his inspiration earlier in this chapter, the short and rotund man in Lycra that formed a stein in the Budweiser archive: Bud Man. This icon was introduced in 1969, and is an unusual superhero when looked at with modern eyes. He had the classic cape and mask but also a bow tie (in reference to the Budweiser logo shape). He didn't get remotely buff until the early 1990s, instead having a beer belly that marked him out as essentially a cosplay dad with an affection for rice lager. Despite this, across different mediums he punched sharks and arm-wrestled gorillas in his role as the "Dauntless Defender of Quality." Clearly the point is to appeal to the childish nostalgia in all adults, while also being in a strange way aspirational: all dads (and let's accept here they are marketing at men) want to be seen as superheroes by their kids. This man, who looks a lot like them but happens to be a superhero, drinks Budweiser. That's all you need to know, and indeed all there is to him.

Duffman is similarly devoid of individual character on the surface, but *The Simpsons*'s writers imbue him with more meaning than the original. It's revealed that every man who has ever been a Duffman has died, in reference to the tragic stories of five Marlboro men. Most remarkably of all, one of the Duff men recognizes his betrayal of his Jewish heritage after doing a Nazi-esque performance at Oktoberfest that goes "If Duffmensch orders you to party, this Reich will last a thousand beers! Oh, ja!" Like so many *Simpsons* jokes, it's funny for very superficial reasons, but you sense the deeper, human satire at its heart. Everyone who has advertised beer, caped or not, has had to play the role of a million people in one, despite being an individual themselves. What you drink does not wholly define you, and yet telling people it does sells millions of units.

Since TV advertising's conception, beer brands have focused on one question to their current or prospective customer—effectively "Are you a Bud Man?" That approach is ripe for parody, but powerful however it's deployed. Bud Man looks different for every brand, from the husbands of Stepfordian wives in the fifties to the lager lads of Carlsberg in the nineties, but the underlying message is the same. Are you like these people, living their best lives? If you are, this is the brand for you. If you aren't, this is the brand for you.

But for me, the greatest advertising campaign of all time did the exact opposite. It said *You are not like everyone else*, and then implied that this might just be your greatest strength.

Good Things

"All you can see is his eyes. They stare blankly, almost in different directions. His mouth moves, like he's trying to remember the ghost of a

song. There's no color, but increasing sound. An urgent, far-off drum-
beat that comes closer and closer as it trips over itself.
He waits, that's what he does."

If you're anything like me, that shot, that beat and those words
give you goose bumps. Every. Damned. Time. It's not the opening of a film or TV show. It's just an ad, one I first watched when
I wasn't even old enough to drink…and yet it's burned into my
subconscious. Some days I can't remember what I had for breakfast by bedtime, but play that Leftfield soundtrack and I'm back
on my parents' green leather sofa, trembling with adrenaline
and wondering what on earth Guinness is.

I was not the only one. "The Surfer," as it's known, went
on to win countless advertising awards, and has been voted the
greatest advert of all time by just about every poll or listicle that
exists. On the surface, it's almost meaningless. After your heartbeat slows, you're left wondering what on earth a bunch of Ha-
waiian surfers have to do with Irish Stout. But that, along with
the incredible aesthetic of the thing, is the genius.

"The Surfer" and the other ads that came in the same late-
1990s campaign was a huge risk: a new approach with a new
agency, a high-concept film just as basic lager and lad culture
were at their peak. Guinness could have gone down the dangerous and now dusty low road that had given brands like Heineken
and Carling so much success, but instead it chose the high one.

Guinness has continually reinvented itself through its history, mostly because it has absolutely no right to be as popular
as it is. At the height of the Porter craze in the nineteenth century it was duking it out with the London breweries to be the
biggest brewery in the world. When the sweeter, quickly made
Mild came along and killed the Porter, most breweries folded or
changed tack, but somehow Guinness endured. It became the
biggest brewery in the world toward the end of the nineteenth
century, and as well as dominating its home market for centuries finally became the UK's biggest beer brand by revenue in

2022. That's nothing compared to its sales in West Africa, which is its biggest market by quite some way.

So how has a dark, thick, charred smooth-flow ale come to dominate a world where everyone seems to drink pale lager? It is, of course, a very complicated question, needing in-depth knowledge about social, political and ecological changes throughout the Western World. Maybe someone will write a book about it one day. But more recently, you can't ignore the power of Guinness's advertising, and how it consistently turns the beer's weaknesses into strengths—how long it takes to pour, its dark color, its heavily roasted flavor. Some of these ads have been so powerful that they've not only made the beer a cultural icon, they've become iconic moments themselves. To find out more, I decided to have my own iconic moment in Dublin.

Those Who Wait

In retrospect, the ski jacket was a mistake. Predictably, it was forecast to rain the entire time I was in Ireland, but in the rush to get my 6:15 a.m. flight I'd only found my biggest waterproof. Hours later, as I lined up a few feet from the bar of Dublin's oldest pub, the sweat was falling faster than the drizzle outside. Good things come to those who wait, I reminded myself.

I've been a fan of Guinness pretty much since I started drinking (we can blame "The Surfer" for that), but as a young man it was rare for anyone in a round to join me on the black stuff, unless it was mid-March and we were all wearing novelty hats. So this was the first time I'd stood in line for a beer in a place where *everyone* was drinking Guinness. That meant that service was slow, and for some reason the bartender wasn't using the sixty or so seconds of settling time to charge people. Instead he was watching, as mesmerized as the rest of us by the way the nitrogen causes that signature surge in the glass—with the bubbles seeming to go downward while the head still grows. Finally I got a pint, and decided to cool off in the outdoor covered area: that liminal space where no one knows if you can smoke or not, so people just hover on the border awkwardly. I found a table in the corner, took the inevitable photo on my phone, and then prepared myself for my first ever sip of Guinness on Irish soil.

Everyone tells you Guinness is better in Dublin—even though every single pint of it drunk in Europe and America is brewed there, to the same recipe. Supposedly it's the care taken by the bar owner, the freshness of the beer, and of course the pour. I'd always avoided or deferred on these discussions, but at last I was going to be able to have an opinion on it. I swallowed and waited for an epiphany...

...that never came. It tasted the same: of burned toast, dried berries, cocoa powder. It was delicious, but still the idea lingered that it could be better. If some pubs are better at Guinness than others in the UK, the same must be true even in Dublin. Maybe I was in the wrong pub I thought, as I looked around. This one had one of those cheesy road signs that tells you how far you are from Moscow or Swindon or whatever. A touristy pub like that will never serve great beer, I told myself.

So I headed off along the river toward Temple Bar: the food, drink and cultural epicenter of modern Dublin. There I met Padraig Fox, whose first name I'm still not a hundred percent sure how to pronounce. Padraig's job seems to connect to pretty much everyone and everything at Guinness, from measuring the head on a pint for an ad to training bar staff. One key part of it was showing off Dublin when important visitors come to town. I couldn't claim to be one of those, but Padraig had agreed to show me the best spots. I assumed we'd visit two or maybe three unique pubs, but I consumed six pints of Guinness as we toured what Padraig considered to be the best pints in Dublin.

After reassuring me (and hopefully all those out there who are spreading the misinformation) that what we drink in the UK is brewed in Dublin and to the same recipe as Ireland, we went through the usual checklist of what determines a great pint—cold cellars, clean tap lines, clean glassware, fresh beer and a good pour. Guinness spends millions on training and tech for pubs to ensure this, but as we went around Temple Bar I started to notice that each place was more beautiful, more characterful than the last. Palace Bar was a Victorian cliché, with huge windows, beautiful mirrors splashed with gorgeous sign writing, and an ornate ceiling. Bowes was like stepping into a 1950s American bar, complete with Art Deco lamps on the bar. Clearly Padraig and I agree on the fact that the context is just as important as the pint itself. As I hauled myself and more than three liters of just-consumed Guinness into bed that night, it dawned on me how that should not have been a surprise. It's the model on which Guinness's brand was built.

My Goodness

Somehow I made it to the brewery the next morning. There was barely room in my stomach for coffee, let alone breakfast, but as I wandered around the Guinness Storehouse Experience I started to feel a little lighter on my feet.

The Guinness tour doesn't actually take you around the brewery. Given that it's the most popular tourist attraction in the city—and indeed Ireland—that would be a lot of foot traffic through a busy factory. I'd also hazard a guess that at least half the people who visit don't actually like Guinness, something evidenced by the number of abandoned pints (or double-parked happy customers) in the rooftop bar, where you collect your free pint as part of the entrance fee.

On my personal tour around the brewing side, I was able to experience the incredible coffeelike aroma of where they roast their own malt, see the immaculately clean brew floor, and the sole, giant tank that holds the world's supply of Guinness 0.0. What I didn't see was a single soul other than me and Padraig. The place is almost entirely automated by computers, telling pumps and robots what to do, as it would have to be to work at this scale.

It was a stark contrast to the buzzing halls of the Storehouse, where sometimes over 5,000 people visit in a day. There they are treated to an interactive museum that makes the most of Guinness's myths and legends, as well as its incredible marketing work. Most of that comes from the brewery's archive, said to contain over 4.5 miles of paper records on top of a digital collection that goes right back to 1759. I wasn't going to be trusted inside (I wouldn't trust myself, to be fair) but some of the highlights were being brought out to me by head archivist Eibhlin Colgan.

The job title of archivist has all sorts of connotations to it. I had visions of a wizened old lady, as old as the archives themselves, with pince-nez glasses and an X-ray stare. Eibhlin was nothing like that, though she had a breathy tone to her voice that implied she literally never stopped being asked about, and talking about, Guinness. Over the next two hours I didn't relent. The internet is awash with Guinness factoids, faux histories and tall tales. To some extent that shows how pervasive it is in culture, but I was determined to separate the brand from the myth. Like all great stories, it doesn't really need to be embellished, though it begins ordinarily enough.

It starts in 1759, with a man called Arthur Guinness, who owned a small brewery in County Kildare. Certain that greater fortunes lay in brewing in a city, he acquired a 9,000-year lease on a four-acre site to the south of Dublin. Around 1770 he started brewing London-style Porter, and was so successful at it that by the time he died in 1803 they had stopped brewing any

other style. By 1820, Guinness was the biggest brewery in Ireland, and it was the biggest brewery in the world by the end of
the century, making more than 1 million barrels of beer a year.
It had its own railway and fire brigade, and had reached 60 acres
in size. Many of the buildings still exist today: some still function as part of the brewery but others are shells left pretty much
as they were. Those with the right kind of pass can even visit
the site of the original brewhouse, which is now where employees store their bikes.

Until the mid-twentieth century, Guinness was a very different drink. For a start there were multiple different versions—
some brewed specially for export, some for the mass market and
some for the upper classes. These are the origins of beers like
Guinness Original, Guinness West Indies Porter and Guinness
Foreign Extra Stout, which is the beer loved in West Africa, although when brewed there it's made with sorghum rather than
barley.

The Guinness most people know starts its story during the
First World War, when barley shortages meant the ABV of the
brewery's main product dropped from around 7% to just over
4%. Guinness embraced the change when war ended, but ran
into a different challenge after the Second World War. In the
fifties, pretty much all Guinness was consumed from the bottle and served at room temperature, but other breweries were
switching to draft beer so pubs could serve it quicker.

The Guinness of old was too effervescent—or *lively*, as bartenders like to call it—to be poured quickly on draft. It was
done in Ireland, but bartenders would have to blend from two
barrels to make it possible, with one under high pressure and
the other much less. Guinness had found itself behind the technology curve.

It was a man called Michael Ash who solved what for nearly
twenty years was known as the Draft Problem. Ash was a

Cambridge-educated mathematician, employed by Guinness as a problem solver. He was actually leading the team trying to improve the shelf life of the bottled beer, and took on the draft problem as a side project that some at the brewery came to call *daft Guinness*. The result, which was patented in 1958, was a two-chamber cask with one holding the beer and another holding a mix of carbon dioxide and nitrogen, which combined when beer was drawn out. Because of its insolubility, the nitrogen formed tiny bubbles that made the beer feel smoother and created a tight, creamlike head that didn't foam over like the carbon dioxide version. How big that head should be, now a matter so important there are wildly popular Instagram accounts dedicated to shaming pubs that get it wrong, was decided somewhat arbitrarily. Talking in 2016, Ash said the team asked managing director Hugh Beaver (remember that name, hard not to) how big it should be. Beaver didn't know.

"We had to decide ourselves that the perfect head was three-eighths of an inch...it just looked right."

Three-eighths of an inch sounds pedantic even before you convert it to metric (that's 9.525 mm), and Guinness is pedantic about it. I'm now the proud owner of an official Guinness Head Measurer, which is basically an L-shaped ruler that (worryingly) measures up to two inches.

Ash's "easy serve" Guinness was released in time for the brewery's 200th anniversary in 1959. It wasn't an overnight success, with many Irish drinkers complaining that the nitrogen muted the flavor, but it gave the beer its signature texture and iconic surge. The old two-barrel system went, but the beer kept its ritual two-part pour: pouring in one go made estimating the final height of the slow-forming head tricky, and also prevented it forming the dome above the rim of the glass that is so fetishized by Guinness gurus.

Made of More

So that's the history of the buildings and the liquid, but that's not even half the story. To unpick how it became such an icon, we need to go back to 1862. This was the year that Guinness started making labels for its bottles, which were being filled not by them but by bar owners all over the world, who ordered the beer by the barrel and decanted it themselves. They were only supplied to trusted bar owners, so having labels proved to consumers they were getting real Guinness.

Until this point, the extent of Guinness's branding had been to carve its name into the top or end of the barrel. For a label it was decided they needed something more recognizable, so Arthur's own signature was chosen along with something equally iconic: these labels were the first items to feature the harp logo.

"The harp has a special place in Irish culture, particularly during the medieval times," says Eibhlin. "The harpist would have been a nomad and it would have been bad luck on the chieftain's house if he didn't invite him inside. He'd then have sung a song about the greatness of the chieftain."

The harp on Guinness bottles, cans, badges and glasses is the Brian Boru harp. This instrument is on display at Trinity College Dublin, being one of just three surviving medieval harps and once owned by Pope Alexander II himself way back in the 1060s. It's so central to Irish identity that in 1921, when Ireland gained independence from England, the new government wanted to use it as the national symbol. Unfortunately, Guinness owned the trademark to it, which is why the Irish national harp faces left, and the Guinness one faces right. I'd love to have been in the room for that particular copyright discussion.

Eibhlin showed me some of the beautiful old harp labels, many of which were even personalized and must have been a real source of pride to those who used them. All the more reason, then, to be baffled by the fact that Guinness barely used its iconography, refusing to do any advertising at all until 1929. And when they did, they didn't exactly commit.

"I call it the Ronseal ad," laughs Eibhlin, "because it literally says *the first ever Guinness advert.*"

We can trace the incredible cultural impact that Guinness went on to have directly to the conversations that led to this ad. Arthur Guinness Jr., the third Arthur Guinness to run the brewery, was extremely nervous and reticent about advertising his beer. After all, they'd never done it before and had still become the biggest brewery in the world. But grain shortages and a financial crisis in its biggest export market of Great Britain meant sales were slumping. Arthur thought the beer spoke for itself, but one brewer convinced him there was no harm in doing a bit more talking via print advertising. Arthur agreed, but insisted that "the advertising should always be as good as the quality of the beer." This is the standard against which all Guinness advertising is still measured.

Advertising was such a success that a few years later the brewery engaged an advertising firm, S. H. Benson, to help with its UK marketing. A young artist called John Gilroy was given the account, and while still coming up with ideas took some time off to visit the circus. There he watched a sea lion balance a ball on its nose, and was amused by the idea of it being a pint instead. He went back to the studio and made the ad, adding a flustered zookeeper he modeled on himself and the phrase *My Goodness, My Guinness.*

The campaign was a huge hit and birthed a menagerie of animal ads that included toucans, ostriches, alligators, kangaroos and more. Gilroy was responsible for several more campaigns, including the equally iconic *Guinness is Good for You* and Gilroy's favorite, *Guinness for Strength*. The health claims for both were, of course, pretty spurious, although Eibhlin says the archives have thousands of letters from doctors who backed them at the time.

Indeed, Guinness is famous for being given to pregnant women and anemic patients long after the campaign ended.

The artworks became so recognizable in themselves that for the queen's coronation in 1953, Gilroy made an ad without the Guinness brand or beer on it at all. It simply shows Gilroy's animals waving Union Jacks and being lifted up by his *Guinness for Strength* man. As far as Guinness can tell, it's the first ad in the world to never mention a brand name or product.

When the brewery started advertising on TV in 1956, it animated Gilroy's work, reaching a new audience with the same imagery. Incredibly though, none of his work was ever used in Ireland where the brewery refused to advertise right up until 1959, when it celebrated its 200th birthday (and its new draft system) with a non-Gilroy campaign ad.

It was decided that the Gilroy era had run its course, but the brewery had come to understand that truly great advertising could stand on its own. Making people buy into the ad as much as the product was powerful, and is a major reason that Guinness continued to prosper as Porter's and Stout's popularity waned. Within just a few decades it was the only large-scale dark beer in most countries. Even in Ireland, breweries like Beamish and Murphy's struggled outside of their homeland of County Cork.

As a result, when advertising became the most important thing a brewery could do outside brewing, Guinness was able to do something no other brewery could—base entire marketing campaigns on the way it looked. To its pale lager competitors, its key characteristics must have looked like disadvantages: the two-stage pour took nearly two minutes (119.5 seconds apparently), and the color could put off anyone not used to such a thing. But it was these features that Guinness focused on during its golden era of TV advertising.

The nineties was definitely not a golden era for beer advertising more generally, however. It was the height of lad culture— with magazines fronted by women as undressed as was allowed, and filled with debauched, masculine tales. In the UK, football hooliganism had been tempered, watered-down and redirected into only slightly more acceptable cultural pursuits, much of it lubricated by liters of macro lager, which finally overtook ale as the beer of choice in the UK in the middle of the decade.

The ads from Budweiser, Carlsberg and Carling focused on boys being boys on nights out, or that special brand of harmless sofa boorishness. Ads included things like *Carlsberg doesn't do nightclubs, but if it did they'd probably be the best in the world* followed by beautiful women throwing themselves at bemused everymen who tear themselves away to order a pint.

The ads were pretty sanitized really, but they all reflected a male gaze that was less than ideal. Looking back at them, though, what really strikes me is the contrast between these broad, everyday life ads and the genre-defining work being done by and for Guinness. In a remarkable period from 1994 to the end of the century, the brewery and two advertising firms produced ads that would change the course of TV advertising forever, and insert an unlikely beer into the subconscious of drinkers everywhere.

It's Good for You

I'm sitting in an office just the other side of the wall from the Guinness Storehouse tour. You can hear the buzz of the crowds, like neighbors having a party. Opposite me is Stephen O'Kelly, the brand director for one of my favorite brands on earth. To be honest I'm a little nervous, but I barely need to ask any questions—I just nudge him in the right direction when he goes off topic. His passion for Guinness, in particular its iconography, is insatiable. So it should be: it's been a part of his career since nearly the start, when he was an intern at Guinness's advertising agency partner at the time.

It was there that he witnessed the creation of Guinness's early

1990s Not Everything in Black and White Makes Sense campaign, where the world was turned on its head for a thirty-
second ad.

"That campaign was a real head snap moment," says Stephen.
"It was the beginning of Guinness starting to think outside being
a beer, and standing for something."

The concept was neat; perhaps the first time that a global
brand had made an attempt at being self-conscious. Guinness
was an outsider, an unusual choice, and it knew it. So while
every other brewery was selling beer through a sense of belonging, Guinness was making a play for people who considered themselves proud individuals. That approach was clearest
in an ad that never got aired because it caused a small political
storm when it was leaked. You see, it may surprise you to learn
that Guinness came very close to being the first brand to air an
ad about a gay couple.

The ad is based in an anonymous terraced house that is in dire
need of a tidy and clean. We see a man (who looks a lot like a
Carlsberg ad kind of guy) adding to the mess, tossing magazines
aside and leaving the bath overflowing, followed by shots of a
marigold-wearing hand that goes around tidying up in a very
American-housewife-in-a-1950s-commercial way. Society and
the setup lead us to assume it's the hand of a woman, but as the
messy man leans in to kiss his partner goodbye on his way to
work, it's revealed both subjects were men.

Today, other than an eye roll from that uncle you don't like
anyway, such a reveal would barely get a reaction, but back
then it was an incredibly bold notion. Knowing it might be
controversial, Guinness and Ogilvy & Mather went ahead with
production, but filmed several alternative endings that left the
situation ambiguous. In the end, the leak saved them the trou-
ble of deciding—the backlash was so furious from the right-
wing press and even some shareholders that the ad was canned.

"I was not senior enough to be in the discussions at the time, but it was really brave for Guinness to pay for that to be made. I guess it was just ahead of its time."

So Guinness bottled it at the last minute, but the success of the rest of the Not Everything in Black and White…showed their marketing department the power of celebrating individuality. It taught them that Guinness's weaknesses could be twisted to become its strengths. And it's that approach that informed the next set of ads, all three of which could make a claim to be the best ad ever devised, and certainly some of the most important.

Sink or Swim

It's worth giving a bit of context here. Snide as I have been about the lager ads of the late nineties, they were working. They were the zeitgeist—if you were an archetypal young man in the UK you loved soccer, you fought about Oasis over Blur, you thought Joey was the best character in *Friends*, and you drank crisp, light, cold pints of generic lager. In fact, it was the midnineties when macro lager overtook Bitter as the UK's most popular beer style.

So it was a dangerous time to be making a dark, heavy, roasty ale. It was also a dangerous time to be changing your marketing approach to highlight just how unlike pale lager you are, and indeed how long it takes to get served a pint.

Which is exactly what Guinness did for its next few ads and the now iconic line, *Good Things Come to Those Who Wait*— although I have to point out that this idiom comes perilously close to Heinz's 1980s tagline of *The Best Things Come to Those Who Wait*. Their ad referred to how long it took for ketchup to come out of a glass bottle, and even featured a pre-*Friends* Matt LeBlanc getting up to some mild parkour as he got some for his hot dog. Heinz won a very prestigious award for the ad, but it pales in comparison to how Guinness ran with the idea of wait-

ing being a powerful thing, making two unique ads joined by
a few remarkable threads.

The first example of Guinness playing on the time it takes
to serve actually came in 1994. The concept of "Anticipation"
is very simple—a man orders a Guinness and tries to be patient
as it's poured and settles. By *tries to be patient* I of course mean
he does a baffling interpretive dance to some mambo music.
The actor, Joe McKinney, is all limbs and Mr. Bean–like facial
expressions, embodying that sense of being unable to sit still
through excitement. I'd love to have been there for the pitch:

"Wait, so he's not in a pub?"

"No..."

"And he's dancing literally the whole time?"

"Yeah."

"Because it takes so long for his beer to be poured."

"Exactly."

"Love it."

The ad was a wild success—such a success in fact that Mc-
Kinney had to move to New York where the ad wasn't broadcast to get work because he kept being typecast. Quite why it
works is hard to unpick, but it has a lot to do with the perfection of the soundtrack. Mambo music, which has its origins in
traditional Cuban orchestral music, seems an unlikely fit for an
advert about an Irish ale, but the song ("Guaglione" as recorded
by Pérez Prado) was clearly picked for its irrepressible, lilting,
navel-jerking feeling of impatience. The song suits the manic
but somehow joyful look of McKinney, and together they are
the essence of anticipation. For the first time in history, not
having a beer was fun, exciting, dramatic. Interestingly, the
original version of "Guaglione" was written by an Italian called
Giuseppe Fanciulli—a strange link to the next ad in Guinness's
golden era of TV ads.

"Anticipation" proved that there was something to the idea
of waiting for your pint. It sent questions bubbling up (or per-

haps down in Guinness's case) about what else people waited for (the perfect wave, perhaps), or what else you could do while you waited for your Guinness. It was that theme they returned to when they switched advertising agency to AMV, and started to challenge the way beer—indeed anything—was advertised on TV.

"Swimblack" was directed by Jonathan Glazer, who at the time was *the* director you wanted to make your music videos— he'd worked with Massive Attack, Radiohead and Blur, and had just made one of the most memorable music videos of all time in Jamiroquai's "Virtual Insanity."

"Swimblack" is essentially a short film with more subtext than a Pinter play. You can see the movie poster and hear the deep voice-over of the trailer: one man's battle against the ravages of time; a tale of glory days he can't let die; the friends who supported him until the end.

It tells the story of an aging Olympic swimmer, Marco, who lives in a nameless but bucolic Italian seaside town. Every year, to prove he is still the town's hero, he open-swims hundreds of yards, racing against the time it takes to pour his favorite beer—Guinness. The whole town turns out, cheering him on and willing him forward from the shore, down the road and right up to the bar. There, bare and barrel-chested, he takes a deep draft into a freeze-frame.

For years I assumed he was that timeless hero, that he won every year. I was breathless by the end, wondering if this was a true story, if I didn't have to grow old after all. I was in my thirties when I realized that everyone's knees start to hurt and that his brother was fixing the race, starting the pour later and later after Marco passed the starting line to ensure he beat it. It was a beautiful white lie that sold a very dark beer, and a message that time is both everything and nothing, depending on your perspective, how thirsty you are and how much your brother loves you.

Interestingly, even though it's a different ad agency, different production house and different director, the mambo music of "Anticipation" stayed. Being Cuban in origin, mambo feels inherently Hispanic, but it's perfect for the Italian scene as well, adding to the feeling of celebration, chaos and anticipation the ad brings to the screen. If the first Mambo ad had an impact on pop music, it was nothing—nothing—compared to the track used in "Swimblack." Written and recorded by Pérez Prado again, "Mambo No. 5" took on a life of its own. Lou Bega's version came out just under a year later, and buoyed by the fact that it was recognizable to anyone with a TV in Britain, it hit number one and sold over a million copies to become the fourth-biggest-selling single of the year in the UK. I feel like there are two kinds of Brits who grew up in the nineties—those who remember "Mambo No. 5" for "Swimblack," and those that actually went out and remember dancing to it. Both will remember the names Monica, Erica, Rita, Tina, Sandra, Mary and Jessica to their dying days.

In Black and White

I'm often asked why Guinness, an international and powerful force, is still loved by the smaller end of the modern brewing industry. Back when craft beer thought it was a revolution rather than an evolution, it was perhaps the only macrobrewery to get a free pass. One obvious answer is that it's the best choice in a bad pub, and a bad pint of Guinness is a rare thing thanks to the work its employees do both at the brewery and with their key customers.

But for me, it was this period of incredible artistic work in the midnineties that cemented its reputation. On a creative level it is still unmatched. "Anticipation" changed the game by side-stepping the biggest issue with beer advertising, something I call the *perfume problem*. There's a reason all perfume ads are baffling, overblown thirty-second blockbusters: because people can't smell the perfume through the TV. Beer advertising suffers from the same limitation, and yet breweries still try to sell their beer using words like *triple malted, double brewed, cold filtered* as if these things taste of anything, or mean anything. I've never actually seen a Guinness ad that references its flavor or aroma. Even its texture, perhaps its USP, is scarcely mentioned.

Guinness's focus on individualism was bold at a time when the discourse in beer advertising was all about belonging. Other breweries were attempting to reinforce identity through lager lad culture, but Guinness was creating its own beer culture—one that welcomed multitudes, individualism, diversity; one that asked why can't beer mean more than a night out and a morning after?

Guinness's continued innovation in how to reach past your taste buds, down your throat to your heart kept on hitting home. The vibrant "Sapeurs of Brazzaville," the thoughtful "Empty Chair" from the Made of More campaign, and most powerfully the Never Alone campaign with Gareth Thomas, the first rugby professional to come out as gay—perhaps even an atonement for not pushing through with the kiss in Not Everything in Black and White Makes Sense.

There were ads that verged on this kind of approach before. Tying food with family, drink with friends, perfume with romance and beer with sport were marketing clichés as early as the 1960s. But Guinness was the first brand, in any industry, whose ads put culture first and left its product as almost a sidenote. It's clear that so many brands and advertising agencies looked at those works of art and considered how they could create a similar effect. Would John Lewis's iconic Christmas ads exist without

Guinness? Would Nike's championing of Colin Kaepernick have happened in a world without Good Things or Made of More?

It must be clear by now that to me, beer is more than a liquid, more than an industry, more than a pastime. More than any other company I can think of, Guinness understands that perspective...and, to be cynical, how to sell beer off the back of it. Whenever I take my first sip of a pint, the shot of Marco—sinewy, aged and dripping with saltwater—fills my mind's eye. I hear the Leftfield track of "The Surfer" thump in my temples. Guinness is indeed made of more.

Culturally aware advertising isn't the end of Guinness's huge contribution to popular discourse, though. In fact, one tangential marketing idea from the 1950s has threatened to outshine the brewery ever since it was conceived. It's driven people to do things that no one ever thought could, or indeed should, be done. I am talking, of course, of the works of former managing director Sir Beaver: creator of *The Guinness Book of Records*.

They Think It's All Plover

The story goes that Sir Hugh Eyre Campbell Beaver, who surely must have some kind of record for the silliest knight's name in British history, came up with the idea for a world records–based publication in 1951 while on a shooting party in Wexford, southern Ireland. He had just missed a shot, and clearly feeling a little defensive became embroiled in an argument over which was the fastest game bird in Europe, the golden plover he had just missed, or the red grouse.

Now, I'm sure we've all embarrassed ourselves at a country estate shooting party at some point, and most people would simply dust themselves off and murder the next animal they saw. But not Sir Beaver. He decided that a book full of such facts would be useful to humanity, and was clearly still talking about the idea (and how fast that particular plover was) when he got back to work. Either tired of or excited by the concept, a colleague introduced Sir Beaver to Norris and Ross McWhirter, two London-based sportswriters who had a side gig in collecting facts and figures for other journalists. They already had a keen interest in records—in fact, Norris was the stadium announcer in Oxford on the day that Roger Bannister broke the four-minute mile. Impressed with their general knowledge (perhaps they agreed with him about the plover, too), they teamed up to produce a tome filled with records from around the world.

As the managing director of Guinness, Sir Beaver was able to fund the enterprise through the brewery, which paid for 1,000 copies to be given away. *The Guinness Book of Records 1955*, was a surprise success, and after a reprint it was decided to update and expand the book every year. Since then, more than 150 million copies have been sold in a hundred countries and over forty languages. The company was sold by Guinness (or rather its owner Diageo) in 2001 for $65 million, and is now owned by Jim Pattison Group, which is the parent company of Ripley's.

It's easy to be cynical about *The Guinness Book of Records*, without which we might never have witnessed such feats as Most Snails on a Face (Fin Keheler from Utah, forty-three snails), Highest Jump by a Guinea Pig (Puckel Martin of Sweden, 20 centimeters), and Most Number of Candles Extinguished by Farting (Gerard Jessie of the Philippines, five candles). But just think about your childhood, and the significance these records had on you growing up. Think of the number of times you've pretended, ironically or otherwise, to be going for a world record. If you're anything like me, a huge amount of your childhood play was based around the idea of breaking one, a notion that's entirely natural today but was conceived by a bad shot who happened to be Guinness's managing director. It taps into the same imaginative plane that superhero stories do—this idea, usually quickly knocked on the head by becoming an adult, that

you are capable of the extraordinary. Think of the excitement
that surrounds things like the Fastest Man on Earth (Usain Bolt
of Jamaica, 100 meters in 9.58 seconds), the mystery around the
World's Oldest Person (Jeanne Clement of France, 122 years and
164 days), the staggering feat of the World's Longest Breath (Bu-
dimir Šobat of Croatia, 24 minutes, 37.36 seconds), or one of
the few records to have stood from the first to the latest edition
of the book, World's Tallest Man (Robert Ludlow of Illinois,
2.72 meters or 8 feet, 11.1 inches). Ten-year-old me wanted to
be all those people, while also being David Beckham.

The Guinness Book of Records definitely attracts the more eccentric people of the world, but it also acts as an annal of humanity's greatest achievements. On the face of it, World's Most
Isolated Man (Alfred M. Worden of the US, 2,234.69 miles) is
a rather bleak record until you realize that it's because he was
orbiting the Moon while his colleagues explored its surface as
part of the Apollo 15 mission. Then there's the World's Youngest Nobel Prize–Winner, Malala Yousafzai, who won the Peace
Prize for her human rights activism—activism so important that
it saw her survive an assassination attempt. We only know about
the United Nation's World Food Programme's incredible feat
of delivering 4.8 billion pounds of food to war-stricken Iraq in
barely six months back in 2003, because of this seemingly superficial book.

Now, it's fair to say that some of these feats would have happened without Guinness's sponsorship of a book listing them.
But it's become the name we associate with all the world's firsts,
highests, lowests, mosts. There are over 65,000 Guinness world
records, and every year the team updates around eighty percent
of them, as thousands of people complete their lifelong dream
of being the best at one thing. Within this annual book is a fantastic snapshot of life on Earth: its strengths and its weaknesses,
its weirdness and its collectivism, its banality and its brilliance.
Nothing underpins my belief about beer's central role in cul-

ture more than the fact that in thousands of years, when our ancestors look into the annals or aliens dig up our lost civilization, they will see it—in all its weird wonder—in a book of facts collected and published...by a brewery.

Chapter 6

Cuisine

Or how beer changed what and how we eat

We established in Chapter 1 how important beer was as food for ancient civilizations, and how it continued to both top up people's diets and function as clean hydration right up until the 1800s. There are countless references to beer as "liquid bread" throughout history, most famously among the brewing monks of Belgium and Germany, where it was used to ward off hunger during Lent.

But beer's impact on what we eat goes well beyond replacing it during tough times, or accompanying food during feasts and times of plenty. Its omnipresence in all cultures means beer and its constituent ingredients—which are only so prevalent globally because they are used in brewing—have found their way into all sorts of foodstuffs, many of which you might have no idea about.

I've been to all kinds of exotic and unusual locations for this book, so bear with me while I take you on a journey to your local supermarket. As we all know by now there will be yeast on that shopping cart handle, on all the fruits and vegetables, in those fridges, on the hands of that guy offering you a free sample in a pill cup. But yeast will also be on the ingredients list, or at least responsible for many of the things you'll be buying. In his book *Cooked*, celebrated sociologist and food writer Michael Pollan says around one-third of the world's diet is produced through fermentation by yeast and/or bacteria, and as he puts it, "It's all the really good stuff." Beer, wine and whiskey are obvious, but how about things like cheese and even cured or aged meats?

Chocolate in all its forms—even Hershey's—is made partly from cocoa nibs, which are ground seeds from the cocoa plant. These seeds are harvested with a thick white pulp on them, and so are left to naturally ferment until the mass is reduced and the tannic flavor it contains eaten away. This is done by myriad bacteria and fungi including brewer's yeast, which really goes to town toward the end of the process as the alcohol builds and kills off competitors (don't get excited, kids, no booze makes it to the final product).

This process might be familiar to any coffee geeks reading this. Coffee beans go through a similar process, which removes a mucus layer from the bean and can also affect final flavor as some of the yeast by-products are absorbed. This is why if you're paying more than $7 for a hand-dripped coffee you might find a reference to something like *anaerobically fermented*, which means the ferment happened without oxygen. This gives the farmer more control, and the potential for the roaster and barista to tease out more flavor, less bitterness and perhaps a little more texture.

If you're looking for foods that actually have beer ingredients in, however, you're more likely to find them around the corner in the breakfast aisle, an unlikely place to think about beer, I grant you—we're going to talk about a lot of beer and food matching in this chapter, but I draw the line at pairing it with Coco Pops. That said, while you shouldn't be having beer with breakfast (unless you're in an airport, that's just tradition), you'll find one of beer's key ingredients in almost every cereal you can buy.

Next time you're in the breakfast aisle, take a look at the ingredients of your favorite cereals. Shreddies, Cheerios, Rice Krispies, Frosted Flakes, Weetabix, even Corn Flakes contain malt extract, a gloopy syrup made using the same barley as used for brewing, malted in the same factories that rely almost entirely on the brewing industry, and mashed like a beer but left unfermented. It adds a sweet, malty depth to whatever it goes into, as well as an abundance of vitamins and minerals thanks to the fact that it's whole-grain. It's heavy with protein, essential amino acids, soluble fibers, vitamins B2, B3 and B6, the minerals iron, calcium and potassium as well as magnesium, manganese and selenium.

We only really know this, and therefore only benefit from the remarkable nutrition of barley, thanks to the fact that it was so uniquely suited to brewing. You see, outside of animal feed and alcohol production, it's not that helpful a grain gastronomically. Wheat has been vital for millennia due to its unique bread-baking properties, while oats have become a staple food around the world thanks to the way they turn to porridge. But barley isn't great at either. Its tough shell makes it hard to dehusk, its lower gluten content makes it bad for bread, and it takes longer to cook than the alternatives. But all those things actually make it great for brewing, and through studying it to improve our beer, we've come to see the huge benefits of its extract form. In fact, it was a key ingredient to one of the most important foodstuffs ever created.

Beer for Babies?

The first ever baby formula was created in 1865 by German chemist Justus von Liebig, who in a strange twist nearly got a mention in Chapter 2 for being one of the biggest critics of Pasteur's theories around yeast.

He was dead wrong on that score, but he was still a brilliant man. It's said that much of his work was inspired by the global famine of 1816, caused by the eruption of Mount Tambora in

Indonesia—the most violent and deadly eruption observed by man. The volcanic winter that followed is known as the Year without Summer, and crops failed across the Northern Hemisphere. Liebig's tireless work on agricultural issues and nitrogen's use in fertilization was in part because of his experiences of famine aged thirteen. He's known as the Father of Fertilizer, which sounds like an insult but is actually recognition of the fact that he has saved millions of lives by making starvation significantly less likely. He also specialized in the processes behind making food extracts as a means to deliver nutrition in a smaller and longer-lasting package. He's credited with making both yeast extract (more on that later) and indeed beef extract—a process that led to the invention of the OXO cube. While delicious and ubiquitous in the world of British cooking, it still didn't have the same impact as his baby formula.

Feeding babies when the mother was unable to (and a wet nurse was not available) was extremely difficult in the mid-1800s. Nutrition was a new science and malnutrition common among infants as a result. The leap had already been made to use animal milk, but in the days before beer had inspired pasteurization and refrigeration, anything but bang-fresh animal milk had as much potential to poison as fortify a baby. Some experts even recommended the baby feed direct from a cow's udder—with one admitting any such cow should be "known for its gentle disposition" before attempting.

Liebig was already known as the foremost expert on nutrition— in fact you could argue he invented the whole discipline—and decided that it should be possible to replicate the mother's milk. Thus, in 1867 he released Liebig's Soluble Food for Babies, made up of cow's milk, wheat and malt flour, and potassium bicarbonate. By the next year it was being manufactured and sold in London by the Liebig's Registered Concentrated Milk Company, and in 1869 it reached the US.

A few years later, a British pharmacist whose name you might recognize moved to America to produce and market his own version. Ten years later James Horlick received a patent for a version that used dried milk, creating the first dried malted milk powder, which was sold as a health drink for "infants and invalids." It was taken up by lots of different people, though, especially explorers who appreciated how light it was to carry while being so nutritious.

Horlicks has since become a household name in many countries, enjoyed as much for its malty flavor as its saturation of B vitamins. It was helped on its way by being one of the few beneficiaries of Prohibition, which created a craze for malted products. Low-alcohol beer wasn't a huge seller for bereft American breweries, so many started producing malt extract and selling it directly to consumers. Its health benefits were championed, and dare I say exaggerated, in a bid to extract profit from their expensive brewhouses. In an ad released shortly before Prohibition, Anheuser-Busch claimed its hop and malt-derived Malt-Nutrine "feeds the life cells—renews in the bloodless and poorly nourished a feeling that new life beats strong within them." If I'd been around in the 1920s I'd have been using it with a bit of bread yeast to make home brew, and the part of me that wonders what a *life cell* is thinks that was probably the true purpose.

Sour to the People

Not every malted drink was designed to be healthy, however, nor is malt extract even the closest foodstuff to beer. For example, have you ever drowned your fries in malt vinegar? If you have, you've essentially poured infected beer on your potatoes.

Malt vinegar is made by inoculating ale with acetobacter, a bacteria that converts the alcohol into acetic acid to create that spiky, malty vinegar that brings sumptuously soggy fast-food french fries to life. Vinegar predates deep-fried food, however. The Babylonians were the first to write extensively about their vinegars, and even called it "beer that wandered into the kitchen."

Much of ancient and medieval Europe was making and using wine vinegars, but brewing nations like the UK were more likely to use beer, and there are references to *alegar* (*sour ale*) in cooking recipes from the fifteenth century. That would likely have been made by embracing beer that had gone wrong, but as brewers got more consistent and vinegar industries professionalized, the production process became intentional. From there, vinegar manufacturers would have started brewing themselves, looking for malt with lots of fermentable sugar (because more sugar meant more alcohol, and more alcohol meant more acid), skipped the hops to make the bacteria's growth as easy as possible, and fermented warmer for the same reason.

Its proximity to brewing was not just in the method—Sarson's, which is the UK's most famous brand of malt vinegar, was produced in Bermondsey from around 1814. Its location right on the approach to where Tower Bridge was later built put it at the center of London's brewing district and almost next door to Barclay Perkins, at the time one of the biggest breweries in the world. By the start of the First World War, Sarson's was producing over a million barrels of vinegar a year, rivaling Barclay Perkins itself for size. That wasn't just down to Brits loving tangy fries, though. Malt vinegar was used for pickling and preserving, which in the days before domestic fridges was vital. It was also a base ingredient for traditional condiments including Worcestershire sauce, HP Sauce and tomato ketchup, though the latter is more likely to be spirit vinegar today for efficiency reasons (spirits have a lot more alcohol, remember).

Having dug into the beautiful, newspaper-wrapped world of chip shops, it feels like the right time—perhaps the only time—to talk about the impact of Britain's national dish: fish and chips. Like pubs, the chippy's omnipresence means it's taken for granted, but when you dig into its history and influence you uncover a wonderful and weird world full of tasty anecdotes. Chippies could make a claim to be the original fast-food concept, with the food generally prepared in advance almost exclusively for takeaway. In the 1930s, fish and chips accounted for around half of all the fish landed in British ports, being sold through around 35,000 shops by a workforce of roughly 70,000. The impact it had, therefore, on the fishing, vinegar and farming industries is immeasurable. As well as a source of employment it was, in the dark times of the late 1920s, an affordable luxury. In his 1937 novel *The Road to Wigan Pier*, George Orwell wrote that "It is quite likely that fish and chips, art-silk stockings, tinned salmon, cut-price chocolate...the movies, the radio, strong tea and the Football Pools [soccer betting pools] have between them averted revolution." Perhaps the government were fans of his work, as fish and chips were one of the few foods not rationed during or after the Second World War.

Beer's link to fish and chips goes beyond vinegar, too, because of what's used to make traditional British battered fish. Most chippies would use water for the batter, but when bought in a pub pretty much anywhere around the world, it's made with beer. There are two key reasons for this: the bubbles increase the surface area for oil to catch and crisp up, and the residual sugar caramelizes to add color and flavor. Chefs could simply head to the bar and grab a few pints every morning when making the batter, and I saw it happen every day when I worked in a pub to fund my degree. Sometimes that particular chef would take one for himself as well, which was a surprise introduction to how the world of cheffing is lubricated.

Today the closest literal tie between food and beer comes from a much more niche UK tradition than its national dish. It's so closely linked that supplies were under pressure during COVID as brewers shuttered for months on end. It's also a product so divisive that you'll find *Marmite* in the English dictionary, where it's defined as something that splits opinion.

Love Not Hate

There's a well-known off-flavor in brewing called autolysis. It happens if the yeast is pushed too hard to ferment, or is left in a tank for too long. Translated literally it means *self-destruction*, and refers to the death of a yeast cell as its walls break down and release its insides. It sounds bleak, and it sounds gross, but it's the way that Marmite is made.

To roughly half the world, Marmite is also gross. To me, it's the start of pretty much every day: black coffee, dark brown toast, too much salted butter, Marmite. I understand why people might hate this tangy, burned form of treacle, but for me the key is not too much Marmite: a skid mark rather than a streak, if you will. If that's still no good, try a little peanut butter on top too—essentially the start of a very British satay sauce. Much as I'd love to, though, I'm not here to convert you to Marmite. I'm here to explain to you how closely it's associated with beer, and the remarkable impact they have had on the world.

You remember Liebig, the Father of Fertilizer who fell out with Pasteur, invented baby formula and conceived the OXO cube? It's quite the résumé. Well, he's also the creator, or perhaps enabler, of Marmite. You see, while he was working out how to make beef extract he also figured out how to make yeast extract. He did so by boiling the yeasty paste found at the bottom of an emptied brewery fermenter. This killed the yeast and released the cells' digestive enzymes to break their proteins down—autolysis.

As far as I can tell, the invention lay mostly dormant until a German sugar merchant by the name of Frederick Wissler married a British girl and came to London. In 1898 he founded the

London Sea Water Supply Co., which appears to have supplied London homes with water from the Channel. I can't think of a single use for this, and clearly no one else could either, because just four years later he founded the Marmite Food Extract Company in Burton instead.

If you've been paying attention you'll know exactly why he left London to follow his new-but-still-salty dream. Burton was the home of Bass, at the time the biggest brewery in the world and therefore the biggest potential supplier of spent yeast. But Wissler's Marmite proved so popular that in 1907 a London factory was needed, and was constructed in a former brewery in Vauxhall where the neighbors immediately began to complain of a vicious but presumably slightly moreish aroma.

It had its big breakthrough in around 1912. At that time, a terrible condition called beriberi was rife among humans in certain countries, causing all kinds of issues from shortness of breath all the way up to paralysis, by way of nerve damage and heart failure. Why it affected certain communities and not others wasn't understood until a Polish-born but London-based biochemist called Casimir Funk read a study showing that Asian people who ate brown rice were less vulnerable to beriberi than those who ate only the fully milled product.

Intrigued, Funk looked at the chemical differences between the rices and tried to isolate the substance responsible. What he isolated was the first vitamin complex ever discovered. Funk wasn't the only one to isolate it, but he gets the plaudits here because he understood the impact so clearly, and came up with the word *vitamin*, combining *vitality* and *amine*, meaning it was derived from ammonia. When the benefits of this vitamin complex came to light, foods that contained it were added to all kinds of treatment plans and diets. Marmite happened to be rich in it, so was included in the rations for soldiers in the First World War to keep beriberi at bay due to their restricted diets. Working in Mumbai, India, in the 1920s, physician and researcher

Lucy Wills was coming up against frequent and sometimes fatal cases of macrocytic anemia in pregnant women. She deduced that it was due to a poor diet, and decided that vitamin B deficiency could be the cause. The most affordable source available to her was...Marmite, and it worked on all of her patients. She left India shortly afterward, but recommended Marmite continue to be given to pregnant women, and ten years later it was even used to treat malnutrition in Ceylon, now Sri Lanka. This was no isolated incident: news spread of the importance of B vitamins in pregnant women and by the 1950s it was being routinely offered to pregnant women across the Western World. It turned out that folic acid (B9) was the compound treating or warding off anemia, and commercialization of this led to the first dedicated prenatal vitamin tablets ever made. So in a convoluted way, Pasteur's great rival, Bass Brewery, and a guy who loved seawater created Pregnacare vitamins...and therefore about eighty percent of the ads on the London Underground.

Marmite itself never caught on in India outside its medicinal use—perhaps its strong umami flavor and saltiness contrasted too much with the local cuisine. Marmite can make a great addition to beef gravies and stews, but less so a korma. In the UK, however, it is one of the most popular breakfast spreads. The latest figures I could find are from 2016, when over 50,000 tons of Marmite were made, all now back in Burton, which equates to roughly 50 million jars (I refuse to acknowledge the existence of the squeezy bottles). To give you an idea of how unique Marmite is to its home nation, more than 42 million of those are consumed in the UK.

Table Beers

Oddly enough, one of the few things you'd never have with your Marmite is a beer. Sure, it's been culturally relegated to a breakfast food and tastes like a deeply flawed beer itself, but you'd think two products so closely associated would love each other. Mind you, as mentioned at the start of this book, until I was eighteen I thought beer and food matching meant a French stubby and whatever my dad found under Pyrex in the microwave.

To me, bad French Pilsner was this wonder drink that could go with beef stew, moussaka, turkey burgers—even the miracle risotto my mom used to make that included no wine or cheese. To be fair, all that's really changed since I grew up (other than learning to actually make risotto) is that I drink better Pilsner. The style itself is indeed a miracle drink that can go with just about any meal, and I think that explains at least a little of its widespread, enduring appeal.

As we've explored, beer was food in and of itself to some extent. The sugar and carbs provided calories for manual workers and extra nutrition when it was scarce. Due to the lack of vitamin C you'd only live a month or so if you stuck to just beer, but if you're in dire straits (not the band, the situation) or fasting it will work as a stopgap.

Unless you're a fasting monk, beer is (and indeed historically was) more likely to be found next to food than in its absence. It's always been beer that you had with a meal at home in all but the most wine-obsessed nations. In the European Middle Ages and right up to the eighteenth century, women were making what was called *small beer* (or sometimes *table beer*) in their kitchens. As pubs and breweries took over national production, households would buy it in instead. Typically no more than 2.5%, these beers were strong enough to keep bacteria at bay, but weak enough to still hydrate you and not get the kids drunk (that's right, they gave it to the children, and so would you if you'd cleaned the diaper of a kid with dysentery). Small beer would be served at breakfast, lunch and dinner, and the tradition was so ingrained in British culture that in the mid-1700s so-called

potboys would venture out from the local inn with mugs full
of beer to sell door-to-door around midday and dinnertime.

If you were eating out, for nearly 300 years pubs had an institution called the Ordinary, essentially a varying British plat du
jour that included all the small beer you could drink "before the
cloth was removed" (i.e., you were done eating). At Christmas,
everywhere from Windsor Castle to dinner at the workhouses
would have tucked into roast beef, plum pudding and what just
about every historical resource I could come across refers to
as *good ale*—I assume this means strong, well-aged stuff rather
than mild and sweeter brews. In another example, it's relatively
well-known that oysters were as important to a Londoner's diet
as beer in the mid-nineteenth century, to the point where they
consumed an average of 230 each a year. Traditionally they were
served with Porter, and you'll still find this match in swanky
wine bars in the City and touristy areas like Borough Market.

It wasn't just the UK where beer and food were inseparable.
Given that monasteries were much more likely to make beer
than wine, special beer was often served on religious holidays
alongside public feasts. April 2 was the day of St. Francis, who
founded the Order of St. Francis of Paola. In Munich, where a
conclave of such monks had settled, they hosted what by many
accounts was an epic feast of beer and food. In 1886, the US con-
sul to Germany, G. Henry Horstmann, wrote: "Close streams
of people, men, women and children, people of all ranks and
of every station in life…from all directions, and the garden and
the immense halls, and even the street adjoining, are swarm-
ing with drinkers." The beer they were hunting down was the
first example of a Doppelbock, a dark and sweet beer that was
likely a little rough due to short lagering times during the winter. I suspect a lot of them were there because April 2 usually
falls toward the end of Lent, and a feast was too exciting a pros-
pect to refuse.

A few decades before that was written, Bavarian King Maximilian I granted licenses to breweries to serve beer in the leafy gardens above their beer cellars, but he decreed that they could not offer table service. This reduced the effect the gardens would have on local inns that didn't have outdoor spaces, but it also ensured even the poorest people could afford to drink in them by bringing their own food. The tradition survives today, and you can bring your own food into Bavarian beer gardens or order at counters to take back to the table.

In America there were plenty of food and beer traditions, despite the fact that until the Germans came Americans were mostly drinking watered-down rum and whiskey. The importance of corn in American diets led to bourbon (which must be fifty-one percent corn to use the name) and American light lager, but also the American curiosity of corn bread. That would have been a staple of American saloons, next to oysters muled across the country in barrels kept cold by the railway technologies and ice-house systems pioneered by breweries. The link was so strong that in many major US cities in the late nineteenth century, taverns were required to serve food in order to gain a liquor license, as a nod to the temperance movement. Initially bartenders resisted the idea of putting aside space for kitchens and buffet carts, but when they realized the sales potential of a free lunch they started to invest more in the idea. Breweries even started chipping in to cover the costs of the food in return for exclusivity across a bar's beer taps. When Chicago's Berghoff café opened in 1898, it obviously served its own beer, but every pour came with a free sandwich.

Going out for food and going out for a beer were essentially the same thing for much of human history. Establishments tended to offer both, even if they specialized in or were famous for one, which is why I always give a wry laugh when beer lovers complain about pubs turning into gastropubs. That was their original role, people.

Anyway, as a result, beer houses of all shapes and sizes have had a huge influence on national cuisines. In fact, most of them were developed there. It would have essentially been home-cooked inventions, created by whoever was in the kitchen, influenced by what was available to them, and carried away in the minds of travelers. It's no accident that the diets of "old-world" countries associated most with beer—the Czech Republic, Belgium, Germany, Denmark, the UK—have a lot in common. They all have dishes that are ostensibly the same, both through cultural immigration and the fact they just accompany beer so well. If I had to sum it up, I'd say *potatoes*, because the beer-swilling nations have been both particularly obsessed and ingenious with this root vegetable. Half a millennium after their introduction to Europe, they are still the first thing on the team sheet when it comes to pub menus. In the UK they're probably mashed or roasted (roasties used to be a common free beer snack, now you'll probably get some salt and vinegar chips), in the Czech Republic it's likely in your goulash's dumplings, in Germany it's a mash or creamy potato salad next to a schnitzel, and in Belgium it's frites under that mound of mayo. Potatoes have this wonderful affinity with beer because they can simultaneously soak up our excesses while being crispy, fluffy, oily and satisfying. They keep well and cook quickly, and absorb whatever flavor you want them to, arguably even better than Europe's other great love—bread...which is of course made with brewer's yeast, so is always of cultural importance in brewing nations.

In fact, I believe that beer has as great an impact on a nation's cuisine as any factors traditionally linked to it—climate, availability, immigration, wealth. There are some nations where, if there hadn't been an abundance of beer, certain national or treasured dishes would never have come into existence. No nation shows this more clearly than the Czech Republic, where so many of the most common dishes can trace their origins back to the *hospodas* (*local pubs*). The classic example is *nakládaný hermelín*, a soft cheese that's pickled in oil with onions and chillies, then served with bread coated in caraway seeds. The cheese, *hermelín*, was invented in the 1920s in a bid to create a Czech Camembert, and was then marinaded to extend its shelf life in bars and restaurants. Made well it can last up to a month, only improving in flavor, and jars of it are found in both traditional and achingly modern Czech beer bars. Its salty, tangy, herbal and oily nature is perfect with a crisp, cold Pilsner.

This nationally loved dish is nothing compared to the aptly named *pivní sýr* (*beer cheese*), which is delivered to the table as a plate of onions, a scoop of mustard and some slightly funky-smelling wobbly cheese. Sometimes it comes with a shot glass of beer, sometimes you sacrifice some of your own, but the idea is you mix the three ingredients, then tip the beer in. The result is a cold, oozy umami soup that acts as much as an extension of your beer as an accompaniment. Texture is provided by mountains of bread, which you can use in a futile attempt to pretend it's edible. My favorite thing about trying it for the first time in a restaurant called Masné Krámy in České Budějovice was not the flavor, and certainly not the texture, but Radim's childish joy at my unconvinced reaction. I decided to order another beer and focus on the bread element. Interestingly, beer rolls or *pivní rohlíky* are a big deal in Czechia—essentially a banana-shaped roll that's given a rich fluffy body and crispy crust by the addition of beer and egg.

So our pub-born love of cold beer, fermented food, and doughy carbs has come to define many of our cultures and cuisines—and yet the relationship between food and beer has broken down significantly since. There are a lot of theories as to how wine took beer's place at the dining table, but pinning it down is tricky because it was so slow to happen. The balance didn't really tip until the 1980s or so, and when it did it was more beer's fault than wine's triumph.

Beer Then Wine's Fine

A major factor in beer's struggles at the dinner table is the path that professional brewing took about a century ago—one we hinted at in the last chapter. The great technological advances in brewing in the late 1800s made pale lager the perfect candidate for Ford-style commercialization: it uses stable ingredients, scales easily, can be made quickly but benefits from longer storage, and was still growing in popularity.

The brewers that this book has celebrated thus far—Carlsberg, Spaten, Anheuser-Busch—exploited this ruthlessly, taking small chips out of their beer's unique character in the name of upscaling, efficiency and stability. The Jacobsens' generosity with their isolated yeast strain is a marvel that changed the lives and drinking experience of millions, but it did have its drawbacks. It's no coincidence that the technological revolution of the late nineteenth century corresponds with the dramatic fall in beer style diversity across the Western World. By the end of the First World War, across much of Europe you could have any color of beer you wanted so long as it was pale yellow.

Along with that came a drop in how much beer people consumed overall—America was sliding inexorably toward Prohibition, and the ABVs of many European beers had dropped irrevocably as barley rationing took its toll. So diversity reduced, beers were watered-down, and quality dipped. Social shifts, such as the understandable conclusion that kids are hard enough work when sober, as well as growing interest in coffee and tea, changed the times and places that we drank beer, hurting all but the most robust and modern brewers.

This caused consolidation on an industrial scale throughout most European countries, with the UK going from around 40,000 breweries in the 1700s to barely a hundred by the 1980s. The story was much the same in the US, and the breweries who mopped up all that volume grew to become behemoths—the largest, AB InBev, uses enough water each year to drain Lake Superior…and then some.

I'm not saying the equivalent commercialization hasn't happened in wine too (believe me, I've drunk Blossom Hill) but there wasn't, in the early twentieth century, a way to really scale grape production or speed up fermentation. Therefore, commercialized wine production failed to take the feet out from under those who stuck to artisan methods. It also didn't pigeonhole the drink to the point that most people assumed all beer was bright yellow, heavily carbonated and lightly scented with honey and lemon. Beer once tasted different in every village, town, city or farm that you went to. Toward the end of the twentieth century, wine started looking diverse simply by coming in two colors.

Talking of diversity, beer's fading relationship with food is also in part due to the brewers who allowed it to become gendered. It happened slowly at first, as monks and businessmen took the role of brewing away from women in the sixteenth and seventeenth centuries, and as drinking started to be done more in pubs than at home in the nineteenth century (a process now mostly reversed). These spaces were predominantly male, to the point where many bars were men-only or segregated. As we saw in the last chapter, while beer ads in the mid-twentieth century were often aimed at women, it was more as domestic buyers rather than consumers. By the late 1980s and early 1990s, the idea that beer was a masculine endeavor was so ingrained that brands were making marketing capital off it. Any idea that beer is, or should be, a "man's drink" has no basis in history, science or psychology, and some brands are learning that to their cost now. When beer goes directly against wine at the dinner table, it's the gender-neutral drink—the industry that hasn't gone out of its way to alienate half the world—that wins.

The wine industry, to its credit, has stepped up to the plate brilliantly. At the University of California, Ann C. Noble developed the hugely influential Wine Aroma Wheel, which compared wine flavors to food. It created the whole idea that wine could taste of blackberries or vanilla, that people could describe an aged champagne as tasting like brioche, or acknowledge that Syrah had a black-pepper character. At the same time, the industry hammered home the basics of wine and food matching, emphasized the consumption of fizzy wine with hors d'oeuvres for celebrations, and managed to convince people it could be worth hundreds and even thousands of dollars. Its pricing and marketing made it aspirational for the middle and lower classes who had been drinking beer for generations.

The reason for winemakers is obvious, but it's logical for chefs too. I once met the great chef Michel Roux Jr., who is a beer lover and had a beer list at his iconic Le Gavroche restaurant loaded with Belgian classics. I asked him why beer had such a small mindshare in fine dining restaurants, and his reply was brisk: "I'd rather sell a £50 bottle of wine than a £5 bottle of beer."

Simple economics might explain why beer fell out of favor at fancier establishments, but wine's greatest accomplishment was to dominate the drinks lists of bars when they started to take food seriously. This, to me, was the biggest sign of beer's reputational fall—it was fresh on the taps, at a fraction of the cost, in its spiritual home, and people were still ordering fermented grape juice.

There are, of course, places where wine hasn't yet won the war. The curry houses of Britain still staunchly serve Indian-branded beers (though mostly brewed in Northampton and Burton); there's a trend for modern American bistros that don't just eschew wine but cover their walls with endless taps of niche beer; it's a bold Czech restaurant that doesn't have either Pilsner Urquell, Staropramen or Budvar front and center on the bar; the wood-paneled, cramped restaurants of Belgium might serve drinks at 10% ABV, but they're definitely beers; the number of cask lines at Tom Kerridge's Hand and Flowers pub in the Chiltern Hills just about outnumbers his Michelin stars, and when I went there I drank four pints with lunch (sorry, everyone).

Interestingly, one of the trendiest locations for modern cuisine is also still beer-obsessed. Perhaps because it's the home of Carlsberg, or perhaps despite it, but if you're a lover of good food and good beer, Copenhagen is a capital city in more than one way.

Michelin Bars

The port city was storming. Sheets of rain came down like sails and the wind blew hard as you crossed the bridges, pushing you treacherously toward the bike lanes.

It was my first night in Copenhagen, and I was hungry, thirsty and cold. I walked down the famous Nyhavn, on the far side so I could take in the seventeenth-century facade of colorful buildings, now accessorized with tourist-trapping signs. At the end, I climbed the steps to the final bridge and braced for impact, hooded head down against the rain. When I looked up it was like I'd been blown back in time. A tall ship loomed through the rain, and behind it an old warehouse resolute and ancient against the wind. This was my destination—the former site of the world's best restaurant and now perhaps the world's most upmarket beer bar.

Make no mistake about it, Barr is a fancy restaurant. But it's unusual in that it has placed beer at the heart of it, in the right atrium to be precise. I should say I was a little cynical going in. I hate that wine has taken beer's place at the dining table, but I'm hesitant whenever people try to treat beer like wine in response. Some beers look, taste and fill such roles, but most do not. I remember a beer-matching dinner when a Pilsner was served to me in a champagne flute by someone who genuinely thought he was changing the world. All he was doing was ensuring I'd need a top-up in about five seconds.

One of the things I love most about beer is that it's cheap and approachable enough that it can be made with incredible ingredients, aged for years in a barrel, refermented in the bottle like champagne and still be served by the pint with chips in a country bar. Thankfully, the folk at Barr seem to understand that. Yes, you could get a beer flight with your tasting menu, and yes it was all expensive imported stuff poured for you from the bottle by a waiter with a white cloth on their arm, but if that kind of service makes you want to run and hide in the bathroom like me, you can just sit at the bar.

I was literally dripping as I entered Barr. It felt strange to go to such a place without a reservation and a small part of me thought I'd be refused entry because I was so wet. I certainly surprised the guy who welcomed me—I must have looked like Shackleton when he was rescued by the tugboat.

"Hi!" he said, almost too enthusiastically.

Caught off guard I part told and part asked, "I'm here for the pub?"

"Then, go ahead," he said with a wave in the right direction and a slight bow.

I headed right, away from the bright kitchen and open-plan restaurant, to what could easily be confused with the galley of a boat. Everywhere was bare wood: from the ceiling, to the beams, to the walls, to the floor, to the tables, to the chairs. It was lit low and warm, the perfect setting for a stormy night like this. I picked a stool at the bar and was immediately offered a place in the restaurant. Clearly the bar also functions as a clearing house for those without reservations, but I explained I was exactly where I wanted to be—by the beer taps. The waiter smiled and brought me a beer menu.

My fear of the place being booked up meant I was the first one in, literally seconds after the doors had opened, so along with the beer menu came two more waiters: one explained that the digital version was more up-to-date, and the other said that they'd just changed a bunch of barrels so everything was going to be as fresh as it gets. I ordered the tasting menu, but declined the beer matching so I could pick for myself, starting with a malty Vienna lager from ÅBEN, a brewery in the meatpacking district of Copenhagen.

The first course took just a few minutes to arrive, and was presented by a chef over the bar as if he were handing me a pint. He explained the dish—butter-poached squid with kohlrabi, spinach, white currant sauce and jalapeño oil—and left me wondering what on earth to drink with it. When I match food and beer I like to look for the missing flavor, the part of the palate that might be missing out. For a burger, it might be bitterness (so think IPA); for a stew it might be acidity (maybe a Flemish Red); for a salad it might be salt or umami (how about a Gose?). Often I look for complementary flavors in a beer style and a dish, and other times I look to contrast them. In all situations I try to match the intensity so one doesn't overpower the other—which is why your macro lager tastes like soda water with your curry house Madras, for instance.

This squid dish, however, hit all five kinds of sensors on my tongue, was as delicate as a flower, and didn't really share any of the classic characteristics of beer. I was beginning to see another reason why beer might rarely taint the white tablecloths of Michelin-starred restaurants. In the end I chose a Czech Pils, and it was perfection—a buttery maltiness matched the squid, the hop oils complemented the chili, and the bitterness added an extra element to the dish without dominating. And then I was in the flow: a spiced red ale with beef tartare and smoky mayo; then a second helping of Vienna lager with Wiener schnitzel— though I ordered a Baltic Porter when I'd finished that, because it went so well with the artfully burned brussels sprouts and horseradish cream on the side. The dessert of stewed apple and quince with kefir ice cream and rosemary caramel was crying out for a velvety, stone-fruit heavy New England IPA.

I was fully on board (not to mention just full) by the end, but I was still conscious that you'd need to be a serious beer geek, aware of and ready to try any style, to really make fine dining and beer match up. With all respect to wine, its flavors are found within much smaller parameters, so the chances of getting things wildly wrong are much smaller. Of course, the flip side is the chances of getting something earth-shatteringly right is also diminished. It was the wider possibility offered by beer that convinced Barr's founder and head chef Thorsten Schmidt, a friend of Noma's René Redzepi, to give over nearly half his restaurant to a pub setup.

"Beer and food hasn't always been a clear connection for me," he says. "In fact, that was one of the reasons I decided to create a bar—to explore the potential of beer in enhancing culinary experiences."

Experimenting with beer might seem a little prosaic to someone like Schmidt, who once prepared space rations for Danish astronaut Andreas Mogensen, until you know his background.

"The idea behind the bar stems from my upbringing in Germany," he says. "My parents would often meet friends and neighbors at the local *Kneipe* for an evening of beer, card games or simply conversations."

A *Kneipe* is the German term for a *local, boozer* or potentially even *dive bar*. No doubt there would have been some food on offer there, but the kind of things you reach for because you've had a skinful and don't really want to go anywhere else to soak it up. So really, Barr is a collision of two very different passions—dark and comfortable beer bars, and white tableclothed fine dining restaurants. If you want to know which is more important to Schmidt, it's worth knowing that Barr is the Norse word for *barley*.

I headed back through the huge oak doors of the restaurant and pulled my hood over my head with two conflicting thoughts. One was whether I could afford to go back the next

night to try the beer matching menu, and another was a sense
of sadness at what beer has missed out on by being cleared from
the dinner table. Food throughout the Western World has gone
through several incredible reinventions in the last few decades,
and brewers only really have themselves to blame for beer's exclusion. It was one of the original drivers of national cuisine,
but like so many artisan pursuits, technology took some of the
artistry away.

Beer is still irrelevant to restaurants in most nations today,
and even I find myself instinctively thinking about wine when
going out for dinner or cooking something special at home. As
craft brewing brings diversity back and great chefs start to see
the potential, I hope more places like Barr will open up. I don't
expect, or even want, beer to supplant wine. I just think it deserves its place on tasting menus, from both a historical and a
flavor point of view. Just don't serve it in a champagne flute.

Chapter 7

Community

Or how beer brings people together

For all my high-brow talk of beer's influence on civilization, the reason it still persists in a world where water is safe to drink, calories are almost too easy to accrue and we drink wine with dinner is the connection it forges. What do we drink at weddings and funerals? Beer. What do we suggest when we bump into an old friend? A beer. How do we celebrate after a good day? Beer. Hate your job? There's a support group for that—it's called "everyone" and we meet on Fridays at the pub.

Beer has this magical ability to cut through whatever life throws at us, to bring us together whatever our differences and find common ground. Take the Christmas truce of 1914. Despite being five months into the most deadly war the world had ever seen, German and British troops all along the front downed their weapons and mingled with the enemy for a day. Most famously, a Scottish regiment took on a German one at soccer, losing 3–2 (but getting their own back the whole time by wearing nothing under their kilts). But further down the line, the troops of British Captain Clifton Stockwell and German Baron Maximillian von Sinner met in no-man's-land to share three barrels of beer and some plum pie. Sadly there are no photos of this event but it was recorded in Sinner's diary, and Stockwell later wrote a poem about it, in which he brutally dismissed the beer donated by the Germans as "indifferent." In fairness to Sinner, it was stolen from the French.

What I love most about this historic moment (other than the shade thrown via the medium of poetry) is that when these men, faced with unspeakable, unimaginable horror with no end in sight, were given one moment of respite, they chose to drink beer and play soccer. Both of these cultural phenomena are often dismissed as "just beer" or "just a game," but they were everything to those men on that day. One day they were dodging bullets, and the next supping beer with the men who held the rifles. What power there is in the pint.

Of course, times don't need to be as dark as that for beer to bring people together. Beer and the places that serve it have been a magnet for humans for millennia. In small quantities, alcohol's effects are immediate, mild and relaxing, helping us connect where social barriers might otherwise stop them. To revisit an old haunt, as the Nobel Prize–winning poet Paul von Heyse observed in his poem "Ode to Hofbräuhaus Bock Beer":

The servant not far from his stabled horses
The bureaucrats from their imperial offices.
Porter, professor, pharmacist, student
[beer] washes away the barriers that divide them

When we celebrate, it helps us achieve unbridled joy. When we commiserate it helps us talk about our feelings. I don't think there should be any shame in admitting, even saluting the fact that it has helped ease our way through life. It doesn't matter whether you live in a metropolis or the outback, hell it doesn't even matter if you don't actually drink yourself, alcohol is at the center of our social lives—and thanks to beer's lower cost, lower ABV and relatively global availability, it has played that role more than any other form of alcohol.

At least that's my theory. To test it, I thought it would be interesting to go somewhere so remote that the nearest brewery was thousands of miles away. That way I'd see firsthand the effort that humans put into getting a pint, and ideally how doing so had either built or changed the culture and sense of community, like the first time Homo sapiens ate some old grain.

I thought I'd found the perfect place: an isolated mining town of 3,000 people that until the 1980s was only reachable by several days on a boat. I then discovered that in 2015, some maniac had taken that society to the next phase of evolution...by building a brewery on the very top of the world.

Cold Up North

You'd think that the hardest part of getting to the Arctic would be the last bit: the small plane, the rugged terrain, the buckling winds, the icy runway.

But no, the biggest snag on my way to Svalbard was the British train strike, which combined with a broken-down truck on the M25 to make me miss my first flight. Shackleton had it tough, but he didn't have to spend four hours on a cheap airport café chair at Gatwick station.

From that point onward, though, my Arctic adventure was easy—almost too easy. Things started to feel like the beginning of a horror movie, with carefree, smooth sailing punctuated by signs that I should turn back everywhere. There was the random search at security, and the grizzled passport controller who asked, "Ever been to Svalbard?" without looking me in the eye. Then there were the deadly silent passengers at the gate, despite what I can only describe as an amassing of crows, flying silently and almost immobile against the wind just outside the airport window. To distract myself I did some more research on Svalbard on my phone, only to learn something that made me feel worse: it's actually *illegal* to die there, because it's too cold for your body to decompose. Obviously you can't predict accidents, but if you're critically ill, you're shipped off. It should have reassured me, but it made the place even more foreboding. Usually, my brain told me, you only outlaw something if it happens too much...

In case it isn't obvious, I was a little anxious about my trip to Longyearbyen, the world's most northerly town. It wasn't just the cold or the polar bears, it was the fact that for four days I would be among the 3,000 or so most northerly people on earth. If I dipped my toes in Longyearbyen's northern shore, I'd be in the top one hundred. As someone who's basically lived within sight of a major highway for most of my life, that isolation feels unnatural. Then there's the fact that in summer the sun never sets, and in winter it never rises. I don't know about you, but the first scientific lesson I ever learned as a kid was that the sun rises and damn well sets. That's what days are, for God's sake. And without days, how do you measure weeks, months, years, or time itself? Where the hell was I going, and why won't anyone else in this damned airport notice the crows?

Still, like everyone in a horror movie, I ignored the signs. I got on the plane.

A World Without Light

Mary-Ann's Polarrigg is right on the edge of town, among the warehouses of the docks. It's supposed to be a former miners' dormitory, but to me it looked like Disney had made a ride out of the murder house at the end of *True Detective* season one. The entrance was a giant timber gate topped with countless sharp antlers, and the buildings were ramshackle collages of corrugated steel and oak. The yard was icy and littered with rubble and dead spruce trees. The word *Recepzion* was written out in sticks, like an SOS sign on a beach. Inside was a little better—think the *Twin Peaks* hotel after the apocalypse—but I decided to just dump my bags and go and find a beer.

Until the airport was built in the 1970s, Svalbard was a good few days' sail from the north coast of Norway. It was discovered in 1596 by a Dutch exploration team, of which only twelve made it home. Since then it's been sporadically populated, first with whalers and their literal bloodbaths, then trappers and finally coal miners. The latter resulted in all sorts of geopolitical wrangling before Norway was finally given dominion, with parts left to Russia and some very powerful private companies. Today there's just one Norwegian mine still operating, with tourism and research the main industries. In fact, in terms of permanent residents, there are possibly more polar bears than people.

Tourism and research both require plenty of modern tech, but they don't necessarily need good roads, paths or lighting. My journey to find a beer involved teetering over a bridge originally built for a gas line, and latterly extended for human traffic. The wood creaked beneath my feet, but I was thirsty and nervously excited to be headed to the "world's most northerly pub."

Any worries that I was walking into a *30 Days of Night* horror-film scenario were quickly allayed by the most mundane and British of comforts: Wi-Fi, contactless payments and Phil Collins on the stereo. I don't know what I expected, but it wasn't the annex of a Radisson Blu Hotel pumping out "Against All Odds."

Thankfully they did serve the local beer, the reason I'd put on thermal underwear for the first time in my life. The Pale Ale was crisp, caramel-tinged and piney, and I immediately wished I'd ordered a pint not a 12 oz. It tasted about as fresh as beer gets, which is to be expected given it was made just a few hundred yards northwest. I wasn't due to visit the brewery until morning, so rather than endure more Phil Collins I headed to the first place that came up when I googled *where to drink in Svalbard*, and happens to be the world's second-most northerly pub.

The Karlsberger Pub, spelled with a *K* for copyright reasons (not joking), has actually been voted one of the coolest bars on the planet on more than one occasion. It's partly for its location, but more for its incredible whiskey and brandy selection. What impressed me most though wasn't the dizzying array of bottles lining the walls, but the way the pub wears its history on its sleeve.

It's owned by former miner Steve Daldorff Torgersen, and has become the town's social hub after dark (or after 5 p.m., because like I say, it's dark for a third of the year). You don't need to be told that a miner owns the place, you just have to walk through the door. Don't get me wrong, it's beautifully decorated, but every inch of it from floor to ceiling has some kind of reference to mining. The centerpiece is a giant copper carriage filled with coal, the ceiling is covered with pallets, pipes and tin signs. Around the walls at eye level are eleven stunning portraits of his former colleagues, some of whom still work underground but more of whom now drink here.

The bar was actually shut when I arrived, but Peter the bar manager opened for me, and while pouring a Svalbard Brewery Pilsner told me to call it KP like a local, not Karlsberger Pub.

"Fake it 'till you make it," he says with a flourish, handing me the beer.

We prop up the bar for an hour, chatting randomly about life in a way that you only really do with strangers in a pub. Peter refills his coffee three times, and relives his twenty-five years in bars. He's not Svalbard-born—few people are—but instead comes from Oslo. He moved here in 2018 with his girlfriend to escape the burnout of city bar work, and is clearly still in love with the place.

"Svalbard isn't for everyone," he says. "City people come here for work in skinny jeans, ankles showing, and don't last a week. But five and a half years later, here we are."

Svalbard is no longer isolated (it's a direct flight to Oslo), but to stay here you can't just live with the wildness, you have to love it. Even at this time of year, October, when the snow is thin and the sun still peers over the peaks, it can be oppres-

sive. The rocky mountains loom over you imperiously, reminding you that they will be there long after any of us. I've never
experienced somewhere so immutable, so obviously hostile,
aside from the open sea. Back in 1956, a Norwegian writer
Liv Balstad wrote that the most vital skill for life in Svalbard
is "the art of resignation." You can have all the airports, lights
and heating you want, but you can't quite escape the feeling
of being at nature's mercy here.

Except in KP. There are no windows, save for those that
look into the whiskey vault, and it's hard to know whether it's
so dimly lit because that's what miners are used to, or because
it helps you detach. Actually, it's about helping drinkers connect with each other.

"There are no distractions in here," says Peter. "Well, there
are smartphones, but mostly it's only about the people."

Peter says that KP hasn't always been the main hangout for
Longyearbyen's nightlifers. When he first moved to Svalbard he
worked at Huset, which is a communal building opened around
seventy years ago to serve as the social hub for the miners. Despite this, it was built at least a mile from the main street, to be
equidistant between the miners' homes near the mountains and
the office and government employees farther up the valley. It
must have worked for a while, but as Longyearbyen started to
expand down by the water and mining lost its hold on the community, its location became more of a drag. Huset was eventually bought out and is now the kind of fancy restaurant this
writer can neither afford nor be bothered to walk to.

So KP has slowly become the heart of this small town, filling up every night whatever the time of year. It's not the kind
of locals bar where tourists would get aggressive side-eye for
coming in, but it has a definite sense of not being specifically for
tourists, unlike the first place I visited. There's even a German-
style *Stammtisch* (*regulars' table*), where only locals are meant to
sit, some of whom are ex-miners or even employees at the final

mine still in operation. Peter has taken to putting a sign on the table every day to avoid any (good-natured) confrontations. The sign says *Reserved for the KP Council*, which seems less a joke and more a semiofficial title. Peter still remembers the time years ago that he had to tell them the price of Carlsberg was going up.

"They're in here most nights," he says. "They are good people, but they always have an opinion. They all feel like they own a bit of the bar."

True to form, when the pub opens, the first person through the door throws his coat casually down at the table, revealing a hoodie with *KP* emblazoned on the back. He orders a Coke and a coffee, but only a few minutes later there's a beer on the table too.

Before my trip to Svalbard, going from mining to hospitality would have seemed an odd flex. My image of a miner's life was a lonely, dark one where people skills would be a distraction. In reality, miners work in teams, which, given the dangerous and claustrophobic nature of the work, means the human bonds are as tight as the carbon to hydrogen in coal. Not only that, but you'd crave the physical and human warmth of a good pub at the end of a day spent underground. After years of relying on bars for your social life and respite from the harshness of Arctic mining, it makes perfect sense to found one. And given that Huset is a 1-mile hike across frozen tundra and the world's most northerly bar feels like a hotel lobby, it makes sense that KP has become the natural choice for everyone here.

But there is something magical about it, too. Of course, there's the coal-dusted faces of the miners staring down on you, and the knowledge that you're closer to the North Pole than you are to the next bar to the south. But equally, there's the soft golden glow of the backlit whiskey cave and the range of locally brewed craft beer that makes it feel a little like an East London speakeasy. It was simultaneously instantly familiar while also being like nowhere I've ever been.

It takes just fifteen minutes for the other tables to be full, mostly ordering pints of Carlsberg or Svalbard Brewery Pilsner. People seem to come in big groups, taking over multiple tables or spilling over and around them. As Peter welcomes them like old friends, I nurse a 7% Stout and contemplate how I'd spend the long evenings if I lived in Svalbard. Very likely I'd be propping up this bar, talking to Peter about our former metropolitan lives while relishing the feeling of being in a town so small you can point right at its heart.

Arctic Night

By the time I left KP it was pitch-black. The street lights in Longyearbyen are bright so polar bears are put off a trip down the main street, but beyond the roads the darkness is almost instant. Worried I was too late to find somewhere for dinner I checked the time, to find it was barely 6 p.m.—the four-month polar night was only a few weeks away, and the sun had clearly set hours ago.

I headed up the hill toward a glowing, big-windowed building—one of the older restaurants in town recommended to me by Peter. Much like KP, the place was buzzing, and I had to take a seat at the bar and crane my neck to take it all in. Every broad oak table was littered with plates and beer glasses, while people sat elbow to elbow on stools and banquettes draped in furs. Antlers formed some of the chandeliers, and there was even a menu printed on a pelt stretched across the wall.

Peter described Kroa as the "closest taste of old Svalbard that's possible" and that extended to the food, saying that if some dishes came off the menu there'd be a riot among the longer-standing locals. I ordered a Svalbard Weissbier and one of those dishes—the klipfish, or salt cod. It's a traditional Norwegian dish, particularly around Christmas time. The name translates

as *cliff fish*, because it was originally dried out on flat rocks by
the sea. Before cooking it's supposed to be soaked in water to
reduce the salinity, but mine didn't taste like the chef had bothered. Thankfully it came with sweet-baked veg and buttery
mash, drizzled with sweet jus and bacon bits. About halfway
through the meal, the bartender delivered a second Weissbier,
as if reading my thoughts.

You can see why klipfish is popular with the locals—it's both a
taste of home and brilliant beer food. The local beer was popular
and Carlsberg was relegated to cans, but there wasn't a second
where one of the bar staff wasn't pouring one into a glass. The
spirits shelf and wine fridge went untouched the whole time I
was there…and I was there a while because I got talking to Ola.
Or rather he got talking to me.

Ola looked like a Victorian strongman gone to seed. As a
structural engineer he'd lived all over the world, but he had
come to Svalbard in March and immediately made himself at
home in Kroa. He knew all the staff, most of the regulars, and
a lot about the culture and politics of the island. He also had
four chihuahuas, which isn't strictly relevant but feels important to make clear.

Ola explained to me that Svalbard is not quite Norway. It is
funded by Norway but actually governs itself, and just under
five percent is still owned by Russia or private interests. Anyone in the world has the right to live and work in Svalbard, and
it's also nearly tax-free, which makes it appealing for shorter
stays if you can find lucrative work here. More importantly for
my story, however, it means that eating and drinking is cheaper
here than most of Norway. That helps explain why both KP and
Kroa were packed to the rafters, and lubricates the fact that during the polar night, drinking in cozy bars is just about as good
as it gets. There's another reason for Longyearbyen's burgeoning food and drink scene, though, one that Ola says most people
won't talk about. He says it's because of "others."

Ola is here to help with some new construction on the east side of town, and says there's a lot being built on the island, even as its main industry (mining) is on the way out. The reason is that even without natural resources, Svalbard is a strategic place to control. To be blunt, it could offer Russia a foothold much closer to the American East Coast, and its location could be crucial to controlling sea access to Russia's Northern Fleet on the Kola Peninsula, which houses its nuclear submarines. Essentially, both Norway and Russia are keen to keep their presence there strong, but not intimidatingly strong—hence the investment being made by the Norwegian government in Longyearbyen.

I can think of a few other good reasons, though. One is the dogsledding, another is the salt fish at Kroa, and the last one is the Weissbier I had with it. After a third beer I bade Ola goodnight and headed toward the polar night and my not-at-all intimidating hotel.

The World's Most Northerly Brewery

Svalbard Brewery is only fifteen minutes' walk from the main drag, but walking into the wind in 21°F that morning made it feel like hours. By the time I arrived at the door, I could neither feel my face nor really move it enough to say hello to Ida Dahl, who manages the brewery. She led me up to the mercifully warm taproom and offered me either a coffee or a beer. I asked for both and took a look around as she poured them.

The taproom opens Fridays and Saturdays, and has had a bit of money put into it. It's cozy, and I bet it draws a crowd. In theory this is the most northerly bar in the world, being at least a few yards closer to the shore than the Radisson Blu, and I ask if that brings anyone in. Ida says she hadn't even looked at it that way, and maybe she should make a sign.

I'm just taking my first sip of the piney, resolutely bitter IPA when Robert Johansen walks through the door. Robert is the maniac I referenced earlier, otherwise known as the founder. Like KP's owner Steve Daldorff Torgersen, he is a former miner and carries himself in the way that people with physical jobs seem to. Heavy, but spritely; powerful, but understated. His voice croaks like there's coal dust in his throat, but it fills the room. He sticks to coffee, and we sit down for a chat by a big window that looks out across the brewery.

Robert moved here in 1982, and was just twenty-two when he started working in Mine 3 near the airport. Just the way he talks about his work makes me claustrophobic—long, dusty days underground in tunnels that are 218 yards long but only 60 cm high. Only around one in five of those who went down the mines lasted six months before they quit and left the archipelago. I shudder at the thought of a life spent partly underground and partly in the Arctic winter. No wonder there's a tax benefit.

For those that could endure the work and weather, Svalbard is a wonderland for adventures. Robert lived for the camaraderie that came with small teams doing dangerous work, and seems to have replicated that on his days off by camping in the wilderness, a place he calls the *bush* despite the complete lack of vegetation.

"We were on the edge," he says. "We were out there every weekend on snowmobiles, and we knew there was no one more north than us."

It wasn't always possible to go adventuring, however. The darkness and climate meant that sometimes going out was either too dangerous or just entirely unappealing. When that happened, there were only a few options—and the most obvious one was drinking. The problem was that if you weren't in a restaurant (of which there was just Huset in the eighties), alcohol was heavily restricted. Due to the obvious danger of mixing alcohol and mining, the population of Svalbard were only allowed twenty-four beers and two bottles of spirits a month. You could have as much wine as you wanted (the law was, after all, made by the management classes), but Robert says none of the miners would touch it. "Miners like beer," he says, matter-of-factly.

To Robert, a case of beer and two bottles of spirits represented one weekend in the bush. Clearly mining makes you thirsty, and that made Huset a busy place.

"It was a company town: no shop to buy bread or anything," he says. "Just one bar, one restaurant, and everyone was there on the weekends."

Everyone ate at the restaurant at Huset, and then almost everyone went to the bar afterward. It was a necessity, a ritual and a pleasure—and meant you could save your meager beer rations for trips out. It's fascinating to me, not so much that alcohol was rationed, but that it was so central to daily life. The mining companies could have provided all sorts of entertainment, some requiring much less administration than getting their entire workforce drunk every week, but they chose a bar. On the one hand there would have likely been a recruiting crisis if there was nowhere to drink on Svalbard, but equally they must have thought that nothing knits a community together like decent food and plenty of beer, and clearly judged it worth the risk. At the top of the world, what better thing can you do than toast to it?

Taking Flight

Clearly a man for whom the phrase *keeping your feet on the ground* means nothing, while working deep underground Robert got a private pilot license. Initially it was just a hobby, a quick way to get to less accessible parts of the island and do the odd supply run to mainland Norway.

But after more than a decade in the mines, the mining company offered him a job as a pilot for them, so he decided to go back to the mainland and train for his commercial license. While there, he found out a friend had started home brewing.

"I'd never tasted home brew and I was skeptical," he remembers. "But it was much better than the industrial types of beer, so I started doing it."

Once he had his license he was split between Tromsø and Svalbard, with plenty of spare time in between flights. He tried all kinds of styles, but really started to relish stronger beers like Imperial Stouts and Barley Wines. His talents meant he started making a lot of friends, and he ended up making 50 liters or around 88 pints per batch.

"That got me thinking about setting something up on Svalbard," he says. "Everything up here was imported. Why couldn't we have something of our own?"

The reason was that the same Svalbard law that restricted how much alcohol you could take home also said that producing alcohol on Svalbard was illegal. Undeterred, in 2009 Robert wrote a letter to the Norwegian government asking for them to reconsider. When nothing happened he started calling, and continued to call once a month for five and a half years, until finally in 2014 the law was changed. Robert hadn't been sitting on his hands waiting, either. He was primed and ready to go, with a brand-new stainless steel brewery built to order and waiting. The first Svalbard Bryggeri beer was released in 2015, made with Arctic glacier water, Finnish malt, American hops, an Italian brew kit and a German brewmaster.

Getting the foreign ingredients wasn't too hard—a supply boat comes every ten days in fact—but dealing with the waste materials was trickier. Exporting the spent grain for processing on the mainland was both wasteful and expensive, but it's what Robert had to do for years because it simply wouldn't decompose in the Arctic. He finally found an alternative though, drying it to the point of it being combustible then using it to fire his boiler. He still has to export plenty of his beer to survive though, because no amount of cruise ship visits and anti-Russian geopolitical population growth could drink the thousands of liters he has to make to get the right economy of scale.

The locals would drink it all if they could, though. To say it's been embraced by the locals would be an understatement. Every bar and restaurant has Svalbard Bryggeri as its main beer, it's in the only food shop in town, and the taproom is full every Friday and Saturday. It must be gratifying to Robert to see the kind of camaraderie he had with his mining colleagues at Huset played out over his beer, and even in his bar. He celebrates his old colleagues and way of life in a limited series of beers, Gruve 3. Named after the mine he worked in and even barrel-aged in the mine itself, these dark and strong beers each bear the name and face of one of the miners who worked there with Robert—with his own one being a 9% bourbon barrel-aged dark ale called Autopilot.

This kind of grounding has made the brewery a source of huge pride to everyone I spoke to—when I explained that I was a beer writer, without fault they lit up like a beacon and proceeded to tell me all about the brewery, and Robert in particular. He's a rough-hewn link to a past that's still important to many on the archipelago, and Svalbard Bryggeri is also the first commercial food product made on the island. The restaurants all serve local whale, seal and reindeer meat, but vegetables, fruits and all other drinks come from elsewhere. Now they have beer not only brewed on the island, but partly using water from the glaciers that cut this landscape and surround the town. It feels like the physical realization of what beer meant to the Svalbard miners—sure the most important thing is that it's alcohol, but it also put their name on a way of forging community, in a place where no person should really live.

The Desi Pub

It was reassuring as a beer writer to see how vital beer, bars and yes, craft brewery taprooms could be to an isolated Arctic community, but you don't need to be miles from civilization to be— or to feel—isolated. There are countless examples of tight-knit communities based around breweries and pubs in the world's metropolises too—including London.

It is a matter of eternal shame that I was a beer writer living in the capital for a decade without knowing about Desi pubs. To some extent, I can be excused: these pubs were not designed for me, though they would all likely welcome me with open arms. These pubs were opened to cater to the people of Indian descent, and in doing so became part of a movement that changed the face of the country.

Migration to the UK from India began in the 1700s, when the East India Company started its effective occupation. Most Indians came to the UK as employees: men hired to fill vacancies on the ships coming home. What they didn't know was that most of them wouldn't be paid nearly enough to afford the return trip. So they, as well as the occasional Indian wife a British man brought home, were forced to settle in England.

By the mid-nineteenth century there was a transient population of around 40,000 Indians in the UK—including one member of parliament. Most, however, came after the breakup of the British Empire in the 1950s, during which the UK offered easy migration to anyone from the Commonwealth countries. Today, there's around 1.8 million British Indians—or Desis as they often refer to themselves. Despite such large numbers, or perhaps because of it, it's not always been a smooth ride for them.

I became aware of Desi pubs thanks to a fellow beer writer, David Jesudason. In his book *Desi Pubs*, he talks about the racism he experienced as a young drinker in British drinking establishments. The first time he ever walked into one, in fact, it was assumed he was a taxi driver there to pick someone up. Growing up in the 1990s, however, he missed the worst extremes of British racism.

When we talk about racism in the West, the most common example used is the experience of African Americans, but when Malcolm X visited Smethwick, a town that's around thirty-seven percent Asian, he declared the racism "worse than America."

He was there in part because of the man responsible for the creation of Desi pubs. Avtar Singh Jouhl came to the UK in 1958, settling in Smethwick and working in the foundries. He was shocked by the treatment he and his fellow Indian migrants received when going out for drinks. The color bar, which segregated pubs into white and nonwhite drinking areas, was in full force in the early sixties and some pubs refused to serve people of color period.

Jouhl quite rightly wanted the concept abolished, so he and some fellow members of the Indian Workers' Association enlisted a few white university students to go into these pubs and buy beer for them. When the beers were handed to the British Indians they were all kicked out. Jouhl used evidence of these events to object to the pub owner's license when it was next up for renewal, then encouraged British Indians to apply to run them instead—and so the Desi pub was born.

According to Jesudason, a Desi pub is one run by a British Indian person that wears its South Asian heritage on its sleeve. It might be through the decor, the food, the music, the events or all these things, but it's essentially a place that any British Indian will feel as if it were designed for them. With that, of course, comes the safety and comfort of belonging, something that would have been hard for people of color to find in public spaces in the midsixties. Although segregation and refusal of service based on ethnicity was made illegal in the Race Relations Acts of 1965 and 1968, segregation in pubs quietly continued all over the UK until the 1990s. This meant the Desi pub's role has remained important to this day. Jesudason says the earliest Desi pub he can find opened in Leicester in 1962, but there are now hundreds, and the most famous of them came to play a vital role in the experience and community of nearly all British Indians who came to the UK after the midnineties.

Glassy Junction opened in 1994, and was an institution in the heavily Asian-influenced Southall, west of London, until it closed in 2012. For just shy of twenty years it was what Jesudason calls "a raucous celebration of Punjabi pub culture," as well as a safe haven for British Indians in a city that was not always welcoming. It was a hub of the community, and a place for South Asians to fully express their identity and heritage without fear of reprisal. No British pubs, or indeed any public space, in London were playing Indian music, celebrating Diwali or serving authentic curries. It became such an important place for immigrants that it was even heard of back in India, as both a brilliant night out and the first port of call for Indian migrants arriving via Heathrow Airport.

From Southall's main street you can see the planes on their final approach, and hear the roar of the turbines, and the idea was that Indian immigrants could head straight from the plane to Glassy Junction for some familiar food, and most likely a beer. If you hadn't had time to exchange your money or were short on pounds sterling, you could even pay in rupees. It's a tradition you'll still find at one of Southall's two surviving Desi pubs, The Scotsman—where a former Glassy Junction chef serves some of London's best curries.

Little India

It would be hard to starve in Southall. As you walk down the main street, pretty much every door leads to a restaurant or food market. The enticing smell of frying onions and heady spices are enough to make you stop midstride—though the classic London aromas of weed and exhaust keep you moving. Anyway, on this wet January afternoon I had a date with a giant naan to get to.

I turn off the main drag and the shop windows immediately give way to driveways and front room windows. Aside from an office with *DESI RADIO* in the window, it looks like any other London estate, probably built in the 1970s and now well lived in and loved. You could say the same for The Scotsman, which is tiled in retro brown and has those odd frosted windows that replaced curtains sometime in the mid-twentieth century. Essentially it looks like any other housing estate local, a breed sadly now more likely to be boarded up and awaiting development into flats.

The biggest clue that this is not one of those pubs is the emblem that hangs just below the pub sign: *DELIVEROO.* There aren't many pubs with food good enough to warrant a delivery option, but The Scotsman definitely has it. Inside, the decor is a joyous mix of London pub, Indian restaurant and 1990s wine bar—with tartan carpets. Layered on top of this mélange are countless pieces of sport memorabilia and images: Pelé stares at you from a pillar, a host of Indian cricket players celebrate on various walls, a few Liverpool players are midflight by the bar, and inexplicably Mike Tyson leers over the table right by the main entrance. Around the corner are two pool tables and some slot machines, the first of either I've seen in a pub for a long time.

It's only when the bartender says *Hello?* in the manner of someone on a phone call with a bad line that I realize I have literally walked in, stood in the middle of the room, and started making mental notes—rather than behaving like a human and going to the bar. I order a Cobra and sheepishly take the menu she offers me. In the grand tradition of Indian restaurants, the menu is vast, but I've done my homework online. I was getting the lamb masala, which I'd seen comes on a huge plate with peppers, onions and tomatoes cooked for hours in the rich, spicy sauce. Most importantly I was going to mop it all up with a jumbo naan.

The bartender looked a little skeptical as I ordered. The Scotsman's naans are famous for being roughly the size of a toddler and arriving at the table hanging from big steel hooks for everyone to tear chunks from. I was not everyone, I was one. But I stuck to my guns. I'd come a long way. I'd earned this.

Just as I sat down with my beer, owner and head chef Shinda Mahal came through the bar to say he'd cook then come out after I'd eaten, so I was left to soak in the Cobra and Indian music videos coming from various screens around the pub. The steaming curry comes first, with the chops piled up and glistening with oil turned red by heavy spicing. Crispy fat clings to the meat as I lift the chops from the sauce, and the word *aromatic* doesn't come close to how they smell. Then out came the enormous naan, held at a distance by the bartender because it was dripping luxuriantly with garlicky butter.

"People usually get their phones out and film it," she says, slightly disappointed by my reaction. But I'd expected this—I'd literally been waiting weeks knowing I was coming. As I ripped my first piece, I felt the perfection of it—soft, doughy and buttery on the top, crispy and charred on the bottom. It soaked up the rich masala sauce, then folded perfectly like Roman-style pizza dough.

I had been assured I could box up anything I didn't finish, but the proud Brit in me said *We don't leave bread behind.* Besides, I thought I was going to make it. I was the encapsulation of the man jumping a gorge: cocky, then terrified, then elated, then ultimately grasping at air as I fell just short. I left what is best described as a normal naan-sized amount, utterly spent and keen to tell Shinda just how special the meal was.

Shinda has a very kind face, and a soft and warm handshake—not something you experience with many chefs. He came to the UK in the late nineties and walked straight into a job at Glassy

Junction, where he started as a bartender before finding his true calling out back in the kitchens. He recalls the time fondly and enthusiastically, and abbreviates it simply to *the Glassy* while we talk.

"It was an all-mixed community," he says. "Everyone was welcome in the Glassy and everyone in Southall knew it, so it was crowded and rowdy, but everyone was respectful."

That last word feels like a reference to the fact that few other pubs in Southall were respectful to Asian people at the time: Southall has often been the target of racists, both amateur and organized. To have a place like the Glassy must have been such a comfort. Still, the work was hectic, and a year later he took the role of head (or rather only) chef at The Scotsman, which was much smaller and quieter than Glassy Junction. It represented an opportunity to put his own stamp on the place, though.

"Before I started, the food was all English, sandwiches only," he says. "Then I started to do Indian food and improve the mix to about 50/50. In 2008 I took over the business, and started doing proper Indian food using all traditional methods."

Shinda took over the pub's lease when the owners decided it wasn't financially viable, but he has ("slowly, slowly") turned it into one of the best known Desi pubs in the country, largely off the strength of his cooking. Despite being uncomfortably full, I can't help but enthuse about just how good my masala and naan were. He's clearly delighted, but I get the sense he knows exactly how good his food is.

"There are a lot of special dishes on the menu. The lamb masala, the lollipops, the Scotty tava—you can't get the same food any other place," he grins. "It's not just Southall people who come but people from other towns. They all know The Scotsman."

The pub is still entirely focused on its local community, however. While I sweated over my lunch and beer, there was a constant stream of locals coming in for a quick plate of chicken lollipops, or something I couldn't quite work out that sizzled right until the plate was empty. Oddly they all seemed to drink Peroni, throwing another nation into the mix. Over seventy-five percent of Southall residents are of Asian descent, and obviously that encompasses myriad races, religions, ages, shared histories and experiences from across the continent. A look at the decor, the various sports teams, the British nuances, the huge menu, and you can see that Shinda is set up for them all—and they all come to The Scotsman.

"We celebrate all my cultures here; we're the local to everyone."

As I nursed the last of my Cobra and willed my body to digest enough of the naan to allow me to walk upright to the station, I marveled at how much light had been found from such dark times. All over the country, British Indians faced with persecution and exclusion hadn't just created spaces for themselves, but kept their spaces open to all. They gave a home to a burgeoning community of Asians in Britain, and have gone on to define the idea of a public space and community—a place that welcomes everyone.

In a time when inner-city pubs the country over are struggling, establishments like The Scotsman are flourishing in their residential estates and satellite town centers. As a result, as David Jesudason points out in his book, they have outlasted many of the outright racist pubs that inspired them.

Chapter 8

Entertainment

Or isn't beer supposed to be fun?

I'm not going to lie: there's a lot more Hitler in this book than I envisaged. In fact, if I'm honest, the original pitch had absolutely no Hitler at all. But it's the beer writer's curse to take very seriously what others don't give a second's thought to.

When I started this career I imagined myself becoming the life and soul of parties, pouring out magnums of rare beers to rapturous applause then regaling people with tales of my incredible adventures. Instead, my wife warns people at social gatherings not to ask me what I'm drinking in case they "set me off," like I'm some jabbering windup toy.

In my defense, the people who make the best beers in the world also take their beer very seriously. They have to, because making such beer requires excruciating attention to detail and is not at all easy. Drinking it, however, is very easy, which is why people tend to enjoy it in the moment rather than analyze it. I do a little too much of both, so while this book is mostly about the incredible and deadly serious social, political, historical and scientific importance of beer, the main reason I actually wrote it is because drinking it is a hell of a lot of fun.

In the last few decades, saying such a thing has become somewhat controversial. There's a lot of hand-wringing about alcohol by lobby groups, politicians and parents, and if we ignore the extremes of these conversations, there are plenty of valid concerns. Drinking to excess is never fun, and regularly drinking to excess is dangerous in the short and long term, to you and those around you. Alcohol and acetaldehyde (which is what our body turns alcohol into) are both class one carcinogens. This puts drinking in the same category as breathing in asbestos, smoking tobacco and bathing in nuclear radiation. But this category also includes bacon and sunlight, two things I'd file next to beer as Worth the Risk.

I'm not being flippant here either. The phrase *everything in moderation* may be a cliché, but there have been hundreds of studies into the effect of alcohol consumption on *all-cause mortality* (i.e., chance of death) that have found that light drinking—up to around three drinks a day—is actually less dangerous than being a lifetime teetotaler. The reasons for this are unclear, and despite the enormous data set collated over decades, plenty of people criticize this so-called J-curve of alcohol's relation to mortality. Critiques include the fact that teetotalers might have underlying health conditions that forced them into abstinence; or that casual drinkers are more likely to be active and wealthy and have access to good health care. None of these addenda have really been investigated, so to critics I say, "Show me the data and I'll throw the J-curve out of the window."

There's one argument in favor of the J-curve, however, that makes me think I'll never see that data. Alcohol and, perhaps more than any other subcategory, beer brings people together. A truly epic metastudy of over ninety separate papers conducted from 1986 to 2022 and involving over 2 million adults, found that social isolation increased the risk of early death by thirty-two percent, and loneliness increased the risk of death by fourteen percent. Simply put, if you hang out with people regularly, you're likely to live longer. Now, teetotalers clearly have social lives; I'm not saying they don't. But most human social occasions are built around alcohol, and always have been. Pubs, bars, restaurants, festivals, dinner parties, sports—all occasions where we've shown beer playing a vital role—reduce isolation

and loneliness. They are the antithesis of it, and there are studies proving that, too.

What those studies don't quite get across, though, is that mod-
erate drinking among friends can result in some of the most
life-affirming moments a person will ever experience. This is
something you see throughout the world and throughout history,
from the straw-drinking Sumerians to scuzzy website photos of
people in clubs in the early 2000s. Despite the fact that most so-
called beer Instagram photos are now carefully arranged shots
of hazy IPAs with the cans artfully blurred behind, such gal-
leries are dwarfed by the number of posts of people just having
fun with their mates, beer in hand. It feels almost intrinsic to
humanity that wherever we go for group leisure time, we either bring or seek beer.

The truth is, if beer wasn't a hell of a lot of fun, it would have
died out pretty much as soon as food had become a certainty and
water flowed from your own tap. Early beers would have been
as funky as hell, and even in the nineties I hated my first sip of
beer—it tasted like earwax. But I persevered because I didn't
hate the way it made me or my friends feel. The gentle buzz
that most beer offers by being (relatively) low in alcohol is a lubricant that greases so many of our social interactions, whether
with friends or strangers.

On my travels I've seen countless examples of beer's ability to
unite, excite and entertain, and some are on an epic scale. If a
wildlife documentary were made about us as a species, a celes-
tial David Attenborough would focus on the gatherings at our
millions of beery water holes—where we play, court, rest and
sustain ourselves in vast numbers every day. The biggest gathering, humanity's wildebeest migration if you will, would be
the one that happens in early autumn on the elevated plains of
Upper Bavaria. You see, there is no event where beer's incredible power to bring people together is better demonstrated than
Oktoberfest.

Gemütlichkeit

If you ask a German what they think of Oktoberfest, the most common answer will also be the simplest: "The beer is overpriced." This did little to deter me before my first visit, because an overpriced beer in Germany is still cheaper than any beer in the UK.

I was, however, a little perturbed by the other responses I got—that it was too busy, too loud, too cheesy, and only really for tourists. I am not a man who likes crowds (they tend to get between me and the bar), and like all tourists, I hate other tourists. But as I snaked my way down the main drag of the Theresienwiese in Munich, where Oktoberfest is held every year, having drunk my fourth liter of 6% lager in the Hacker-Pschorr tent, and screamed the chorus of Robbie Williams's "Angels" arm in arm with a man I'd only met as the intro started, I decided that the crowds—and maybe even the tourists—are what makes Oktoberfest so special.

It was a magical event from its very conception, which was basically as the reception for the 1810 wedding of the Princess Therese von Sachsen-Hildburghausen to the then crown prince of Bavaria, who later became King Louis I. That year, the Bavarian royal family, who as we know understood that the way to a Bavarian's heart was through their beer belly, organized a horse race just outside the city walls so the common folk could celebrate. It was such a good party that they did it the next year—and the following 215 years too, albeit with short breaks for world wars and global pandemics. Over that time it has become the biggest festival in the world, beer-related or not, with an incomprehensible 7.2 million revelers in 2023—about 450,000 a day.

As any German will tell you, that amount of people means serious money, and it has become something of a profiteering exercise. Until 1919, any brewery could pour there, but with the state bankrupt after the First World War, the six biggest breweries stumped up the cash needed to get it running again, with the stipulation that they'd be the only ones serving beer. Since then they've made up some slightly nonsensical rules about who can and can't pour beer during the festival, which conveniently leads to the same six breweries hosting every year—Spaten, Hofbräu, Löwenbräu, Paulaner, Hacker-Pschorr and Augustiner.

While in Munich to research Chapter 2, I also visited Giesinger Bräu, a small lager brewery with the burning desire to pour at Oktoberfest. To do so they have jumped through every hoop created for them: despite not wanting a classic Helles, they brewed one because the big six demanded it. They bought a filter to filter it, because the big six demanded it. They even dug a well 166 yards into the earth to extract the groundwater under Munich rather than using the town supply, because the big six demanded it. On the wall just behind their fermentation tanks is a mural saying *Poured at Oktoberfest*, with every year since 2014 written and then crossed out. The costs are into the millions, and 2024 was recently crossed out and 2025 added. We may have to wait at least another year to see the brewery at Oktoberfest, but there's no reason you should pause if you see their beer anywhere else—it's excellent.

At Oktoberfest itself, most drinkers, including myself four liters in, don't give the cartel element a second's thought. Everything that people expect—camp music, good beer, heavy food—is supplied in absurd quantities. More than half a million chickens are eaten and around 7 million liters of beer consumed. If that doesn't get the scale of the party across then consider that in 2019 more than 600 people ended up with alcohol poisoning, another 6,000 people needed medical treatment, and 4,000 items ended up in lost property (I think my dignity is in there somewhere).

You could argue that the last thing the party needs is another brewery, but the beers are roughly the same and so are the tents, with the exception of Augustiner Festhalle (which looks like someone at the brewery got their Christmas decorations out early). The tent also has its own butchers for its meat, and serves its Festbier from wooden barrels, which gives it a creamier feel and lower carbonation—ideal when you're drinking four liters of the stuff.

For various reasons, mostly that in a former job I helped import the stuff, I usually end up in the Hacker-Pschorr Festzelt. Here you enjoy your caramel, licorice and lemon-tinged beer under the bright blue of a painted ceiling and the words *Himmel der Bayern—Heaven of the Bavarians*. It is difficult to express the euphoria you feel in a place the size of a football stadium, where everyone is gently buzzed and drinking in what is likely a once-in-a-lifetime experience. There are people so far away you can't make out their faces, but they are in the same tent, drinking the same beer, listening to the same music, and experiencing it in a very similar way to you. It is intoxicating even without the booze element. The only way I can describe it is the contrast between being at a comedy night versus watching the Netflix special. You laugh harder, smile broader, feel better while experiencing exactly the same jokes that you would if you watched a recording at home. Oktoberfest Jonny LOVES Robbie Williams, Jonny at home with a can of Paulaner Oktoberfest thinks "Millennium" has a certain nostalgia but finds Robbie's general *oeuvre* pretty derivative.

My point is, Oktoberfest proves that beer is inherently magnetic and fun, and its combination of liter glasses and overly broad music is found independently all over the world.

Brazilian Oktoberfest

Munich's Oktoberfest may have been the first, but it's far from the only beer festival with an oompah backing track. There are, in fact, thousands of them every autumn, all over the world.

Some are cynical cash-ins that offer little more than a rented marquee, white-labeled lager and a Europop playlist from the depths of Spotify. But others are, in their own way, no less authentic or fun than the original—usually because Germans had a hand in them.

As we learned in Chapter 3, just a few years after the first great party on the Theresienwiese in 1810, people began to abandon Germany and Bavaria in huge numbers: 10 million emigrated by the start of the First World War. Many of these people were affluent and educated, so with them went Germany's architecture, music and cuisine—as well as its brewing knowledge and drinking culture. At least half of them headed for the USA, but others ended up in more surprising corners of the world. On my travels I've seen German culture everywhere from South Africa to eastern China, given away by the presence of Bavarian lodgelike buildings, an affinity for roasted pork and schnitzels, and of course plenty of lager.

Despite voluntarily leaving their homeland, these German migrants hung tight to their roots, and wherever they settled their impact is still clear today. The second biggest Oktoberfest celebration is held in Blumenau, a south Brazilian city founded by a German pharmacist in 1850. It's a remarkable place that wears its German heritage as proudly as a Bavarian wears lederhosen in September. The city is crisscrossed with the Bavarian white plaster and wooden beams, whether it's a high-rise or a cottage. In the older part of town, this pattern dominates entirely, as do people of German origin—and it's reflected in all parts of its culture. There are beer gardens and German restaurants everywhere, and even a brewing museum.

The city held its first Oktoberfest in 1984, but instead of celebrating a wedding it was organized to raise money after a devastating flood. Since then it has grown to welcome nearly 1 million people each year, and its Germanic connection has made it perhaps the most authentic outside Germany—albeit with its own Brazilian twists. Unlike Munich, where the festivities are mostly confined to the Theresienwiese for the sanity of the long-suffering locals, Blumenau's Bavarian architecture sets the scene for lots of costumes and parades, something the Brazilians know a thing or two about.

The main party happens in the Parque Vila Germânica, a permanent fairground and faux-Alpine city that, at 430,556 square feet, is one of the largest public parks in Brazil. Revelers in German dress get in free to enjoy the rides, beer tents and music as they tuck into bratwurst, pork knuckles and pretzels. The latter are served with cinnamon sugar rather than the traditional salt, which sounds delicious but doesn't quite suit the beer. Speaking of which, instead of a traditional 6% Oktoberfest beer, you mostly drink Brahma…

Brazil's best-selling beer owes a debt to Europe as well, being the invention of a Swiss immigrant called Joseph Villiger, but at the end of the day it's just another macro beer—and not a very good one at that.

Just like the original, Blumenau's Oktoberfest isn't solely focused on beer. What's in the glass is a lubricant for a festival that echoes the campness of the Munich original while adding a carnival feel. Beer doesn't just bring people together, it can work as a blurring line between cultures. A Brazilian Oktoberfest sounds like a bizarre notion, but in reality it's a perfect combination of two national identities that are famous for their open-invite parties.

But Blumenau is not, in fact, the most unlikely setting for an Oktoberfest. That title goes to the Qingdao International Beer Festival, colloquially known as Asian Oktoberfest.

Asian Oktoberfest

With a population of over 1.4 billion people, it's inevitable that China would be home to the biggest beer brand in the world, the oddly named Snow, but its love of beer is really cemented by the fact that it's also home to the second biggest: Tsingtao.

While Snow barely leaves the People's Republic, you'll know Tsingtao as the most common option at your local Chinese restaurant, and while the beer is nothing to write home about (my parents are bored of those letters anyway), its history and location is fascinating.

Tsingtao is an alternative spelling of the brewery's hometown, Qingdao, which lies on the eastern coast of China in Jiaozhou Bay. In the nineteenth century, China was the subject of constant invasions by Western powers, with Britain and Portugal controlling large parts of it. Jiaozhou Bay, however, was controlled by the Germans, albeit only for sixteen years. It was also not your usual invasion—Germany simply coerced the Qing Dynasty into leasing the country about 500 square kilometers after the killing of two German missionaries in 1897. It lost the territory when Japan invaded in 1914, but it had already stamped its culture throughout the region, especially in the thriving port city of Qingdao.

As this is Germany we're talking about, that meant opening several breweries. First came Brauerei Landmann-Kell, founded by a German clockmaker and optician called Gottfried Landmann in 1901. He went as far as to bring over German brewmaster Ludwig Kell to make the beers, but the brewery failed within its first two years. This was likely down to the fact that locals mostly boycotted German businesses, but archives also show that Landmann paid for plenty of ads for his clock and optics shop, but none for his fledgling brewery. After seeing success with a brew pub in Shanghai, another German called Carl Gomoll founded a wheat beer brewery in Qingdao. This one did a lot better, only closing when the Japanese muscled their way in.

Tsingtao Brewery could have gone the same way. It was founded in 1903 by a group of English and German merchants based in Shanghai. Opening just a month after Landmann-Kell went out of business, it thrived by focusing on sales to Western immigrants and setting up networks throughout eastern China. Barely a decade later, however, history intervened and Japan gained control of Qingdao. Liquidators were called in and the brewery was sold to Dai Nippon Brewery. It remained a Japanese concern right up until 1945, when Japan surrendered to the Allies. The brewery was sold to a private investor before being nationalized under the laws of Chinese Communism four years later. For the next thirty years it produced beer for the State, before being privatized again in 1990. The new owners wasted no time in recalling its German heritage, and the very next year saw the first Qingdao International Beer Festival—or Asian Oktoberfest.

Barely two decades later, I decided to visit the coastal metropolis to experience beer culture on the other side of the world and visit the Oktoberfest farthest from its home. Within a few hours of stepping off the plane, however, I started to doubt whether I'd actually make it to the festival.

Ganbei!

"Ganbei!" we cried one more time, raising our glasses of beer. I had been told before the trip that this was the local word for *cheers*—but next to me, a man's voice broke with emotion, while a woman to his right had hidden her drink from view. Back home, saying *cheers* is merely good manners, but in China it means business. When the call goes up, you don't have to just take a sip, you're supposed to *finish* your drink—even if the waiter has just filled it to the brim.

You'd think the Chinese would therefore treat the word with respect, but it was thrown around with abandon during dinner with some locals on the first night of my trip. Each cry of *ganbei* was met with less enthusiasm, until we sounded like schoolchildren saying good morning to a principal. In between, we were invited to take part in drinking competitions, just in case we got too comfortable. While we were catching our breath and running to the loo, we were served delicious seafood fresh off the boats in the Yellow Sea, deliciously crispy eggplant coated in sticky chili sauce, and spongy buns filled with sweet red beans. Then, abruptly, the Chinese contingent rose and started shaking hands.

"What do you mean they're going home?" I demanded of my guide. It was barely dark outside and we had just spent the past two hours downing our drinks so as to not offend. I'd taken every dish with two hands and a bowed head, and used my chopsticks with skills only found in those brought up eating Chinese takeaways and drinking French Piss, glued to Saturday night *Baywatch*. Why, just ninety minutes into dinner, were they heading to bed? As it turns out, that was just the custom. In China, the beer protocol seems to be *Drink hard, drink fast, be in bed by nine*. If I was going to make it to Oktoberfest in a few days, I was going to need to start hiding my beers as well.

Qingdao is known locally as Beer Town. Even when you're not inadvertently being drunk under the table by strangers at a restaurant, Tsingtao is absolutely everywhere. Most unusually, every street corner shop had bags of beer hanging like cotton candy at the fair. When I say *bags of beer* I don't mean bags of bottles or cans—I mean bags literally filled with beer. The ones hanging were just for show, but you could purchase them freshly poured to take away—all you needed was a straw. I guess the need for cold beer is so strong in this hot, humid place that simply opening a bottle or can is too taxing.

Walking among the bag-sipping locals, the mix of identities is as striking as it is surprising. Despite being occupied by Japan for twice as long, it's the German influence that's most obvious. The city is famous for its beautiful red-tiled roofs and oak beam buildings, as well as a twin-towered century-old Catholic church right at its heart. It makes for an utterly unique urban

space, one that couldn't be more different from Beijing, where
I stayed for a few days on the way to the coast. Beijing is shut
off—everything happens several stories up, in glass skyscrapers
that reach into the haze of pollution and humidity. Qingdao has
its fair share of monster high-rises, but its German architecture
sits proudly among it. Despite local opposition during the occupation, the Germans were intent on making their mark and
at some point its culture has gone from an unwelcome influence to happy nostalgia. Sometimes though, the Chinese end
up a little wide of the mark...as I found out the following night
at the festival.

There are infinitely more pole dancers and techno DJs at
Qingdao International Beer Festival, and a few more topless
middle-aged men (though this is a close-run thing). Asian Oktoberfest is essentially a knockoff, the beer version of shrink-
wrapped, poorly printed counterfeit DVDs. At Oktoberfest you
drink in tents branded by the historic six breweries of Munich,
but at Qingdao International Beer Festival, I swear I drank Tsingtao in the "Pulanade" tent. Maybe the beer was getting to
me, or maybe it was as close as the organizers dared to get to
Paulaner.

For all the lack of authenticity though, there is an earnestness
to the Asian version that you can't help but admire. Some of the
locals are exceptionally drunk, but they are also delighted to be
so, dancing, singing and swaying with a lust for life you only
really see in September in Munich. Venturing into the biggest
tent, I chose a table right in the middle of the action to soak in
the thumping electro music and beer poured direct from towers on the table, served so cold it gave me brain freeze. Initially
a little overawed and skeptical, the *ganbei*s started to take their
joyous toll and I loosened up. I'd expected something more akin
to the real Munich Oktoberfest, but that would only be authentic to a small part of Qingdao. A festival that took its German
history and mixed it in with Chinese drinking culture and ka-

raoke booths created something more true to the region. Everything that made me cringe at first became the things I applauded
loudest, such as the balding, potbellied topless man dancing on a
balcony; the lady doing the worst karaoke version of "Livin' on
a Prayer" I have ever heard; and the man who turned up purely
in a Speedo and looked every inch like he might take that off,
too. I have been to hundreds of beer festivals all over the world,
and this was unlike anything I have ever witnessed.

I'm not certain I'd recommend going to Qingdao International Beer Festival, but I can't deny that it still managed to
conjure that feeling of what the Germans call *Gemütlichkeit*—
of warm fuzziness and good cheer. I'm not sure that's particularly down to the festival itself, but more the inevitability of
beer in combination with friends, music and food. The fact that
we see these things united over the world, especially if some
Germans have passed through at some point in history, proves
that drinking festivals are alluring and entertaining on a kind
of carnal level.

Sometimes, though, you don't really need the people bit.
Sometimes the beer itself can be fun. As in the actual liquid.

The craft beer revolution has done wonders for small business
and diversity in the beer industry, bringing the experimentation
that was a necessary part of brewing for the first 12,000 years
back. In reaction to the proliferation of pale lager, breweries have
once again started playing around with fruits, souring bacteria,
spices and unusual ingredients. Obviously this isn't a bid to make
the best of what's available any more, but to push the boundaries of what can be made by barley, hops, yeast and water, and in
doing so to excite beer drinkers and attract new ones.

There's a lot of snobbery about these kinds of beers, but not
every brew has to be analyzed and dissected; not everything has
to have a deeper meaning and a rich history; not every sip has
to be a religious experience. Some of the most fun beers I've
ever tried, however, were brewed in a church.

Lead Us Into Temptation

Sometimes I feel like many beer writers celebrated the 500-year anniversary of the Reinheitsgebot in 2016 by signing up to it, such is the snootiness with which modern small-batch beer is considered.

Craft beer, whatever that really means, was in a strange time in the mid-2010s. Thirty years had passed since the American craft brewing revolution, when home brewers all over the country took their hobbies full-time and showed a whole nation that beer didn't all have to taste the same. American IPA, the beer that had sent microbrewing over the barricades with its bitterness and bold hop-driven aroma, was being forced into retreat by an army of sweeter, fuller-bodied styles. Mostly it was the New England IPA, a hazy, velvety and juicy reinvention. Many beer writers dismissed the haze as laziness (clear beer always used to be a sign of proper maturation) and claimed it was a fad: it's now craft's flagship style. Then there was the fruited sour beer, which at its most extreme resembles an alcoholic smoothie and is labeled *heretical* by the same critics. Finally there was the rise of Imperial Stouts with all manner of unusual ingredients— initially vanilla, coffee and chocolate, but as we'll learn, things have evolved (or devolved, depending on your point of view) from there.

On occasion, the worst of craft beer's excesses do worry me, but only out of the concern that people might think it's all craft beer has to offer. Otherwise, I embrace the absurdity of it all by reminding myself that this is hardly the first time beer has gone off the rails. When hops were first used there must have been some highly cynical brewsters, and the same for the German brewers who added rice and maize when they got to the USA. The first Oyster Stout, supposedly brewed with oyster shells to aid clarity and add salinity, would have no doubt raised some eyebrows among Londoners...though hopefully they left some room on their foreheads to go even higher for Meat Stout—a strong dark ale with beef extract, made by a small Lancashire brewery called Mercers in the early twentieth century. Then of course there's every lambic beer that's ever been made with fruit, and the sickly, bright green woodruff syrups traditionally added to Berlinerweisses in northern Germany.

Put simply, if you think brewers have only just started pushing the boundaries of what humans should and shouldn't drink, you don't know your beer history. And if you don't like the way these experiments are going, I suggest you steer clear of any churches in the Stockholm suburbs...

Just a few miles north of the historic city center is Sundbyberg. It feels like any other Scandi satellite town—clean, practical, spacious and relaxed—and there was a time that you would have said the same for the church on the corner of Espanaden and Sturegatan. Its beige, almost featureless exterior is about as austere as a church gets, but confusingly, along the front is a bubble-font sign that says *Omnipollo*.

Inside, the ceiling, walls, pillars and windows are as they have always been. Even the organ is still in place. But crammed in between them is an epic stainless steel brewery. The tanks are where the pews should be, lined up toward the now-missing altar in a ghostly tableau of communion. Just below the height of their manway hatches, a mezzanine floor goes around the whole church, making the taproom space. Instead of bread and stale wine, it's smashburgers and 11% dark beers served from slushie machines. Up there, people can eat and drink while they bask in the light from the stained glass, peering up at the projection of a smiley face above the sanctuary.

I'm still taking it all in as Omnipollo founder Henok Fentie comes over with a pint of lager unlike anything I have ever seen. The head is even more compact than the one I had in the Budvar cellars, and it towers above the rim of the glass by at least an inch. Still, I'm more surprised that I'm being handed a Pilsner.

"I never thought we'd be able to produce and sell lager in any meaningful way at all, but it seems like it's happening," he says, his face inexplicably clear of foam despite taking a big sip. For almost any other brewer who has opened in the last 200 years, that would seem like a very strange statement—lager has been the biggest selling beer style in the world for generations—but Henok's brewery is famous for making the antithesis of pale lager. As I wipe the froth clinging to my nose, I note that, even when brewing a classic German Pilsner, Henok has to find a way to break tradition.

Omnipollo is a former cuckoo brewery, which is to say it used to brew exclusively at other people's places. This gives them the flexibility to try all sorts of different techniques and styles at breweries more set up for them. If I had to describe their beers in one word, I'd have to go for *fun*, but Pilsner is not fun. You have fun drinking it, sure, but its production and its flavors are decidedly serious. Omnipollo takes many things seriously, but beer is rarely one of them.

It was founded in 2007 by obsessive home brewer Henok and artist Karl Grandin, who had a vision of brewing modern craft beer and dressing it up as Pop Art. The idea was to change the wider public's perception of beer as a commercial, everyday endeavor and to show the artistry that goes into it.

From the beginning, Henok shied away from styles that would appeal to broad audiences, however. The first beer was an American-hopped Saison, probably considered sacrilege by both Belgian beer lovers and hopheads in the US. But this was the early 2010s, when craft brewers were working in batches so small that it was hard not to sell out of it. It gave the industry (and indeed some YouTubers covering the scene, ahem) the false notion that beer could be whatever you wanted it to be; that the sky was the limit. Most breweries learned pretty quickly that this was not the case: that some people's expectations were hard to change, and that running a brewery was an expensive endeavor.

From the outside it looks like Henok and Karl learned none of those lessons. Perhaps it's because they didn't have the overheads that a physical brewery has, or because they had set up contracts with breweries all over the world so had a wider base to sell to, or because they never bought into the traditions of supply and demand, but Omnipollo mostly makes exactly whatever the hell it wants.

Henok was early on the New England IPA train, introducing the concept to lots of countries thanks to his ability to brew fresh batches all over the world. As he flew around the world to do collaborations with some of his favorite breweries, he soaked up the culture, processes and flavors. It was this approach, combined with his childhood ambition of being a pastry chef, that led him down the path that most people associate Omnipollo with, one they mostly dug themselves: the unholy, rocky path that leads to Pastry Stouts.

"It became clear that if we're working with exports, we had to make something that made sense to ship from Europe to LA," says Henok. "We were exporting an idea as much as the hops, malt, yeast or whatever."

If you're unfamiliar with Pastry Stout, the headline is that it's a very strong, dark beer that's brewed to be exceptionally sweet, then conditioned over various beer-adjacent ingredients. Most commonly it's coffee, or cacao, or coconut—flavors that would clearly work with a dark, chocolaty, nutty noted beer. Some breweries take it a little further by adding less expected things like marshmallow, cinnamon, bananas and even chili peppers, then aging them in spirit barrels to add further flavor and complexity. Omnipollo has done pretty much all that, in some cases in one beer, but they have also taken the technical brewing side to a whole new extreme.

As we know, the alcohol in beer is a by-product of yeast eating the malt sugars. The more sugar there is at the start of fermentation, the stronger the beer is likely to be. But Omnipollo fudges the math a little. They specifically brew beer with such high levels of sugar that the yeast essentially poisons itself with the alcohol content before it can ferment it all. This means that some Omnipollo Stouts have more sugar in them at the *end* than many very strong beers have at the start.

Extracting that amount of sugar from barley, at the scale that Omnipollo does it, is a remarkable technical feat. It requires an incredible amount of malt in the mash, and a ten-hour boil to reduce the liquor down. After fermentation there might still be around 250 g of sugar in a pint. Now, I don't care what anyone says, that makes Omnipollo Stouts delicious. I wouldn't consider myself a man with a sweet tooth, but it takes a real fun sponge to deny the joy of sugary alcohol, especially when it's paired with delicious things like coconut or coffee—and Omnipollo knows how to source their flavorings.

Getting Buzzed

We're in a taxi, driving around a commercial port complex just outside of Stockholm. The driver is lost, we're obviously not from here, and patience is running thin. All I know is that we're late and we're headed to one of the most exclusive coffee roasters in the world—Standout Coffee.

We finally arrive a little flustered and are greeted by Alexander Ruas, a former Swedish barista champion and cofounder of Standout. He welcomes us into a small warehouse where we're hit by a wall of rich roasting coffee aroma. On the walls are beautiful artworks that reference beer and coffee, and by the windows are two state-of-the-art-looking roasters. Not much production is going on, though. An employee is weighing and packaging beans, and Alex has clearly been doing emails. It feels more like a design agency than a coffee roastery.

That makes more sense as Alex explains the nature of Standout. He only buys beans from farmers who have supplied coffee to national barista champions—essentially, he buys the coffee that has been deemed the best in the world. If that sounds a bit cynical, they do so by getting to know these in-demand farmers personally, and working so closely with them that Alex knows them all by their first names.

I'm actually here to pick a coffee myself, for a collaboration Coffee Stout that Henok and I are working on, and Alex has three kettles and filters ready for me to try his selections. My ability to talk about artisan coffee is the same as my ability to help a lost Uber driver in Stockholm, so I'm pretty nervous about making a fool of myself. I'd asked Henok for advice, and all he'd said was, "Don't let Alex lead you"—which was frustrating because that was my exact plan. I needn't have worried. The flavors may be different, but the language is the same between beer and coffee, and Alex and I enjoyed tasting our way through the three he thought might work for our beer, finally deciding on a big, roasty Brazilian bean loaded with nuttiness and caramel. With the tasting over, Alex shows me a large, hemplike bag full of beans, and explains how the beans were sourced by Henok himself on a visit to a coffee bean farm in South Sudan for Alex to roast for all his Imperial Stouts. It seems Henok puts more attention, pride and absurdly sunken costs into his coffee than most brewers do into their hops and barley.

Back at the brewery, Henok takes me on a tour of the tanks, taking little pours from each to see if it's worth giving me a try. He's most excited about a beer he's made with another famous Pastry Stout producer in the US, Moksa. This beer has been in bourbon barrels and conditioned over literal tons of toasted coconut.

"Fudgy," says Henok simply.

It's the kind of aroma that can't help but bring a smile to your face. It's more Bounty bar than Bountys are, with waves of sweet vanilla and decadent bourbon booze leaping out. It's simultaneously a kids' party and a dinner party nightcap in a glass.

The way it's made seems less fun. In the corner of the brewery where the entrance to the vestry used to be is a small conditioning tank. Welded into the side of it is basically a boat motor, capable of spinning whatever liquid is put in the tank at breakneck speed. To infuse Omnipollo beer with flavors, the brewers load the middle of the tank with sacks of whatever ingredient they're using today—coconut, coffee, hazelnuts, cocoa, sometimes even hops. It's laborious, intensive and requires a level of hands-on sanitary care you don't often see in breweries of this size. A lot of beer geeks and beer writers assume such breweries are using extracts and flavorings, and to be fair, Henok has to do so with some of his beers, but it's usually a last resort.

"If there is a way to make a beer taste better but doesn't have a very romantic story to it I'll definitely use it," Henok tells me. "But we have naturally moved toward more natural ingredients because we've had better results."

By now we're back up at the taproom bar, and Henok is preparing his biggest party trick—one that has now been copied by other fun-orientated breweries. Omnipollo themselves copied it, but from the most unlikely source: Sapporo Brewing. Karl was in Japan and was served an ice-cold pint of Sapporo that had been topped with frozen slushied beer. Baffled but delighted, he sent a photo back to Henok, who leaped on the idea. They were already producing beers with the flavors of ice cream; how good would it be to create the texture too?

Creating that texture isn't easy though. As Henok has learned, to get a really creamy head you need high sugar content and high alcohol, and as a result a really low temperature in your slushie machine. Even so, it can take hours to create small enough crystals that it feels like rapidly melting ice cream rather than very cold crumble. When it works, though, it's about as much fun as you can have while drinking a beer. Omnipollo has a beer garden in the center of Stockholm during summer where they serve their beer ice cream hybrids in cones and pots, and they regularly bring a slushie machine to festivals, where beer geeks line up for a creamy-topped Pastry Stout or sour.

I've seen beer geeks and writers tut and fret about such things and to be honest, I've done it as well. But doing so is the very definition of gatekeeping, and means we've lost sight of the most basic joy of beer—that it's fun to drink.

Beer has had some very significant impacts on the world, good and bad, but we're not supposed to think about that while we drink it. It should all melt away like the slushie on a Stout when you're a few deep with friends. The effort, invention, energy and art that goes into making an Omnipollo beer should never be in doubt, but the brewery's philosophy isn't to dwell on that, nor should the drinker. As we drank some final beers and waited for my taxi to the airport, Karl washed away the last of my cynicism.

"Just because you take making beer seriously, it doesn't mean you have to take drinking it seriously."

There was a beat, before Henok added, "There were marshmallows in that Pilsner by the way. We didn't tell you that."

Just Not Cricket

Sometimes it doesn't matter how exciting or sugary your beer is, a Friday night just doesn't take off like you thought it would while daydreaming at your desk at 4 p.m. In those moments, bored humans have turned to one of the greatest assets we have over the rest of the animal kingdom—imagination. The humble bar or drinking game has been with us for as long as we've been drinking, and new ones are still being invented.

There was a time in my life so carefree and easy that when I was bored, I'd text a few friends one simple question: "Pub?" As a student I had two friends for which the answer was almost always yes. On one of those occasions we invented a quite brilliant game, which for reasons I can't recall we named Kaboos (if you google it, it seems to be some kind of Lebanese bread). Anyway, it was a warm day and we were sitting outside at a round wooden table; the kind with a hole in the middle for a brewery-branded umbrella to go through. With conversation in a lull, one of my friends flicked a two-pence coin at the hole, and to our general astonishment and joy it went right through. Cue hundreds of attempts to do it again and four rounds later, we realized we should probably go home.

There have been countless games invented at the pub. Some don't survive the night (RIP Kaboos) and others become local curiosities—cultural quirks like skittles, Aunt Sally, bar billiards, ringing the bull, quoits. A few, however, have become internationally recognized sports. Both the pubs I worked in as a teenager had keen darts teams that filled the place on quiet weeknights, and there's something joyous about the game's competitive but very social nature. Snooker evolved out of a particular form of pub billiards, but was formalized in a British Army mess tent in Jabalpur (likely over a few beers), India. One sport outranks them both in popularity, however, and while it wasn't invented in a pub, its modern rules were written there.

I never thought I'd read a book about cricket, let alone write one that talked about it. I have played the game competitively once in my life, at school, and I was out for a golden duck (that's with the first ball, folks). I then proceeded to bowl an over with four wides, before I was quickly relegated to the farthest boundary. I was twelve at the time, and ever since I've always protested (a little too much) that the sport is boring. However, I'm swallowing my pride because no book about beer and its impact on the world could be complete without talking about the sport to some extent. They are inextricably linked, and have been for at least 400 years.

Cricket's origins are murky to say the least. Given that the joy of whacking a ball with a stick is essentially preprogrammed into humans, knowing exactly when it turned into the quirky, unpredictable game of cricket is hard. Variations of it are found all over the world, and one of them even evolved into cricket's American cousin, baseball. The version of cricket we play today seems to have been formulated by working-class men of the sixteenth century in southeast England. The chalky North and South Downs had lots of flat (and public) ground for pitches, but there was also plenty of wood and expertise for making the bats and stumps in the Weald. The relative wealth of the lower classes and indeed the usually tolerable weather of the region also played a part in a day-long, largely sedentary sport catching on. Most important though, by the mid-1700s—around the time that cricket really began to resemble what we snore through today—the region's pubs had changed their business models.

The village pubs of southeast England had come to realize that they could sell a lot more beer if they organized ancillary events. With the dreariness of Puritanism pretty much dead and a little secularism sneaking in, weekends and religious holidays were getting less church-heavy and a lot more pub-based. Some of the earliest mentions of cricket, including one from 1622, come from prosecutions against men for playing cricket on Sundays. Barely a hundred years later, pubs were hosting weekend sporting and entertainment in their gardens or sponsoring ones nearby: feasts, morris dances, wrestling matches, plowing competitions, footraces, sack races, horse racing and games of cricket.

Anyone who's ever watched a cricket game—whether I'm playing or not—might be driven to drink, but it is the perfect sport for inebriated spectating. It lasts a few hours at least, has a slow build to some often very tight finishes, and offers both the players and spectators plenty of opportunities for heckling and betting. As a result, by the eighteenth century, cricket was attracting huge crowds to larger pub gardens and fields. In 1769 an incredible 20,000 people watched the Caterham Club, recorded as "Surrey" as a whole, lose to a small village team you might have heard of.

Hambledon is a leafy place in Hampshire, about 6 miles north of Portsmouth. In the mid-1700s its cricket club played home matches on a common sheep pasture called Broadhalfpenny Down, on the corner of which was an uninspiring sounding pub called The Hut. It was here that the laws of Renaissance cricket were redrafted into the game we know today.

Back then, The Hut was run by one Richard Nyren, who was Hambledon Cricket Club captain and ran the place much like the club pavilion. Given that Hambledon club matches regularly brought in over 10,000 spectators, it must have been quite a business model for him.

Clearly though, Nyren wasn't in it for the money. He was himself a fantastic all-rounder cricketer, and on his team he also had John Small, regarded as the greatest batsman of the eighteenth century. Together with a roster of talented men from surrounding villages, Hambledon became a household name, playing fifty-two matches against "the rest of England" (essentially the best from all the other clubs in the country) and winning twenty-nine times.

Such success gave the team power to dictate the laws of the game as it developed, and to their credit they made changes to improve cricket rather than their own fortunes. Nyren was passionate about the spirit of the game, and defiant in the protection of its laws. His son John Nyren later published a book about the club's exploits, and records a few examples of Nyren and Small standing up to nobles and landed gentry when matters of the law were at stake.

Between John's writing and a few other records, we can stitch together how modern cricket came to be. Essentially it seems that the prodigious skill of the Hambledon team and those who dared to play them were exposing some flaws in the original rules, first written in 1744 at the Royal Artillery Company in East London. Those rules and customs had a few pretty striking differences to today's. First, the bat was thin at the top, getting wider toward the bottom and curving like a hockey stick. Second, there was no middle stump, just two outer ones and the bail on top.

The first rule, or rather custom, was changed at speed in 1771. Hambledon had just endured its worst season ever and the club's very future was in doubt, so the final game against Surrey on September 23 was a must-win. Imagine the outrage when Surrey batsman Shock White walked out onto the field, presumably suppressing an insufferable smirk, with a bat wider than the stumps. Within the laws of 1744 there was nothing about bat width, and in theory White should have been allowed to play. Thankfully the spirit of cricket prevailed and some Hambledon players produced a carpenter's plane to shave down White's bat (I'm not sure why someone couldn't have just lent him a different one).

Hambledon went on to win (by just one run), but two days later over a few pints at The Hut, Nyren, Small and another player called Thomas Brett signed minutes that limited the size of a bat in their matches to 4.25 inches—a limit that stands today. Not only that, but they created an iron grid with which to measure any bat they doubted met the criteria. In the same meeting they also decided an exact weight for the ball, presumably in case White turned up next season with a cannonball.

The two-stump wicket was changed in 1775, again at The Hut but not because of a match at Broadhalfpenny Down. This time Hambledon were playing "the rest of England" in Kent, in a match where the winner would take home the modern equivalent of £40,000. With an achievable run chase ahead and Small at the crease, Hambledon must have been feeling pretty confident.

That feeling would have been enhanced when famous bowler Lumpy Stevens launched a ball right between the two stumps, failing to knock off the bails. Such a thing was not unheard of, but it was exceptionally rare. So it was even more remarkable when it happened not one more time, but two more times, by which point poor Lumpy must have been tearing his hair out. He was forced to endure another three hours with Small at the crease, during which the batsman eked out the fourteen runs Hambledon needed for the victory.

With their pockets full of cash and beers in their hands, Nyren decided something should be done about the issue, and Hambledon signed into law a third stump. Although the wicket has changed in size a little since, this was the last major rule change made to the game, and the final rules written down by the Marylebone Cricket Club (who play at Lord's) in 1816 are broadly the same as Hambledon's and the ones used today to humiliate twelve-year-old school kids.

This is a wonderful story of idyllic England in the eighteenth century, but you could try to argue that beer and pubs played a relatively small role. Doing so, however, misses the point that there was only cricket on Broadhalfpenny Down because of the community created by the pub. It didn't just bring players and Nyren, it brought people, beer, food and attention to the games, which financed perhaps the most important club in the game's history. It provided a place to manage the club, its reputation, and its rules, as well as a focal point even on the days when cricket was not being played. In his book *The Glory Days of Cricket: The Extraordinary Story of Broadhalfpenny Down*, former cricketer and historian Ashley Mote calls Nyren's old pub the "pavilion to the whole cricket world."

The audience's feasting and drinking are still vital to the modern game of cricket, as inspired by the pubs of the day. Breaks in play are still quaintly called *lunch* and *tea*, and while in the professional game it probably means a banana and an energy drink, to amateurs (and spectators) it more likely means a hearty meal and a few beers. Most amateur cricket clubs around the UK are either attached to a local pub or sponsored by one, and even if the association isn't official, you can guarantee after a game at least a few players will be going for a couple of jars. The connection is eternal in hundreds of the UK's pub names and signs—the Cricketers, the Cricketers' Arms, the Jolly Cricketers, the Merry Cricketers and the Royal Cricketers. There are pubs named after famous cricketers too: The Graces, Fiery Fred and The Thomas Lord Inn. If you're ever in Hambledon you can still visit The Hut, now called the Bat & Ball, and even see the minutes of that 1771 meeting, signed by Nyren himself. For a hundred years, the pub also featured the iron bat measure, though it now lives somewhere less likely to be nicked by a drunken cricket nerd. I couldn't work out exactly where it is, so I can only assume it's in that giant warehouse at the end of the first Indiana Jones film, next to the Ark of the Covenant.

The endless invention of the inebriated and inspired beer drinkers knows no limits, and it's not just the arbiters of international sports that have made world-changing declarations in pubs, either. Great scientific developments have been announced there too—including the structure of DNA.

Chapter 9

The Future

Or how beer will continue to change—and even save—humanity

Speak to most beer experts, beer lovers and barflies and they'll tell you the future of beer looks a little bleak.

Since I started (legally) drinking in 2005, the UK has lost at least 13,000 of its pubs. That's pretty much one-quarter. As a nation we drink around 5 million liters less beer a year than we did back then, and about forty percent of people between eighteen and twenty-five consider themselves teetotal. As a result, the rise of low-alcohol beer in bottle and can—which has been prophesied every year by supposed industry analysts since the early 2000s—is finally happening.

In my early twenties I was deeply skeptical of this trend. If I wanted a beer, I didn't want a pale imitation that tasted like someone had spiked it with Perrier. I wanted a real beer, a beer that gave me a buzz and, as the ad at the Duff factory put it, filled my Q zone with goodness. As a toddler-dad pushing forty, though, it's fair to say the appeal of a few beers without the hangover has started to hit home. But the future of beer can't be low alcohol. It just can't. As much as the brighter start and lower calories help me balance my life, writing this book has shown me that a key element of beer is the inebriation: there's barely a sentence that doesn't show that pretty compellingly.

Even if low-alcohol beer tasted as good as the full-strength stuff, people would still drink the full-strength stuff. I haven't got any scientific studies to prove that, nor any adjacent examples to imply it, because alcohol is unique in the human world. I'm fairly certain that Coca-Cola will pretty much kill off real Coke in favor of Coke Zero eventually (unless global warming kills us all first), and if Marlboro invented a cigarette that didn't wipe five minutes off your life, there's no doubt customers would switch. But those vices don't bring people together like alcohol does, unless we mean forcing smokers into a damp corner by the bins. Beer's intoxicating nature is a key lubricant for society, and no temperance movement is going to convince me otherwise. Just look at America's Prohibition—people still drank sixty-six percent as much alcohol as they did before, even when it was a literal crime to consume it. Beer is life, and life finds a way.

So if low-alcohol beer is to forever remain an important but small part of the beer industry and life in general, where does beer go from here? I'm fairly certain we will always look to the past—the great lagers and hoppy beers that have flooded our society are here to stay in some form and volume, but to assume they will always dominate might be naive. There are challenges outside of healthy young people's habits and my 5 a.m. starts to consider. Global warming puts beer's ingredients under threat, while as a category it is losing ground to wine and canned cocktails in many social circles and spaces. More generally, we must remember that people's tastes change: there was a time in the late 1700s when the idea of a new beer style ever rivaling the popularity of Porter was unthinkable, but within 120 years, Porter was just a curiosity. The same will likely happen to pale lager at some point. Macro lager is not necessarily the logical conclusion of beer, and assuming it is would be to ignore history—it's dominated for less than 200 of beer's 13,000-year reign. So, what comes next?

Back to the Future

Sometimes to go forward, you have to go back, which is why I'm finishing this book at one of the first places we visited.

Carlsberg is far from the oldest or longest-running brewery covered in this book, but next to Spaten I consider it the most important. Even if its main product is as dull, safe and predictable as a Coldplay album, in all its other activities Carlsberg has kept JC and Carl's spirit of invention alive.

I learned a lot in the Carlsberg Laboratory and archive, but the moment that will stay with me longest actually happened once the official interviews were over. Just like any public tour, mine ended with a few beers, which I shared with the two men in charge of Carlsberg's innovation arm. In most breweries the pilot plant is an excuse for the brewers to have some fun, to experiment with ingredients and recipes on a scale where an accountant won't be knocking on their door if it goes wrong. Remarkably, Carlsberg's is basically a working model of the main brewhouse, built with such attention to detail that brewers can even dial up the pressure in the fermenting tanks to replicate the weight of thousands of liters of beer all on top of one another in the main plant.

With its principal role being to help with the technological challenges of brewing session lager on a biblical scale, I wasn't expecting much for the pilot range: perhaps some historic recipes from the archive, some unusual yeast strains isolated for their efficiency, or some new hop varieties that were agronomically resilient. In short, nothing I haven't tried at countless other breweries. I was dead wrong.

I've always believed that craft brewing's strength is its willingness to push boundaries—whether that's in tech, tradition or ingredients—in search of something new. But no craft brewery I have been to is pushing things as far as Carlsberg, the producer of a lager even they once acknowledged is "probably not" the best in the world.

I'd just left the archive, where I'd held a genuine yeast slide book put together by Emil C. Hansen and seen beautiful sketches he'd made of Carlsberg's different yeast strains (his work as a vagrant painter finally paid off). I was taken back down to what used to be the main lab, which reminds me of the dated classroom where I did my best to ignore my chemistry and biology lessons at school. We'd been through it on the tour and seen the bench decked out with Emil's equipment where he supposedly made many of his breakthroughs. In my absence, the workbenches in the middle, where JC once peered over shoulders and offered his entirely uninvited opinion, had been laid out with an ice bucket full of beer, glasses of various shapes and sizes, and some curious-looking grains in jars.

The tasting was led by the pilot plant's head brewer Erik Lund and Carlsberg's head of science Zoran Gojkovic, who took great delight in confounding my expectations for well over an hour. Zoran is a man with many opinions on the future of beer (including a worry that if we only drink low-alcohol beer "How will people get born?!") and a healthy skepticism that craft brewing's love of hops will last. Both these considerations play into the fact that none of the beers I tasted were remotely low alcohol (in fact they mostly pushed 10%), and some of them had no hops at all.

"A few hundred craft brewers in Denmark compete for about 1.7 percent of the market," he says. "They make the beer as well as we could, and we all use roughly the same malt, hops and yeasts. So we don't brew hoppy styles."

Few of the beers made in the pilot plant leave it, but some of its biggest successes do. One of those is Tears of Enzo, which caused a stir in the press when it was stocked at Copenhagen's two–Michelin starred Alchemist…at $340 a bottle. The name is a nod to Enzo Ferrari because the beer is reddish-pink, like someone washed an F40 on the hot cycle. It's made by using a special variety of barley with a black husk which, when watered down in a beer mash, turns out to be red. Combined with a few different yeasts and bacteria to create acidity, its fruitier character starts to resemble rose or even blush champagne, with soft tannins and raspberry, cherry and cranberry notes.

I'd argue that brewing a sour red beer, putting it in a champagne bottle and charging nearly $350 will restrict your market more than releasing a Hazy IPA into a crowded market, but the pilot plant's discoveries have wider ambitions and implications. In the case of Tears of Enzo, it's competing with wine without having to radically change ingredients or processes—as well as allowing them to brew a genuinely red-colored Pilsner for Liverpool FC, which the brewery sponsors.

Some of the other beers had more important ramifications, however. One came from a plain, unlabeled brown bottle that was so nondescript Erik wasn't certain he was pouring the right beer, until it cascaded into the glass. Nearly colorless, with the lightest yellow-green hue that made it look like white wine, this beer smelled like grappa—the boozy Italian spirit made from spent grapes that has a nutty, tequilalike note. This beer wasn't made from barley but a wild African crop called fonio. Found predominantly in West Africa, where it's thought to have been one of the first cultivated grains, it has some unusual properties. It's pretty drought-resistant, can grow from seed to harvest in just eight weeks, and is gluten-free. As such, it's touted as a possible solution to several issues, from the challenges of climate change to the increase in celiac disease.

It's notable that the main thrust of Carlsberg's research and development is around sustainability. In some ways it worries me that most beer innovation going forward will be addressing existential problems (Will we lose beer's newfound focus on exciting and diverse flavors, and does that matter if the world is ending anyway?). But on another level it's in character with beer's history. It has always provided nourishment, inspired problem-solving, and pushed on culture. As ever, our reliance on beer is forcing us to look at wider issues and opportunities, but actually it is beer's constituent ingredients that might have the most impact—ingredients we may have left behind if it weren't for our obsession with brewing. In fact one of them, the incredible microbe we've kept by our side for millennia because of its ability to produce alcohol, might just save the planet.

In Our DNA

1996 was a big year for the world. Personally, I got a week off school to go to Disney World Florida and watched Gazza chip Colin Hendry at the Euros. But while I was living my best life, some more important people were changing theirs—and indeed everyone else's.

The incredible work of these 600 or so people didn't get the same press as Dolly the Sheep, who stole the scientific headlines that year by erroneously being named the first animal clone (scientists had actually been doing it since the 1950s, albeit not with a nucleus from a mammary gland or childishly named after Dolly Parton's mammary glands). The breakthrough I'm talking about did involve a nucleus, though, and indeed the thing that made Dolly who she was—Deoxyribonucleic acid, or DNA.

DNA was actually discovered in the mid-1860s by one Friedrich Miescher, but its structure and significance weren't fully understood until Cambridge scientists Francis Crick and James Watson pooled their resources with Cambridge graduate Rosalind Franklin in the 1950s. I'm happy to report that Crick (to Watson's surprise) announced their breakthrough in a pub, The Eagle on Bene't Street, Cambridge, and did so by saying they had discovered the "secret of life." Crick isn't the only person to have stood up in a pub and declared such a thing—I think I did it when I first tried Scampi Fries—but he might be the first person to actually be right.

DNA is like our own, personal computer code. It's found in all our cells, and is made up of genes. We inherit half from our fathers and half from our mothers, and they determine how our cells act—which results in things like our skin color, hair color and eye color, as well as helping shape our personalities. As you can imagine, DNA is a complicated beast, so reading and recording an entire double helix of DNA was the next, truly vast task. It took until 1976 to sequence the first genome (a simple bacterium called Bacteriophage MS2) and another twenty years before scientists sequenced the first truly significant organism… take one guess at what they picked.

In October 1996, scientists announced they had sequenced the genome of brewer's yeast. This was a huge deal, not just because it was only the fifth thing to be sequenced but because it was the first eukaryote. Eukaryotes are organisms with a nucleus in their cells, which allows them to carry out more intricate tasks and reactions than cells without. It essentially means they are more complex organisms—all animals and plants are eukaryotes.

The most obvious reason why yeast was chosen is that it's still a single-celled organism: as complex goes, it's as simple as it gets. The thing is that in 1990s-genome-sequencing world, *simple* meant manually reading 12 million lines of DNA, so it took 600 scientists ten years, and cost around $40 million. Scientists had to start somewhere, but for that kind of investment there needed to be a payoff. Thirty years later we're realizing the reward might be saving the world, but before that we need to talk about the incredible use that brewer's yeast is being put to in the modern world already—now that we can genetically modify it.

Modern or Modified

Now, there's not enough beer in the world to convince me to get into an ethical discussion about genetic modification. Despite being a very scientific area, most opinions are guided by emotions. All I will say is that, as you're about to learn, genetically modified products are absolutely everywhere already. The discussion has been had, a decision has been made, and neither you nor I was part of it.

The reality is that if a product is not genetically modified itself, something that has been genetically modified may well still have been used to make it. I include beer in that, because yeast labs all over the US are already modifying brewer's yeast to create new aromas, minimize off-flavors, and speed up fermentation. In fact, as a species we're nearly at the point where if you want to avoid ever interacting with genetic modification, you're going to need to move to a commune. It's also worth noting that with this being the case, our ecosystems are yet to collapse and a giant GMO tomato hasn't taken over New York Stay Puft Marshmallow Man–style. Not yet anyway.

Seeing as yeast has been our close companion since civilization began, it's natural we turned to it for perhaps our greatest accomplishment. But it's the practical applications of brewer's yeast that made it such an obvious candidate for sequencing. Its vital role in drink and food production is well-documented already in this book, but yeast had been co-opted into several other roles by the 1990s—most of them in the pharmaceutical industry.

Until the eighties, all insulin given to diabetics was taken from the pancreases of dead pigs. Besides the ick factor and colossal carbon footprint, there were implications for anyone who follows a kosher, pescatarian, vegetarian or vegan diet. In 1982, genetic engineering of an E. coli bacteria produced synthetic insulin, but it wasn't a very efficient process because the insulin was produced inside the cells and needed extracting. So in 1987 the same thing was achieved using brewer's yeast, which secreted the insulin into the sugary broth, making it easier to harvest. Today around half of all insulin is created by E. coli and the other half by yeast, and thankfully both are scalable—since 1980 cases of diabetes have more than quadrupled.

So how is it done? Well, the true detail of genetic modification is the kind of thing that makes a drinks writer go cross-eyed, but it's easy to explain the general process. Someone significantly cleverer than me identifies the gene responsible for telling a cell how to do a certain action. That gene can be copied and inserted into another organism's cell(s). Sometimes you need to insert multiple genes because one gene can't do the entire process you're looking for but will work in a sequence called a pathway.

Now, in theory you could change any eukaryotic cell to do anything you want, but ideally you'd work with one that already has a similar function to your end goal because it minimizes the number of genes you need to create the right pathway. Yeast eats sugar and spits out chemicals, so all you need to do is find a way to change the chemicals it makes. Yeast is a simple and malleable eukaryote that's able to accept changes to its DNA easier than most, and our close relationship means we understand it better than pretty much any other cell on earth.

As a result, yeast has come to be used as the ultimate factory worker for all kinds of medicines. The human papillomavirus (HPV) and hepatitis B vaccines are produced by genetically modified yeast, and work is being done to convert it to produce codeine and morphine—or as Nicholas P. Money calls it in his amazing book *The Rise of Yeast*, "home-brew heroin." There are several new COVID-19 vaccines being produced using yeast, to help combat the fact that at the time of writing, around 1 billion people remain unvaccinated. Yeast vaccines are highly scalable, and some of them only require refrigeration, rather than the deep-freezing required for the original COVID vaccines.

Most vital of all is the creation of a synthetic and scalable anti-malarial drug, which has saved millions from one of the world's deadliest diseases. The original antimalarial, Artemisinin, was discovered by Chinese scientist Tu Youyou in a sweet worm-wood that had been used for millennia to treat fevers in Chinese medicine, but its natural, biological origin meant the price was high, competition fierce and supplies sensitive to agricultural issues. Unfortunately, the people most at risk of malaria happen to be those least able to afford any relevant drugs, so the Bill & Melinda Gates Foundation gave a grant to find a synthetic ver-sion in 2004. Eight years later, a genetically modified yeast was created by adding the genes from wormwood that encoded the right enzyme production. Today that drug, made by Amyris, is the most important antimalarial, and therefore one of the world's most important drugs.

Beyond Baby Food

Aside from disease, one of the other great challenges human-ity faces is malnutrition—and it's likely to get worse thanks to global warming. With its scalable nature, yeasts capable of pro-ducing edible by-products could feed those already struggling to get enough to eat, and indeed help every corner of the world as we face up to the consequences of our CO2 emissions.

It's almost a cliché to say that one of the best things we can personally do for the planet is to reduce the amount of meat we consume, but doing so is exceptionally hard. Our food systems, economies and cultures are almost exclusively built around an-imal protein, and cutting loose from that is a real challenge. I was vegetarian for around two years through concerns about the planet and animal welfare, but when my wife was pregnant we slipped up biblically as her body craved all kinds of deli-cious meaty things. We told ourselves we'd resolve it once the baby arrived, but our daughter was born with severe allergies to several foods—an increasingly common issue. Try being a vegetarian without soy, wheat or nuts, folks, and you'll see how difficult a meat-free future might be.

As always though, our millennia-old friend yeast might come budding to the rescue. The same genetic modifications that can be used to produce all kinds of drugs can also produce food-stuffs, and there are several examples already on the market. Impossible Foods Inc., one of the largest vegan meat producers in the world, uses genetically modified brewer's yeast to create a compound called heme. Heme gives blood its red color and helps carry oxygen in living organisms, so it's found in all animal muscle tissue. In an interview with the American Society for Microbiology, Impossible's founder Pat Brown said that when cooked, heme is responsible for catalyzing "abundant, simple nutrients into this explosion of hundreds of diverse volatile odorant molecules. When you experience them, together they add up unmistakably to the smell and taste of meat." The company's yeast-derived version is in all their vegan burgers, but whether it's close enough to convince people to make the switch for most of their meaty needs is questionable. It's also significantly more expensive to produce than what other vegetarian burger manufacturers are doing, which is simply adding yeast extract for that umami hit.

Beef isn't the only agricultural product that is being looked at by biotech firms. The world drinks over 700 million liters of milk every year, and that's just people getting creamy mustaches: it doesn't include the incredible amount used in cheese making, yogurt making and other dairy-heavy products. The water use and burden on the land is incredible, and could be considerably lightened if one of the several companies trying to produce yeast-brewed milk manages to get its costs down. A few firms have already made milks that are indistinguishable chemically from what comes from a cow's teat, but we're still a long way from this being commercially viable. There are also ethical questions around whether milk made using a yeast with animal genes in it is vegan, but if uptake is high, the potential impact on the planet could be immeasurable. Which might be more than can be said for biofuels.

Who Paid You?

When I conceived this book, I thought that this whole chapter would be about biofuels. As I rolled up my sleeves and started diving into the topic, I was sure I'd find that biofuel was going to be our savior. After all, it's essentially fuel we can grow in a field, and what's more environmentally friendly than growing plants? Well, as it turns out, lots of things are.

Biofuels are fuels where the energy comes from living matter. Most of the world's biofuel is derived from corn, with sugarcane and soybean making up the rest. For the first two (soy-derived biodiesel is a very different thing), the process is a little like making beer. The sucrose in the corn kernels or sugarcane is fermented using brewer's yeast, then filtered and distilled until it's 200 proof, or pure ethanol. It's then blended with gasoline and sold as fuel for your car, tractor, plane or emergency generator in your Armageddon shelter. In the US, if you drive a car capable of using flex-fuel you could be using up to 81% bioderived ethanol, while in the UK pretty much all cars drive on E10 fuel, which is shorthand for a biofuel content of 10%.

Biofuel companies, governments and car manufacturers make all sorts of claims about removing millions of tons of CO_2 from the atmosphere (or rather not releasing them in the first place), and how this is a move away from nonrenewable energy sources. But the truth is murkier than that because tracking the amount of energy, and indeed CO_2 emissions, needed to *produce* biofuel is very difficult indeed.

The first thing to point out is that burning biofuel releases CO_2 like pure gasoline does, albeit a little less. The "carbon neutrality" comes from the fact that during its life, the sugar-cane or corn energy source will have absorbed and "offset" that CO_2. Hopefully you can see the flaws in that. For a start, the fuels we use are not pure ethanol—we're still burning carbon we found in the ground. Corn is also not an ideal crop because its sugar needs breaking down by enzymes to be fermentable by yeast, and this is a costly extra step.

Finally, there's the incredible impact that monocultures can have on the environment. According to the US Department of Agriculture, the country grew around 300,000 square miles of corn in 2022—that's an area bigger than France—and the same of soy. Just think about the scale of that for a second. I saw it myself on the train from Chicago to St. Louis—five hours of nothing but soybeans and ironically a town called Normal right in the middle of it. In *The Rise of Yeast*, Money talks about the cornfields of his home on the Ohio-Indiana border, where local species have been wiped out by pesticides and streams clogged with algae as the fish left the oxygen-depleted waters. Diversity is fundamental to the health of our world, and any kind of reliance on production at this scale and concentration is detrimental.

Most importantly though, the process of growing these crops is far from carbon neutral. Arable farming contributes two percent of all carbon emissions. It comes from the intensive use of buildings and heavy machinery, the disturbance of carbon stores in the soil, and through the use of fertilizers on an almost continental scale. These great swathes of biofuel crops are not replacing other farm fields: they are creating new ones all across the USA and in the world's second biggest biofuel producer, Brazil. The amount of grassland loss and deforestation is incomprehensible, as is the release of CO_2 from these vital carbon stores.

As I said, bringing all these various impacts into a study that definitively tells us biofuels are better than fossil ones is very difficult. Whenever you see claims that they are (or indeed that they definitely aren't), it's important you follow the money to see who has paid for that conclusion and how they came about it.

Before you say fuck it and buy a diesel car, or indeed invest your pension in solar panels, it's worth saying that just because the scientific consensus is…well, just because there isn't one, that doesn't mean biofuels are a waste of space and corn on the cob. All technologies have to start somewhere, and there are huge advances on the horizon that could turn biofuels from marginal improvement to planet-saver…

Given that the main issue is the amount of land, energy and emissions that go into growing the living matter, it comes down to a question of efficiency. If we can get significantly more energy out of a single corn plant, we can reduce the burden, and there is a hell of a lot of research going into doing just that. The most obvious target is all the waste matter—the stems, leaves and tassels. These all contain sugars in the form of cellulose, which standard brewer's yeast can't eat. Genetically engineering a yeast to chop through the cellulose could open up these waste resources and massively increase the efficiency of corn-derived ethanol. Alternatively we could look to other microbes and co-ferment these energy sources like lambic, or indeed the mucus of coffee beans. There have been studies into using white rot fungi to break down cellulose like it does a rotting tree, then using yeast mopping up the available sugars. If one of these approaches works, there's the potential for it to be used not just for corn waste but all agricultural waste—we could potentially fuel the planet using the offcuts of the food we grow, offsetting our emissions through the very act of growing them.

Of course, we know that yeast's propensity to produce alcohol means other microbes can rarely live in harmony with it, so our best chance with the technology now at our fingertips is to create a perfect GM version that can do all these things. There are huge challenges ahead, but such potential makes biofuel once again look like the answer we've all been searching for. So you can either breathe a tentative sigh of relief as you fill up your hybrid, or start googling who paid me to write this chapter.

As Close As We've Come

Even if yeast isn't the answer to climate change, it has already changed enough lives in another way to earn its stripes as a world-saving superhero. I'm not just talking of Pasteur's work, or yeast's role in producing antimalarial drugs. Due to its eukaryotic nature and complex DNA, yeast is a vital window to what our own cells look and act like.

This means that people studying the human body at a cellular level often start with yeast. If you're looking at how a human cell might respond to a certain stimulus or mutation, or a virus or bacteria, you can observe how a yeast cell does and assume that a human one will react similarly. It's incredible that the same organism that helped civilization form, survive and thrive happens to have so much in common with us. And together it's hoped we might find a cure for one of the only things on earth that kills more people than malaria—cancer.

Most cancer is caused by mutations of our genes. Very simply, when cells divide, occasionally certain messages in our DNA can get mixed up. Usually this is harmless, but sometimes cells can start to divide unchecked. This is most likely when we have lots of mutations, because there's more chance that one of them will be harmful. That's why cancer is more prevalent in older people, as well as those who have damaged their body in some way—through smoking, using sunbeds, taking a hike near Chernobyl, or um…drinking alcohol. Some genes are more likely to cause mutations whatever we do, and we can inherit them from our parents.

Yeast has got involved in the fight against cancer in many

ways. Sometimes it's direct: a study in 2017 showed that combining brewer's yeast with chemotherapy drug paclitaxel can improve the efficacy of the latter in breast cancer—brewer's yeast is actually also capable of producing the precursor to paclitaxel. But yeast is also of huge help to researchers in the area of cancer cell growth. For hereditary cancers we can insert human genes into yeast to see which might cause mutation, and how they go about doing so.

We also know that cancer cells grow aggressively fast, requiring huge amounts of glucose to do so. There is a fallacy that eating sugar can cause or encourage tumor growth, which has led to the idea that people suffering from cancer should reduce the amount of sugar and carbohydrate they consume. According to Cancer Research UK there are no studies that back this, and it's dangerous to do so when going through treatments like chemotherapy. Still, cancer's reliance on glucose is a huge area of study for cancer scientists. What if it were possible to only fuel healthy cells, or to shut down cancer cells' glucose stores? These scientists need a malleable, simple organism to experiment with, and guess what other organism thrives on that very simple sugar? Yeast does, and it metabolizes it in the same way as cancer cells, which is a different way to healthy human cells. So medical scientists can learn about the metabolism of cancer cells, and potentially how to starve and slow them down, by studying brewer's yeast.

The Momentum of History

There are likely some people reading this and thinking that it's not beer making these incredible steps—and it's true. The yeasts used in these advances have never and will never see the addition of hops or malt, though a beer that prevents malaria could definitely catch on in West Africa.

It's clear to me, though, that all these advances are still the result of our millennia-long love of beer. The only reason we've studied yeast, isolated its various strains and bred its most effective spores is because of its ability to create alcohol and taste delicious at the same time. We only know what yeast is capable of because we've kept it closer than perhaps any other living organism on earth. In *Cooked*, Michael Pollan entertains the argument that fermentation could be considered as important to human development as the discovery of fire. By writing this book it's clear that I believe this wholeheartedly.

In the research for this book I spoke to Patrick Gibney, a genetic scientist who quite recently set up his own lab at Cornell University looking at research topics that span eukaryotic cell biology to wine microbiology. During his time he's worked on all kinds of genetic modification of yeast, as well as its application in technology and medicine. The fact he finally ended up working on yeasts producing alcohol is kind of inevitable—it's just the reverse of the journey yeast itself has taken. We had a few email conversations and an epically long call for this chapter, during which he used a phrase that has stuck with me since—*the momentum of history*. It speaks to this idea that our relationship with brewer's yeast is kind of unstoppable, an almost unnatural selection made by humans. The more we know about it, the more it helps us; the more it helps us, the more we want to know about it. We're stuck in this feedback loop that is forever intensifying our reliance on this tiny microbe. As Pollan puts it, we're locked in "a dance of biocultural symbiosis," both reliant on each other for survival. At the start, the yeast was probably in control, but now the tables have completely turned. The demands we make of it are ever increasing and have already passed the point of its natural limitations. Still it has proven malleable enough for us to adapt it physically, right up to the point where it may be its undoing.

Genetic modification has allowed us to bend yeast strains to our will, but the final step will be to create our own: a strain of yeast made partly or wholly of genes that humans have 3D printed and clipped together like Lego. The Synthetic Yeast Genome Project is a global consortium of geneticists that has been working on an entirely man-made yeast genome since 2006, and in 2023 they announced that they'd reached halfway. To get so far is a titanic human achievement—there are 6,275 genes in a yeast cell.

With such a biblical (or should that be heretical?) task, they've had to edit on the fly. You see, about five percent of those 6,275 genes have no function, and even more aren't useful, so rather than recreate the genome gene by gene, scientists have been removing or ignoring genes they don't want. This will make editing it further even easier, and to that end the team has also included several hundred short DNA sequences that can prompt sections to rearrange themselves for different pathways.

This leads us to the *why?* Aside from the potential for a fully editable bionic yeast, the biggest benefit is that through building the genomes, we have learned things about the way that DNA works that we would never have considered by simply studying it. For example, we all know how our houses stand up—foundations, structural walls, wood and brick materials, insulation. But if we had to build our own we'd immediately come across issues we'd not considered, complications we can't work around, techniques we'd never learned. Synthetic genomes represent an entirely new way of studying the biological world, moving past simply observing and describing, and learning by doing. By building.

Without Beer

And so it seems that 13,000 years after we had our first conscious encounter with brewer's yeast, 6,000 years after it helped quench the thirst of our first civilizations, and 150 years after we finally understood its nature, a microbe we can't even see with the naked eye is to remain one of the most important driving forces in our lives.

There are obviously many great advances happening with other organisms that may change our world, and many of the discoveries made in this book owe so much to other sciences, other people, and even other drinks. But none of them could claim to have their hand in so much of what humanity has gained through history. Sometimes I lie awake at night wondering about alternate universes where Pasteur had no beer to investigate so millions died as germ theory took another century, or Prohibition spread to Europe and Hitler had no beer halls to spout his hate in. I lose hours thinking about realities where the pubs of the Czech Republic are famous for serving great wine, and churches in Stockholm still exclusively serve God. Those people might never know what comes to those who wait, and Lou Bega is just David Lubega Balemezi, the son of a Munich-based biologist. Producers in Hollywood aren't exactly lining up for the disaster movie where beer was never invented, but the changes would be as dramatic as any that have been made so far—the body count would certainly be the highest.

On a personal level, without beer, my dad's daily routine would have been subtly different and my life entirely altered—and even if you're not a drinks writer, I bet you could say the same for yours. Anthropologists are yet to find a society ancient or modern that has not brewed at some point in its history, and in the modern world it is one of the few, inarguable things that unites us. As the Christmas truce of 1914 shows, there are few things that would cause us to refuse a beer with someone.

Just like the effects of alcohol leave no part of our body untouched, so beer has affected every element of our society, and the more we drink of it, the deeper that impact is. Alcohol, and for some reason beer in particular, is increasingly seen as a malign force in the world. There's no denying it's an underlying and sometimes direct cause of problems both societal and individual. But I hope that this book could be handed to even the most hardened antialcohol campaigner—or God forbid even a wine writer—and they would be forced to admit that without beer the human world would be a much simpler, much sadder and much less brilliant place. If it were here at all.

★ ★ ★ ★ ★

Glossary

This is a book about how beer made us, not how we made beer. Inevitably though, to understand some of the terms, processes and indeed implications in the book, knowing how we do make beer might help.

Rather than slow down the (riveting) text, below is a simple introduction to the brewing process, followed by a short glossary of niche and technical terms that you'll come across in the book.

The Modern Brewing Process

Modern beer has four core ingredients—yeast, hops, water and grain (usually barley, but others can be used).

The first step is to germinate that grain. This means encouraging it to grow shoots, which releases sugars we'll need later. The grain is then dried in a kiln at varying temperatures and times to create different flavors from Jacob's crackers and digestive biscuits to coffee and dark chocolate. This process as a whole is referred to as *malting*.

Now the brewing can begin. The malt is combined with warm water, which activates enzymes that break down and release the malt sugars into the water to create a sticky liquid called wort. This wort is then boiled (usually for an hour) to sanitize it, and hops are added at different stages to add flavor, aroma and bitterness. Hops are also a natural preservative, so they help stop the beer going off.

The beer is then cooled to somewhere between 46°F and 104°F and transferred to a fermenting vessel, where the yeast is pitched at the temperature that yeast strain prefers. The sugar in the wort is consumed by the ever-multiplying yeast, which produces alcohol, CO_2 and lots of different aromatic compounds as by-products. More hops or indeed any delicious ingredient can be added at this point to infuse the beer with more flavor.

The yeast works until either all the available sugar is consumed or the alcohol content of the beer gets too high for the yeast to keep multiplying. At this point, many beers go through a *cold conditioning* phase, being held near freezing to round out flavors. The beer is now basically ready, but it might have more CO_2 added to increase the carbonation; be filtered to ensure a clean and consistent product; and be pasteurized to ensure it doesn't spoil. The beer is then packaged in whatever vessel the brewer has chosen—mostly likely keg, cask, bottle or can.

That's about it. Depending on your experience it might sound pretty simple or incredibly complicated, but with the number of chemical reactions going on, I can assure you it is the latter. Beer recipes are relatively simple—it's the process that makes the biggest difference in how a beer turns out, which is why refining it is responsible for so many of the discoveries covered in this book.

Technical Terms
In This Book

Ale

In the nineteenth century and earlier, ale simply meant beer with hops in—beer was usually beer without hops (I know). In modern times we use *ale* to refer to beers made with a warm-loving *ale* strain of yeast—also known as Saccharomyces cerevisiae, one of the most important characters in this book.

Beer

A fermented beverage made using malted grain, hops, yeast and water. Historically it might also refer to a fermented beverage made using malted grain, yeast and water...but little or no hops.

Berlinerweisse

A sour wheat ale historically made in northern Germany. It's traditionally served with woodruff-flavored syrup in its home region, but around the world it's more likely to be used as a canvas for huge additions of fruit.

Bitter

The beer style that followed Mild in Britain as it went out of fashion in the mid-twentieth century. Bitters have a long history and vary greatly according to the brewery and the region—they could be almost black or as pale as a Pilsner, but all should have some fruity notes from the yeast and a good hop bitterness to balance the strong malt character.

Brettanomyces

A species of yeast similar to Saccharomyces, known for its more funky flavors and aromas (pineapple, scrumpy, hay, manure). Historically a key flavor component in well-aged British beer, but now more famous for its contribution to American and Belgian wild ales.

Brewer's yeast

Scientifically known as Saccharomyces cerevisiae, this common strain of yeast is used to make pretty much all beer, bread and wine—and has thousands of different strains.

Cask beer

A name given to real ale served from a barrel, usually from a hand pump on the bar.

Craft beer

An increasingly unhelpful term usually used to denote small breweries making modern American-style beer. I, however, use the term to denote any brewery that intends to make the absolute best beer possible in a race to the top, rather than the bottom.

Dry hopping

The technique of adding hops during the fermentation, conditioning or even transportation phase of brewing.

Fermentation

The chemical breakdown of a substance by bacteria, yeasts or other microorganisms. In this book I almost exclusively use it to refer to the actions of brewer's yeast on malt sugar in beer.

Fruited sour

An evolution of the Berlinerweisses of Germany. Usually a low-alcohol wheat beer soured with bacteria to make it fresh and lemony, then fermented or conditioned with whole fruit or puree in various quantities.

Gose

A sour wheat ale historically made in northern Germany—specifically Goslar. It differs from the Berlinerweisse because it's traditionally also brewed with salt and coriander seeds.

Helles

A pale style of lager invented at Spaten brewery in the 1890s, in response to Czech Pilsner's popularity. It has low bitterness, but keeps the richer body of the Czech Pilsner with notes of honey and lemon.

Hops

The flowers of the hop plant, which is typically grown in temperate climates. They were originally used in beer as a preservative because they contained oils that restricted bacterial growth. However, they are now used for their remarkable aromatic and flavor characteristics, as well as their well-known bitter flavor.

Imperial Stout

An extra-strong version of a Stout Porter, usually brewed for export (particularly to the Russian Court, which leads to the occasional use of the name Russian Imperial Stout) but not exclusively. In modern times these beers are often aged in spirit barrels, and laced with other ingredients such as coffee, chocolate, coconut and more.

IPA (India Pale Ale), English

A pale style of ale from the late eighteenth century that was brewed specially to be sent to India, using lots more hops than usual as a preservative. Hops were even added to the casks that went on the boats. Eventually the style gained popularity in the UK as well.

IPA, New England

An evolution of the American IPA that added wheat and oats for a rich, smooth and heavily hazy body, dialed down the bitterness, and used a combination of British ale yeast and huge dry hops to create juicy, tropical aromas and flavors.

IPA, West Coast

Also sometimes referred to as American IPA, West Coast IPA is an American adaptation of the British IPA using hops from the Pacific Northwest of America. This replaces the spice and hedge-row fruits of English IPA with pine, resin, grapefruit and even tropical fruits. Typically the bitterness was increased and drinking fresh (rather than aging) was encouraged.

Keg

A pressurized container used to store, transport and serve beer using CO_2 (and sometimes nitrogen, like in Guinness).

Lager

The name for a large family of beers made using lager yeast—which prefers to ferment colder than ale yeast. These beers also almost all undergo an extended cold conditioning phase, known as *lagering* (from the German *lagern*, which means to store).

Lambic

A historic Belgian beer style that according to EU law can only be called Lambic if it comes from the Pajottenland (essentially the Senne valley just southwest of Brussels). It's naturally cooled and infected with wild yeasts and cultures in the air and barrels it is fermented in to create a beer with strong Brett character as well as sourness. This is balanced by wheat and barley flavors, blending between barrels at the brewery, and often fruits that are added in the final conditioning phase.

Macro lager

A slightly pejorative term for generic pale lager brewed by international conglomerates all over the world, usually using maize or rice as well as barley. Most are loosely based on the Pilsners of late nineteenth-century Germany and Bohemia but some are more like Vienna lagers.

Märzen

An amber, crisp and delicious style of beer invented by Gabriel Sedlmayr II on his return home to Munich after a gap year exploring European breweries with Anton Dreher. It got its name from typically being brewed in March (*März* being German for *March*) and lagered in caves over the summer.

Mashing

The technical term for the brewing process where the malt is combined with warm water to release the sugars needed for fermentation.

Mild

Originally a term for young beer, Mild as a style took over as Porter went into decline. Most Milds were dark, sweeter and drunk fresh—a lot like those still brewed today.

Pilsner

A pale style of lager first brewed at Pilsner Urquell in Czechia in 1842 that is the origin of all the global lager brands today. There are two main kinds—Czech style with a richer caramel and brioche tinged body, floral aroma and strong bitterness, and German style which is lighter, more cracker-like and crisp.

Porter

A dark, slightly smoky ale invented by London brewers responding to a change in tax law that made pale malt more expensive to use. Darker malts were smoky and needed aging to round out that flavor, so the beers were well hopped to ensure it didn't spoil while it matured. It would have likely shown some Brett character, adding funk to the roasty aromas and flavors. More modern examples should still be hoppy and fruity, but lack the smoky and Brett character (unless advertised!).

RateBeer

A beer rating website that started in the early 2000s when the internet was in its infancy. Used by beer geeks to track their beers and review them, and by breweries as a way to create hype while researching what kinds of beers sell. Responsible for the mad Westvleteren rush of 2005.

Real ale

Beer that has been naturally carbonated by undergoing fermentation in a sealed container that it is subsequently poured from. This could be a cask or even a bottle or can.

Saison

A beer style with a murky history, supposedly based on beers brewed for seasonal workers on the farms of Belgium and France during harvest. Modern saisons, however, are based on Saison Dupont, a strong blond beer brewed in Belgium that has notes of clove, banana, pear and brioche.

Small beer

A term used historically to denote beer of very low alcohol—strong enough to ensure it is bacteria- and virus-free but low enough to be consumed all day long without getting inebriated.

Stout

Originally simply a strong Porter, Stouts are now their own category thanks to Guinness and how the beer's ABV dropped in the early twentieth century. Sometimes called Irish Dry Stout, it's a dry and very roasty beer that puts very dark malts at the fore.

Table beer

Essentially a synonym for *small beer*, taking its name from the fact it would have often been seen at the dinner table in people's homes.

Untappd

A rating app for beer lovers, where geeks can check in and rate their beers out of five. Hated by most breweries (in the same way that Tripadvisor is hated by restaurants) but an important marketing tool nonetheless. Some shops and bars will buy their beers based on their Untappd ratings, and customers certainly do.

Vienna lager

An amber, crisp and delicious style of beer invented by Anton Dreher on his return home to Austria after a gap year exploring European breweries with Gabriel Sedlmayr II. Similar to Sedlmayr's Märzen beer.

Wort

The word used by brewers for unfermented beer—that is, the sugary sticky stuff that the yeast is pitched into.

Cheers To...

I am not a historian, anthropologist, scientist, brewer or chef, so a book like this could not come together without the incredible talent, hard work and generosity of some very lovely people.

I want to heartily thank everyone who appears in this book, as well as the many who helped behind the scenes. In no particular order they are Andreas Krennmeir, Bryan Alberts, Charles Denby, Beate Neubauer, Nicholas P. Money, Pat Gibney, John W. Arthur, Tracy Lauer, Kasper Larsson, Alex White, Mark Rasmussen, Breandán Kearney, Ned Palmer, Troika Brodsky, David Luxton, Rebecca Winfield, Ed Faulkner, Felice McKeown, Peter Joseph, my man Mike in Luxor, Rich Mallett and Mark Dredge.

I also want to thank some of the people whose previous work inspired and informed this book. In particular they are David Jesudason, Jeffrey S. Gaab, Kristof and Kirsten Glamann, Annette von Altenbockum, Jef Van den Steen, Wolfgang Behringer, Pete Brown and Martyn Cornell.

Finally, as with every book I've written, I have to thank my wonderful wife Heather for her love, enthusiasm and understanding, my parents for supporting my madcap career choice, and Brad for being my travel buddy for so many of these adventures. Lastly, massive thanks to Rich, Rich and Ed who have been my beer-drinking partners for twenty years, and hopefully at least twenty more.

Further Reading

If you were intrigued or skeptical about any of the events in this book, I heartily recommend you read all of the amazing books below.

Munich: Hofbräuhaus & History—Beer, Culture & Politics, Jeffrey S. Gaab

Beer, John W. Arthur

The Rise of Yeast, Nicholas P. Money

Die Spaten-Brauerei, Wolfgang Behringer

Desi Pubs, David Jesudason

A Brief History of Lager, Mark Dredge

Trappist: The Seven Magnificent Beers, Jef Van den Steen

Index

Villemin, Jean-Antoine, 78, 79

Villiger, Joseph, 244

Vilshofen, Bavaria, 106

vinegars, 195–7

"Virtual Insanity" (Jamiroquai), 183

vitamins, 193, 195, 199–201
    B, 193, 195, 200
    C, 201

vodka, 64, 65

Wagner, John, 141

Watson, James, 270

weddings, 215

Weetabix, 192–3

Weihenstephan, 39

Weilheim, Bavaria, 106

Weimar Republic (1918–33), 101

Weissbier, 102–7, 110–11, 223–5

West Africa, 170, 174, 269, 280

Western Brewer, The, 151

Westmalle Abbey, Belgium, 42, 43, 45, 46

Westvleteren, Belgium, 43–8

Wetherspoons, 91

Wexford, County Wexford, 186

wheat, 18–19, 30, 33, 34, 38, 40, 52, 63, 77, 99, 101, 125–6, 193, 194
    Weissbier, 102–7, 110–11, 223–5

whiskey, 61, 140–2, 192, 203, 220

Whitbread, 67

White, Thomas "Shock," 261

wild rosemary, 100

Wilhelm V, Duke of Bavaria, 109, 110

Wilkinson, Toby, 35

Williams, Robbie, 240, 242

Willis Tower, Chicago, 148

Wills, Lucy, 200

Windsor Castle, Berkshire, 202

wine, 9, 12, 19, 38, 39, 61, 65–7, 75, 77, 78, 80, 192, 205, 207–8, 212, 266

wine vinegars, 196

Wissler, Frederick, 198–9

Wittal, Martin, 53, 60–1

Wittelsbach dynasty, 35, 97–110

Wolf, Peter, 105, 110

women, 38, 40, 201, 207
    advertising and, 162, 178, 179, 207
    pregnancy, 100, 178, 200

Worcestershire sauce, 196

Worden, Alfred, 188

workers' rights, 94

World Cup, 164

World Food Programme, 188

World Series, 161, 163

World's Fair (1893), 147

yarrow, 100

yeast, 12, 13, 15, 20, 21, 25, 33, 43, 46, 61–8, 99, 105, 123, 195, 206
    alcohol and, 62, 76, 278, 281
    autolysis, 198
    cuisine and, 191–2
    extract, 194
    genetics and, 271–5, 278–82
    Hansen and, 75–7